CCNA Self-Study
Guide, 2e
(Exam 640-801)

CCNA Self-Study
Guide, 2e
(Exam 640-801)

THOMSON

DELMAR LEARNING ™

Australia • Canada • Mexico • Singapore • Spain • United Kingdom • United States

THOMSON
™
DELMAR LEARNING

CCNA Self-Study Guide (Exam 640-801)

Anthony Chiarella

Vice President, Technology and Trades SBU:
Alar Elken

Editorial Director:
Sandy Clark

Senior Acquisitions Editor:
Stephen Helba

Senior Development Editor:
Michelle Ruelos Cannistraci

Marketing Director:
David Garza

Channel Manager:
Dennis Williams

Marketing Coordinator:
Stacey Wiktorek

Production Director:
Mary Ellen Black

Production Manager:
Larry Main

Production Editor:
Benj Gleeksman

Editorial Assistant:
Dawn Daugherty

Art/Design Coordinator:
Francis Hogan

For permission to use material from the text or product, contact us by
Tel. (800) 730-2214
Fax (800) 730-2215
www.thomsonrights.com

Library of Congress Cataloging-in-Publication Data

Chiarella, Anthony.
  CCNA self-study guide : exam 640-801 / Anthony Chiarella.—2nd ed.
      p. cm.
  Rev. ed. of : CISCO CCNA self study guide. c2003.
  Includes index.
  ISBN 1-4180-0574-6
 1. Electronic data processing personnel—Certification. 2. Computer networks—Examinations—Study guides.   I. Chiarella, Anthony. CISCO CCNA self study guide.   II. Title.
  QA76.3.C46 2005
  004.6—dc22   2005011963

NOTICE TO THE READER

Publisher does not warrant or guarantee any of the products described herein or perform any independent analysis in connection with any of the product information contained herein. Publisher does not assume, and expressly disclaims, any obligation to obtain and include information other than that provided to it by the manufacturer.

The reader is expressly warned to consider and adopt all safety precautions that might be indicated by the activities herein and to avoid all potential hazards. By following the instructions contained herein, the reader willingly assumes all risks in connection with such instructions.

The publisher makes no representation or warranties of any kind, including but not limited to, the warranties of fitness for particular purpose or merchantability, nor are any such representations implied with respect to the material set forth herein, and the publisher takes no responsibility with respect to such material. The publisher shall not be liable for any special, consequential, or exemplary damages resulting, in whole or part, from the readers' use of, or reliance upon, this material.

CONTENTS

CHAPTER 1 Internetworking Models and Communication Standards

CHAPTER 2   Transmission Control Protocol/Internet Protocol (TCP/IP)

CHAPTER 3   Configuring and Managing a Cisco Router

CHAPTER 4   IP Routing (RIP and IGRP)

CHAPTER 5   IP Routing (OSPF and EIGRP)

CHAPTER 8   Layer 2 Switching in a Local Area Network

INTENDED AUDIENCE

Whether you are a student studying Cisco for the first time or a Cisco professional who has yet to become a CCNA, this book is for you. The goal of this technical reference guide is to assist you in taking the Cisco Certified Network Associate (CCNA) Exam 640-801. Helpful test tips and questions throughout the study guide will further prepare you for the CCNA Exam. There is great demand for Cisco certified professionals in the world today and this book is aimed at guiding you through the exam to help you meet that demand.

PREREQUISITES

To best use this study guide, you should have some previous knowledge of networking concepts. You should already have a basic understanding of the data communication process before using this book to study for the CCNA Exam. This book will prepare you successfully for the topics of the exam. However, there are not many labs to assist you. Cisco's test format requires that you be familiar with the interface of a Cisco router to administer it. Because of this, it is highly recommended that you practice the commands listed in this book on an actual router or router simulation program.

WHY I WROTE THIS BOOK

Many Cisco study guides are comprehensive books that are sometimes used as courseware to teach the CCNA objectives. My book, on the other hand, is written in such a way that you will be able to use it as a supplement to any Cisco training course that attempts to prepare you for the 640-801 Exam. However, you do not need to be a student preparing for the exam to read this book. You can be an uncertified Cisco professional looking for a simple-to-read, to-the-point study guide to boost your earning potential. As we all know, a certification can be the difference between you and "the other guy" when going for a promotion.

When I set out to write this book I had one goal in mind: getting my readers certified. I have taken many certified technical exams and know how to study for them and pass them. One method I use to study for exams is to find all the information in a book that I feel is pertinent and write it down in a separate notebook. Then I study from the notebook. This is essentially what I did for you. In this book, I pass my test-taking study habits on to you.

The chapters in this book are clear, concise, and to the point. The technical information in this book is geared toward the test topics stated on Cisco's Web site.

TEXTBOOK OUTLINE

This textbook begins with a thorough discussion of the Open Systems Interconnect (OSI) reference model. In Chapter 2, Transmission Control Protocol/Internet Protocol (TCP/IP), you will get a fundamental understanding of TCP/IP, which happens to be the most widely used protocol in the world today. Chapter 3, Configuring and Managing a Cisco Router, will introduce you to the router. You will learn about the hardware components, the operating system, and the configuration commands used to support it. You will also be provided with a spreadsheet of commands to help you memorize commands before taking the exam.

Chapter 4, IP Routing (RIP and IGRP), is an introduction to routing the Internet Protocol (IP). Chapter 5, IP Routing (OSPF and EIGRP), describes additional IP routing protocols. Chapter 6, Access Lists, covers access lists and how to filter data coming into and going out of a router. Chapter 7, Routing in a Wide Area Network, discusses routing over wide area network (WAN) links and includes information on several WAN protocols. Finally, Chapter 8, Switching in a Local Area Network, presents and reinforces the configuration methods used to manage a layer 2 switch. Appendix A contains a list of abbreviated commands and Appendix B is a preparation guide for Cisco's new testing format. It has several scenarios for you to run through to familiarize you with the new exam. The answers to all Knowledge Test questions are located in Appendix C.

FEATURES

Each chapter begins with a list of **Topics**, followed by the **Introduction**, which provides an overview of the chapter. At the end of each chapter a **Knowledge Test** containing 20 questions will allow you to quiz yourself as you go through the book. You should take the test after you read the chapter and again after you finish the textbook to see how well you retain the material. As a side note, write your answers down on a separate sheet of paper so the answers are not next to the questions the next time you take the Knowledge Test. Appendix C contains the answers to these test questions. The textbook also contains a **Glossary** for hard-to-remember terms with simplified definitions. I have included a command study sheet that will work as a studying tool as well as a reference sheet when working on a router. This is a comprehensive list of commands that will definitely help as you study for the exam. I believe that most commands that can be used to test your knowledge of the CCNA topics are shown in Table 3.1 in Chapter 3. If you know the commands, then you know the answers to the simulated questions.

TEST TIPS are located throughout the book to grab your attention while reading. They will generally appear after a subject that I feel is more likely to be on the exam than others. However, I have also started several sections with a *TEST TIP* to forewarn you that the material about to be read is important.

HOW TO USE THE TEXTBOOK

Italics are used throughout the textbook to introduce new terms (followed by a definition) and to represent Cisco router commands, beginning in Chapter 3. When a router command is listed in the text of a paragraph it will be *italicized* and then explained further. There may be an example as well. In most of the examples, I will show you a screenshot of the command being typed and then explain which portion of the command is required and which arguments are optional in the text that follows. If there are brackets with options separated by "|" symbol, that means one of the options is mandatory but only one can be selected. For example, if the command shows [cisco|ietf], one of these options must be used.

ACKNOWLEDGMENTS

Many people are involved in the creation and distribution of any and every book out there. To be able to give thanks to those who have helped in so many ways is very important. I would like to begin with thanking my family for supporting me in all of my endeavors including, but not limited to, writing books and screenplays, running a business, and teaching a full schedule. I would also like to thank the folks at Thomson Delmar Learning for providing me with the opportunity that is only given to a select a few. To be specific, I have to start by thanking "My Favorite Editor, Michelle Ruelos Cannistraci" (who by some amazing feat has been able to deal with me for almost four years now) and "My Favorite Production Editor, Stacy Masucci" (who was not involved in the 2nd edition, but was a key player in teaching me the ropes of the production process). All the Acquisition Editors I have worked with showed great flexibility with me and trusted my opinion on so many occasions. They include Greg Clayton, Dave Garza, and most recently Steve Helba. I'd also like to thank the Production Editor who has worked on this edition, Benj Gleeksman. Last but certainly not least, I have to thank you for believing in me enough to spend your hard-earned money on one of my creations. I wish you the best of luck in your studies and hope this book helps you earn the title of Cisco Certified Network Associate.

The author and Delmar Learning wish to thank the following reviewers for their ideas and suggestions during the development of this book.

Eugene Broda, Hillsborough Community College, Tampa, FL
Bruce Jost, Jefferson Community College, Louisville, KY
Charles Lange, DeVry University, New Brunswick, NJ
John Morgan, DeVry University, Irving, TX
Dave Patzarian, Albany Vo-Tech, Albany, NY
Alan Runge, DeVry University, Kansas City, MO

ABOUT THE AUTHOR

Anthony Chiarella currently teaches at several colleges in upstate New York. He teaches classes from basic computer architecture through WAN services and design. He holds dual platform engineering certifications from Microsoft (MCSE NT 4.0 and Win 2K), as well as Novell (CNE NetWare 5.0 and 5.1), and is certified in several other technologies, including Cisco (CCNA), Citrix (CCA), A+, Security+, and N+. Chiarella has been certified as a trainer by Microsoft (MCT) and an instructor by Novell (CNI) and holds the Certified Technical Trainer (CTT+) certification. He earned both his BS and MA from the State University of New York, Empire State College. Anthony is the President of TJC Consulting, which is a small network integration firm. Other responsibilities include taking on the role as technical advisor for Delmar Learning's *PC Repair, Maintenance, & Upgrading for A+ Certification* video series. Other works include *Network+ Self-Study Guide* and *Internetworking with Cisco and Microsoft Technologies,* both available from Delmar Learning.

INTRODUCTION

This section describes the CCNA Exam, where to register for it, and the benefits of becoming a CCNA. The exam topics for the CCNA Exam 640-801 and a listing of other certifications offered by Cisco Systems are covered within this section as well.

REGISTRATION

Certification exams are open to the public, and there are no training requirements to consider when preparing for certification. Training in a specific field is recommended if you have not been exposed to the subject matter you plan on becoming certified in. The *CCNA Exam 640-801* can be taken at any Thomson Prometric or Pearson VUE testing center. To register for the exam with Prometric, visit www.prometric.com. To register for the exam with Pearson VUE, visit www.vue.com. Be sure to register for the correct exam, which is the CCNA 640-801 Exam. The exam is computer based and will be given at a testing center near you. The exam consists of 55 to 65 questions, and you will have 90 minutes to complete it. With this exam, Cisco's testing format utilizes Computer Simulations, Drag-And-Drop, Type The Answer Here, Choose Multiple, and Choose One Answer Questions. To familiarize yourself with the format of some questions, use the Knowledge Tests at the end of each chapter in this book. Also included are several appendixes, such as Appendix B, which will prepare you for the format and consists of several skill-based questions as you will see on the exam. This appendix also offers instructions on how to prepare for those types of questions. You can go to www.cisco.com to view the testing format.

CERTIFICATION

Cisco offers three levels of certification: associate level, professional level, and expert level. Each is available in various tracks such as Routing and Switching, Network Security, and Service Provider. Cisco also offers Cisco Qualified Specialist certifications that pertain to specific technologies. When certified at the associate or professional level, the certification is valid for three years. At the end of three years, you must recertify to maintain your certification. The only instance when you would not need to recertify is when you go from one certification level to the next. For example, if you become a Cisco Certified Network Associate (CCNA) and two years later you complete the Cisco

Certified Network Professional (CCNP) certification, your CCNA is automatically upgraded with your professional level certification. The expert level certification, which consists of the Cisco Certified Internetwork Expert (CCIE) certification, is only valid for two years. For more information on recertification, visit www.cisco.com.

ASSOCIATE LEVEL

Currently there are two certifications to achieve the associate level certification: Cisco Certified Network Associate (CCNA) and Cisco Certified Design Associate (CCDA). To see the updated exams offered by Cisco, visit www.cisco.com. Each of these certifications is valid for three years. Recertifying or advancing to the next level allows you to maintain your certification status. Jobs available at the associate level consist of engineer help desk support, level 1 integrators, engineers, and field technicians, as well as entry-level LAN administrators who work in small firms. CCNAs have a strong foundational knowledge of networking design, installation, and support for organizations with networks that consist of approximately 100 nodes. CCNAs are capable of installing, configuring, and administering Cisco routers and switches in a multiprotocol internetwork. Cisco also offers the CCNA certification in a series of exams if the candidate does not want to take the 640-801. The two exams that are available include the 640-811 and the 640-821. By passing both of those exams, you would have achieved the same result as passing the 640-801.

PROFESSIONAL LEVEL

The professional level certifications are more difficult to attain and consist of a series of certification exams that include the prerequisite associate level exams. The certifications consist of the Cisco Certified Network Professional (CCNP), Cisco Certified Design Professional (CCDP); Cisco Certified Internetwork Professional (CCIP); and the Cisco Certified Security Professional (CCSP). The jobs available at the professional level consist of senior network engineers and senior network consultants. With a professional level certification, you will have an advanced knowledge of networking design, installation, support, and administration for medium to large organizations.

EXPERT LEVEL

Expert level certification for Cisco is the most difficult to attain and consists of three parts: first is to meet the professional level requirements; the second is a computer-based exam; and, finally, to become a Cisco Certified Internetwork Expert (CCIE) there is a requirement to complete and pass a hands-on lab, which consists of building and troubleshooting a network at a location specified by Cisco. Expert-level certification opens many doors for a job candidate. Positions held by CCIEs include, but are not limited to, level 3 engineers, consultants, designers, and analysts. The CCIE certification is the premier certification in the network industry. To learn more about certifications offered by Cisco Systems, Inc., visit www.cisco.com.

TOPICS

The topics for the 640-801 are listed next by the chapter they are covered in. Cisco has announced that the following list is a guideline for the content that is likely to be on the exam. There may be additional topics on the exam not listed in the Cisco guidelines. However, if you understand and are comfortable with the topics covered in the following lists, you stand an excellent chance of passing the exam.

CHAPTER 1

The following topics are discussed in Chapter 1.

- Design a simple LAN using Cisco Technology.
- Implement a LAN.
- Utilize the OSI model as a guide for systematic network troubleshooting.
- Troubleshoot a device as part of a working network.
- Describe network communications using layered models.
- Compare and contrast key characteristics of LAN environments.
- Describe the components of network devices.

CHAPTER 2

The following topics are discussed in Chapter 2.

- Design an IP addressing scheme to meet design requirements.
- Configure IP addresses, subnet masks, and gateway addresses on routers and hosts.
- Implement a LAN.
- Troubleshoot IP addressing and host configuration.
- Troubleshoot a device as part of a working network.
- Evaluate TCP/IP communication process and its associated protocols.

CHAPTER 3

The following topics are discussed in Chapter 3.

- Configure IP addresses, subnet masks, and gateway addresses on routers and hosts.

- Configure a router for additional administrative functionality.

- Manage system image and device configuration files.

- Perform an initial configuration on a router.

- Troubleshoot a device as part of a working network.

CHAPTER 4

The following topics are discussed in Chapter 4.

- Select an appropriate routing protocol based on user requirements.

- Design a simple internetwork using Cisco technology.

- Configure routing protocols given user requirements.

- Troubleshoot routing protocols.

- Troubleshoot a device as part of a working network.

- Evaluate the characteristics of routing protocols.

CHAPTER 5

The following topics are discussed in Chapter 5.

- Select an appropriate routing protocol based on user requirements.

- Design a simple internetwork using Cisco technology.

- Configure routing protocols given user requirements.

- Troubleshoot routing protocols.

- Troubleshoot a device as part of a working network.

- Evaluate the characteristics of routing protocols.

CHAPTER 6

The following topics are discussed in Chapter 6.

- Develop an access list to meet user specifications.

- Implement access lists.

- Troubleshoot an access list.

- Evaluate rules for packet control.

CHAPTER 7

The following topics are discussed in Chapter 7.

- Choose WAN services to meet customer requirements.

- Implement simple WAN protocols.
- Perform simple WAN troubleshooting.
- Evaluate key characteristics of WANs.

CHAPTER 8

The following topics are discussed in Chapter 8.

- Design a simple LAN using Cisco technology.
- Configure a switch with VLANS and interswitch communication.
- Implement a LAN.
- Customize a switch configuration to meet specified network requirements.
- Perform an initial configuration on a switch.
- Perform LAN and VLAN troubleshooting.
- Troubleshoot a device as part of a working network.
- Describe the Spanning Tree process.

CHAPTER 1

Internetworking Models and Communication Standards

OBJECTIVES

The following topics are discussed in Chapter 1:

- Design a simple LAN using Cisco Technology.
- Implement a LAN.
- Utilize the OSI model as a guide for systematic network troubleshooting.
- Troubleshoot a device as part of a working network.
- Describe network communications using layered models.
- Compare and contrast key characteristics of LAN environments.
- Describe the components of network devices.

INTRODUCTION

This chapter describes internetworking models and communication standards. An internetworking model is a conceptual framework that is normally used as a guideline when designing hardware or software used in the data-communication process. Two models are described in this chapter: *Cisco's three-layered hierarchical* model and the *Open Systems Interconnect Reference* model, or *OSI* model. Communication standards are also described, along with their governing bodies such as the Institute of Electrical and Electronics Engineers (IEEE) and the American National Standards Institute (ANSI).

Test Tip: Cisco expects all CCNA candidates to have a thorough understanding of the OSI model.

1.1 THE LAYERED MODEL

This section briefly discusses why the data communications industry has adopted a layered approach to internetworking and describes two internetworking models that pertain to the CCNA Exam. Both models are conceptual frameworks available to networking professionals and vendors to be used as developmental guides. (See Figure 1.1 and Figure 1.2.)

Before discussing how these models facilitate network communication, it is important to understand that they are not physical components and cannot be seen or touched. However, these internetworking models provide the blueprints of the current internetworking infrastructure.

Each model is designed in a modular fashion, with one module built on top of the module below it. The **OSI model** was developed in the late 1970s by the International Standards Organization (ISO) and consists of *seven layers*. The **Cisco three-layered hierarchical model** has *three layers*. The models consist of a layered format for several reasons. Three of the primary reasons are

- **Interoperability (Plug-and-Play).** A layered model is used to define standards so multiple vendors' network products can work together. In other words, if a company created a hardware component at the second layer of the OSI model, it should be able to work with a third-layer component created by a separate company.

7	Application	**A**ll	**A**way
6	Presentation	**P**eople	**P**izza
5	Session	**S**eem	**S**ausage
4	Transport	**T**o	**T**hrow
3	Network	**N**eed	**N**ot
2	Data-Link	**D**ata	**D**o
1	Physical	**P**rocessing	**P**lease

Figure 1.1 *Seven-layered OSI model with tips to remember it*

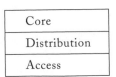

Figure 1.2 *Cisco's three-layered hierarchical model*

- **Division.** A layered model allows for the division of complex interrelated network processes into simpler categories. For example, it is easier to develop and manage one process (such as routing) at one layer than at seven layers.

- **Modular Design.** A layered model allows the processes and activities of a protocol or device at one layer to be redeveloped or redesigned without having to redevelop or redesign the processes that operate at other layers of the model.

A layered model also provides a logical process flow by defining tasks and roles at various levels to accomplish communication.

 Test Tip: An easy way to remember why we use a layered model is Interoperability, Division, Modular Design.

1.2   CISCO'S THREE-LAYERED HIERARCHICAL MODEL

Cisco uses a layered model to define a business's internetworking needs. The model simplifies designing, implementing, and managing networks. It consists of three layers (refer to Figure 1.2), which are described next.

ACCESS, DISTRIBUTION, AND CORE LAYERS

The first layer is the *access* layer, which represents the end users in an organization. End users' data transmissions access the network at this layer. The second layer is the *distribution* layer, which defines local routing and local security policies. It also determines the quickest and least expensive route that data will travel to get to their destination. The third layer is the *core* layer, which takes the data and the path information from the distribution layer and switches or routes the traffic to its destination. The core layer also represents the enterprise services in a network (network services such as e-mail) that are available to all end users.

Following is an example that will help you visualize Cisco's three-layered hierarchical model. User A, located in Boston, Massachusetts, creates an e-mail to send to User B in Albany, New York. User A's workstation, which is located in a switched LAN, represents the access layer. Once User A attempts to send the e-mail, the distribution layer determines whether User A's workstation has permission to send the e-mail. It also determines the quickest and least costly route (also known as the best path) to get the e-mail to the Albany, New York office. The data are then forwarded to the core layer with a designated path. The core layer makes the connection to the remote router and delivers the e-mail. At that time, the e-mail travels through the model down to User B's workstation (see Figure 1.3).

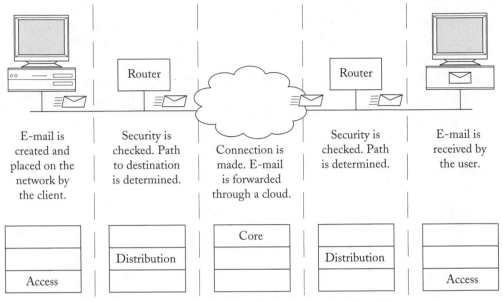

Figure 1.3 *Data flow through Cisco's three-layered model*

1.3 OPEN SYSTEMS INTERCONNECT REFERENCE MODEL

The OSI model consists of seven layers: *physical, data-link, network, transport, session, presentation,* and *application.* Each layer has a different role to play in the communication process. When designing network *protocols,* the vendor must decide at which layer of the OSI model the protocol will fit best. A protocol is essentially the language and control information that computers and network devices use to transfer data between one another.

Each layer of the OSI model is detailed in this chapter. However, before discussing each layer of the model, you should understand how each of the seven layers transfers data to the layers below it (*encapsulation*) and to the layers above it (*de-encapsulation*). This section also discusses how each OSI layer entity communicates with its peer OSI layer entity in another device on the network, which is known as *peer layer communication.*

ENCAPSULATION AND DE-ENCAPSULATION

Encapsulation and de-encapsulation are processes that data go through during network communication. Each layer in the OSI model has a separate responsibility during the communications process. Before user data can be sent onto the wire in a network, the sending or source device is responsible for encapsulating the data.

This process is invisible to the end user and consists of adding control, address information, or both to the data at each layer in the form of *headers* and *trailers*. A header consists of information placed at the beginning of a data stream. A trailer consists of information placed at the end of a data stream. When the data is taken off the wire, the receiving or destination device must de-encapsulate the data by stripping off the control and address information, layer by layer, before presenting the data to the user.

Encapsulation

Encapsulation facilitates communication between two networking components. For example, a user is attempting to access a file on a network file server using a file transfer protocol (FTP) application. The FTP request acts as the application data for this example and is considered a protocol data unit (PDU) or, simply, "data" in the encapsulation process.

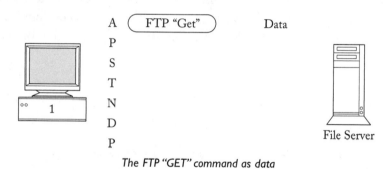

The FTP "GET" command as data

The FTP "GET" command, which is ultimately an application layer protocol command, is passed down to the presentation layer. The presentation layer adds information to the data stating what presentation layer protocol the user's computer is using.

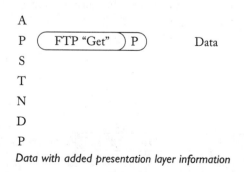

Data with added presentation layer information

The data is then passed down to the session layer, which adds control information.

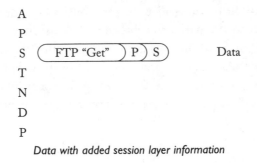

A
P
S   FTP "Get"   P   S   Data
T
N
D
P

Data with added session layer information

Next, the data is given to the transport layer, where the protocol responsible for delivery encapsulates the packet. The data has been a continuous stream until this point and will not undergo a physical change. In networking, the data stream cannot be continuous and has to be broken up into chunks of data so all computers on the wire have a chance to communicate. If the data stream is not broken up, communication would be next to impossible for any machine except the machine that is communicating at that exact moment. At the transport layer, the data stream is converted (or encapsulated) into *segments*.

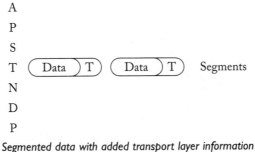

A
P
S
T   Data T   Data T   Segments
N
D
P

Segmented data with added transport layer information

The segmented data is then passed down to the network layer, which encapsulates the segment into a *packet* or *datagram*.

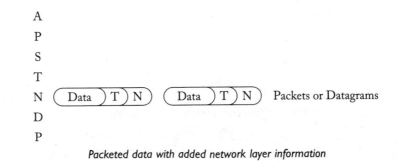

A
P
S
T
N   Data T N   Data T N   Packets or Datagrams
D
P

Packeted data with added network layer information

The data, now in the form of a packet, is passed down to the data-link layer. The data-link layer encapsulates the packet into a *frame* and then passes it down to the physical layer, which transmits it across the wire as a series of bits (ones [1s] and 0s [0s]).

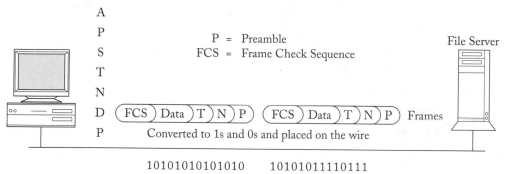

Framed data with added data-link layer information

De-Encapsulation

The 1s and 0s are de-encapsulated when they get to the destination machine. The de-encapsulation process is the exact opposite of the encapsulation process. The control information that was added to the data is now stripped off at the same layer in which the sending machine added it. The 1s and 0s enter at the physical layer and are handed up to the data-link layer and converted back into a frame. The frame is then stripped of its control and address information and the remaining data are handed up to the network layer as a packet. The network layer strips its control information off and passes the remaining data up to the transport layer as a segment. The transport layer strips its control information off and then passes the remaining data up to the *upper layers* of the OSI model, which consist of the session, presentation, and application layers. The upper layers of the OSI model get the data in the form of a continuous stream of data (as though it had never changed).

 Test Tip: Encapsulation and de-encapsulation are five-step processes that occur at the respective layers in the OSI model: Layers 7, 6, 5 = Data (or PDU); Layer 4 = Segment; Layer 3 = Packet (or Datagram); Layer 2 = Frame; Layer 1 = Bits.

Peer Layer Communication

Peer layer communication is the process of communication between each of the seven OSI layers in one machine and their peer OSI layers in another machine; for example, data-link layer to data-link layer, network layer to network layer, and so on. The only layer of the OSI model that communicates physically with its peer layer is the physical layer. This is because the two machines are connected to one another by physical layer components such as the wire and connectors (see Figure 1.4). Each of

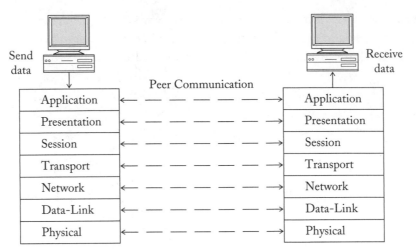

Figure 1.4 *OSI peer layer communication*

the other six layers participates in virtual communication. That is, the data is de-encapsulated, and each layer reads the control and address information that was added to the data by its peer layer. Each layer believes it is directly connected with its peer layer; however, it is not. Rather, a virtual connection is shared by the two layers in separate machines.

1.4 PHYSICAL LAYER (LAYER 1)

When vendors develop hardware or software for network communication, the product is normally designed to map to one or more layers of the OSI model. The products that map to the lower layers of the model are not as intelligent as those that map to the higher layers. The physical layer, which is at the bottom of the OSI model, is the least intelligent layer. Therefore, devices that map to the physical layer have the least intelligence. Most physical layer devices are only responsible for generating or repeating signals. Devices at higher layers in the model can actually decide—based on certain factors—whether or not to send certain data, and if so, where to send it.

Layer 1 of the OSI model defines the electrical, mechanical, and functional specifications for activating and deactivating the physical connectivity between machines on the network. The physical layer does not guarantee that communication between machines on a network will be successful. It does, however, guarantee that a path is available for the 1s and 0s to travel over.

SIGNAL AND WIRING STANDARDS

Signal and wiring standards are both components described at the physical layer of the OSI model. Signaling standards are discussed first, followed by wiring standards.

Signaling Standards

Signaling methods for transmitting data are defined at the physical layer, specifically, broadband and baseband. *Broadband* is an analog signaling method that uses frequencies to send and receive data. Multiple broadband signals can reside on the same carrier (cable). *Baseband* is a digital signaling method that uses digital signals to send and receive data. In a baseband transmission, only one signal at a time can be on the wire.

Wiring Standards

The physical layer defines wiring standards for the physical topology of a network. For example, the standards for an Ethernet network include, but are not limited to, 10BaseT, 10Base2, 10Base5, 100BaseTX, 100BaseFX, 1000BaseCX, 1000BaseSX, 1000BaseLX, and 1000BaseT. These standards are as follows:

- 10BaseT sends data at a rate of 10 Mbps using a baseband transmission over category 3 unshielded twisted-pair (UTP) wire. Each cable segment can be no more than 100 meters. Each connection is point to point, connecting to a central location such as a hub or a switch. The physical topology is a star. An RJ-45 connector is used to connect a node to the wire.

- 10Base2 sends data at a rate of 10 Mbps using a baseband transmission, and each cable segment can be 185 meters in length with a total of 30 nodes on the segment. It also is known as thinnet or thin Ethernet because it uses a thin coaxial cable (RG58u). It requires 50 ohms of resistance on each end of the wire. The physical topology is a bus. A British naval connector (BNC) is used to connect a node to the wire.

- 10Base5 sends data at a rate of 10 Mbps using a baseband transmission, and each cable segment can be 500 meters in length with a total of 100 nodes on the segment. It also is known as thicknet or thick Ethernet because it uses a thicker coaxial cable (RG8 or RG11) than does 10Base2. 10Base5 is implemented as a network backbone. The physical topology is a bus. To connect a node to the wire, an auxiliary unit interface (AUI) is used from the node to a transceiver connected directly to the wire.

- 100BaseTX sends data at a rate of 100 Mbps using a baseband transmission over category 5 UTP wire. Each cable segment can be no more than 100 meters. Each connection is point to point, connecting to a central location such as a hub or a switch. The physical topology is a star. An RJ-45 connector is used to connect a node to the wire.

- 100BaseFX sends data at a rate of 100 Mbps using a baseband transmission over fiber-optic wire. Cable segments can be up to 400 meters long. The physical topology is point to point. A duplex media interface connector ST (MIC) is used to connect a node to the wire.

- 1000BaseCX was designed for very short distances (only 25 meters) over shielded copper cable.

- 1000BaseSX carries a signal for 550 meters and is implemented for short backbone connections over fiber-optic multimode cable.

- 1000BaseLX carries a signal for 5 kilometers and is used for backbone connections longer than 1000BaseSX. It uses fiber-optic single-mode cable.

- 1000BaseT (802.3ab) uses four pairs of category 5 UTP. Each cable run is limited to 100 meters. Physical topology is a star, with each cable ending at a central device.

PHYSICAL TOPOLOGIES

There are four major physical topologies to be aware of: bus, ring, star, and mesh (see Figure 1.5). The word *topology* simply means configuration. In the *bus topology*, all nodes (a *node* is any component on a network) are connected to one cable called a

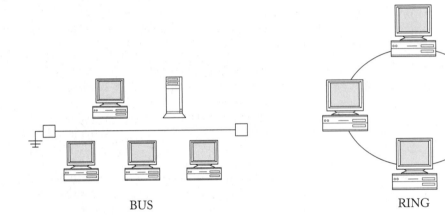

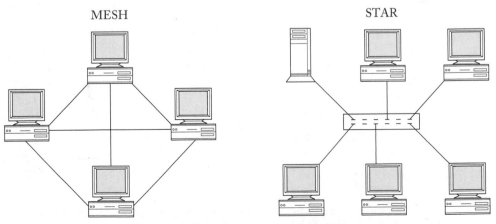

Figure 1.5 *Four physical network topologies*

trunk or a *backbone*. In a *ring topology*, all network components are connected to one cable in a ring. In a *star topology*, all devices on the network are connected to a central point. In a *mesh topology*, every component has a connection with every other component, providing redundancy. Mesh topologies, however, can be expensive to implement.

Another physical topology to be aware of is the *wireless topology*. In a wireless network, nodes use wireless network adapters that send signals to wireless access points (WAP) (see Figure 1.5a).

Figure 1.5a *Wireless network*

WAPs can forward signals to other WAPs or they can bring the signal to the backbone cable of a destination network (see Figure 1.5b).

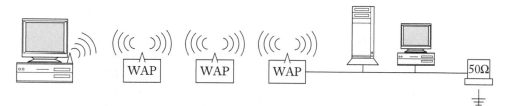

Figure 1.5b *Wireless network with multiple WAPs*

1.5 DATA-LINK LAYER (LAYER 2)

The data-link layer of the OSI model is the second layer of the model and is subdivided into two sublayers: the *logical link control sublayer (LLC)* and the *media access control (MAC) sublayer*.

LOGICAL LINK CONTROL

The LLC sublayer describes how data will get from the second layer of the OSI model to higher layers in the OSI model. It does this by defining *service access points (SAP)* or *subnetwork access points (SNAP)*. SAPs and SNAPs act as pointers to upper layer protocols and depend on the applications the system is running. The LLC sublayer is independent of the media being used.

MEDIA ACCESS CONTROL

The MAC sublayer of the data-link layer defines how 1s and 0s are placed on the network. It specifies the rules that all network adapter boards must follow when attempting to communicate. These specifications are known as *media access methods* and the main three types are

- **Contention.** Data is transmitted onto the wire on a first-come, first-serve basis.
- **Token passing.** Data is only transmitted when the transmitting device has control of the token circulating the network.
- **Polling.** Nodes transmit on the wire when polled by the centralized device.

The MAC sublayer of the data-link layer also defines physical addressing. Every network interface card (NIC) is given a unique address called a MAC address, also known as a physical, data-link, or layer 2 address. The MAC address is considered the physical address because it is physically burned into the NIC's ROM. This address, defined by the IEEE, is 48 bits long and is represented by 12 hexadecimal digits. A MAC address has two sections. The first section of the number is the organization unit identifier (OUI). The OUI consists of the first six hexadecimal digits and is assigned to companies that produce NICs. The second portion of the address consists of the second six hexadecimal digits and is assigned to the individual NIC by its manufacturer (see Figure 1.6).

Additional responsibilities of the MAC sublayer include line discipline, flow control, fragmentation, error control, error notification, and error detection.

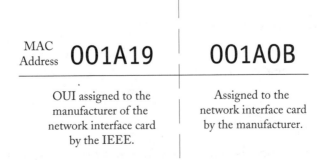

Figure 1.6 *The two portions of a MAC address*

LOGICAL TOPOLOGIES

Logical topologies are defined within the data-link layer. A *logical topology* is the method that data uses when traveling from one node to the next on a wire. The two logical topologies to be concerned with are bus and ring.

Logical Bus Topology

The *logical bus topology* states that when data is placed on the network cable, it travels to all nodes connected to that segment. Every machine is responsible for de-encapsulating the packet up to the data-link layer to determine whether or not it is the intended destination of the frame. If it is not, the node simply ignores the frame. If it is the correct destination, the node processes the frame further.

Logical Ring Topology

In the *logical ring topology*, a frame called a token is generated and placed on the network. The token travels around the ring from node to node, giving each station an opportunity to communicate. When a machine that needs to communicate receives the token, it appends the token with its data. The token and the data are then placed back on the wire and again sent from node to node until the token and the data reach the destination node. After the destination machine reads the data, it retransmits the token onto the wire. The token is passed around the ring to the original sending station, which releases the token for the next node to have the opportunity to transmit on the wire. In traditional ring topologies, only one token was allowed on the network at any given time. However, more recent versions of this technology allow multiple tokens to be on the ring at once.

Knowing how logical topologies and physical topologies can work together is important. For example, 10BaseT uses a physical star topology and a logical bus topology. Hence, it is a logical bus running over a physical star (or a star-wired bus). 10Base2 and 10Base5 use a physical bus with a logical bus to communicate (see Figure 1.7).

PREAMBLE AND CYCLIC REDUNDANCY CHECK

Based on the protocol being used, the data-link layer may have additional responsibilities in the encapsulation process. Several popular protocol implementations add a set of 1s and 0s to the beginning of the PDU called a *preamble* and a trailer called a *field check sequence (FCS)*. Inside a frame's FCS field is a *cyclic redundancy check (CRC)* that is used to verify the integrity of a frame.

Preamble

The preamble notifies the receiving machine that a frame is coming. At that point, the receiving machine prepares its memory buffers to accept the data.

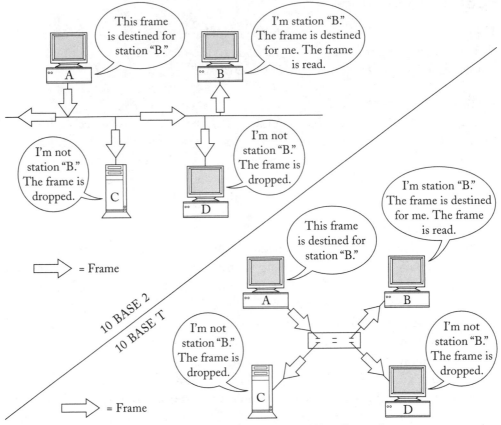

Figure 1.7 *Data flow in 10Base2 and 10BaseT networks*

Cyclic Redundancy Check

The CRC is a mathematical algorithm run through every frame processed by the data-link layer. The CRC is specific to the lower-layer protocol that is being used on the network. For example, if your network is using Ethernet frames, all NICs will be configured to read and write CRCs that will be understood by all Ethernet NICs in the network. Once the data-link layer receives a frame, it checks the CRC by running the exact mathematical algorithm that was run on the frame by the sending device. If the values of the two match, the frame is processed further. If the values do not match, the frame was either corrupt or not compatible with the receiving machine's lower layer protocol and will be discarded. A request for a new frame may be issued.

IEEE STANDARDS AND ANSI

Several organized groups monitor the standardization of networking technologies. The IEEE has had a large impact on data-link layer standards and is discussed next. ANSI also is discussed in this section of the book.

IEEE Standards

The Institute of Electrical and Electronics Engineers (IEEE) is a professional organization that sets forth standards within the computing field, the communications field, and many others. In February 1980, the IEEE laid forth Project 802. Several data-link layer standards were defined in this project:

802.1   Internetworking

802.2   Logical Link Control

802.3   Ethernet

802.4   Token Bus

802.5   Token Ring

802.6   Metropolitan Area Network (MAN)

802.7   Broadband Technical Advisory Group

802.8   Fiber Optic Technical Advisory Group

802.9   Integrated Voice and Data Networks

802.10 Network Security

802.11 Wireless Networks

802.12 Demand Priority LAN

 Test Tip: You should have the following memorized: 802.3 = Ethernet; 802.2 = LLC; 802.5 = Token Ring; 802.11 = Wireless.

ANSI Standards

ANSI (American National Standards Institute) is a professional group made up of volunteers dedicated to the development of communication standards. ANSI develops U.S. standards and represents the United States in international standards. ANSI is the American division of the ISO, which is the group that developed the OSI model.

1.6 NETWORK LAYER (LAYER 3)

The network layer of the OSI model defines processes to transmit data between independent networks by using and assigning logical addressing.

NETWORK LAYER PACKETS

The packets that the network layer creates to fulfill its communication responsibilities conform to one of two general types: data or discovery. A *data packet* contains information being sent from one user on a network to another user on a separate network (see Figure 1.8). These packets contain user information such as upper-layer application data. Examples include data related to a user's e-mail or file transfers.

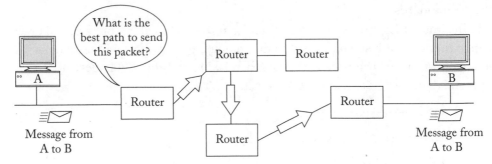

Figure 1.8 *Data packet traveling from network to network*

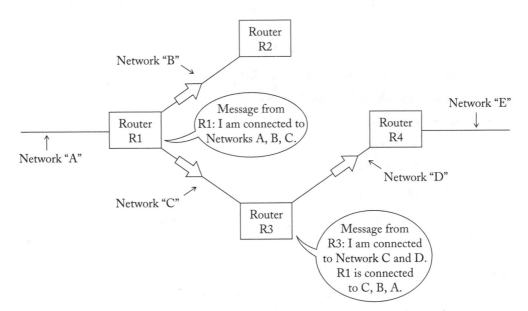

Figure 1.9 *Discovery packet stating what networks the sending router knows about*

The *discovery* or *update packet* is created by and sent to and from routers to gather and update information about what networks each router in the internetwork knows about and is connected to (see Figure 1.9). This information tells a router how to build its *routing table*. A routing table has entries for all known networks in an internetwork.

ROUTING TABLE

A routing table is created by the information exchanged between routers. When a router receives a packet that must be forwarded to another network, it examines its routing table to determine the best path to send the data. The best path is normally determined by the lowest cost route based on the *metric* of the entry in the routing table. The metric is determined by one or more variables: for example, the number of hops

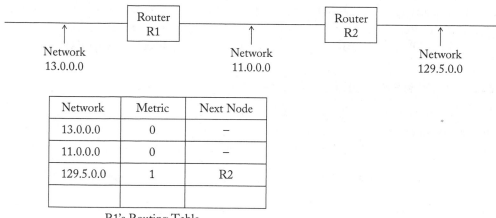

R1's Routing Table

Figure 1.10 *Multiple router configuration with routing tables*

it will take to get to the destination network (a *hop* is the process of traveling through a router), the line speed of the link, and the time it will take to travel over the link to the destination router.

Figure 1.10 shows a router that is directly connected to networks 11.0.0.0 and 13.0.0.0. They have hop counts of 0. To get to network 11.0.0.0, it will use the first serial interface in the router (Serial 0 or S0). The same router can send packets to network 129.5.0.0 through the same interface even though it is not a directly connected network. The packet, however, must be processed by another router that is directly connected to the 129.5.0.0 network. Network 129.5.0.0 is represented in the routing table as being one hop away (see Figure 1.10).

NETWORK ADDRESS

Routers send packets to their destination based on the best path available (lowest metric) in the routing table. To do this the router must know the packet's destination. The network layer provides this information through addressing. However, the addresses used here are considered logical addresses. A logical address is sometimes referred to as a network, protocol, hierarchical, or layer 3 address. Network addresses are assigned by an administrator and are not permanent. Therefore, the characteristics of a network address and a MAC address are different. A logical address can be changed by an administrator, whereas a MAC address cannot.

Logical addressing has two portions: one for the network ID and one for the host ID. The network layer is primarily concerned with the network ID portion of the address. That is why network addresses are recorded in routing tables. When the network layer of a user's PC is encapsulating the data sent from the transport layer, it adds the source and destination network IDs of the communicating hosts to the packet. When the packet gets to the router, the router examines the destination address and then compares it to its routing table to determine the best route to send the packet to its final destination.

1.7   TRANSPORT LAYER (LAYER 4)

The transport layer of the OSI model is primarily responsible for establishing end-to-end sessions between two stations. The logical connections (sessions) created between two nodes can use connection-oriented or connectionless communication methods.

CONNECTION-ORIENTED AND CONNECTIONLESS COMMUNICATION

Connection-oriented and connectionless communication can happen at several layers of the OSI model. The requirement for the CCNA Exam is to know how each works at the transport layer.

Connection-Oriented Communication

Connection-oriented communication is the process of using error-correction procedures to provide reliable, guaranteed delivery of segments between peer transport layers. A connection-oriented session goes through three phases: session establishment, data transfer, and session disconnect. The first phase, session establishment, occurs when a sending node requests to set up a communication session with another node in the network. After the session has been established by the two nodes, the second phase begins. During the data transfer phase, the nodes transmit data and use control mechanisms to ensure data are not lost and communication is successful. The final phase consists of the two nodes agreeing to disconnect the session.

Connection-oriented communication consists of the following:

- **Sequencing.** Sequencing of segments at the transport layer allows the segments to be placed back into the correct order when they get to the peer transport layer. It also allows for the retransmission of data if a segment is lost during the communication process.

- **Flow Control.** Flow control provides several functions to the nodes of a connection-oriented session. The three basic methods of flow control are:
  - *Buffering.* The process of allocating memory to hold data as they come into the device until they can be processed. Too much data can cause buffer overflow.
  - *Congestion avoidance.* A technique normally used when a buffer is being overflowed. The receiving device issues a source-quench packet to tell the sending device to send less data.
  - *Windowing.* The process in which the sending and receiving nodes agree on a specified number of segments that can be transmitted in each transmission throughout the connection-oriented session.

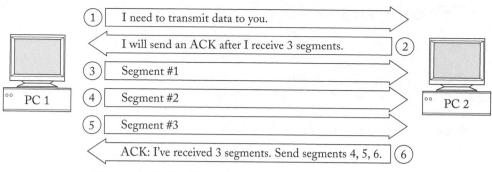

Figure 1.11 *Two PCs communicating with ACKs using windowing*

- **Acknowledgments (ACK).** An ACK is a portion of segment that confirms whether or not data have successfully made it to their destination (it is sent to the original source device by the original destination device). In a connection-oriented session, ACKs are sent confirming the receipt of every segment and are based on the sequence number of a segment. Because ACKs can consume a large part of a network's bandwidth, windowing is used to cut down on the amount of ACKs sent. The window is normally continued so several segments that can be received by the destination machine before it has to reply with an ACK. For example, if PC 1 and PC 2 agree on a window size of three segments, PC 1 would send PC 2 three segments before PC 2 would respond with one ACK (see Figure 1.11). If one of the three segments did not make it to PC 2, it would either request retransmission of that single segment or the entire window of segments.

Connectionless Communication

The primary difference between connection-oriented and connectionless communication is that *connectionless communication* does not establish a session before communication occurs. In connectionless communication, segments are sent to the destination machine with the hope that they make it there. This is a best-effort, nonguaranteed delivery method.

End users do not have the choice of using a connection-oriented or connectionless protocol. This choice is normally written into the code of the networked application being used. For example, if an end user is transferring files, the application would more often than not use a connection-oriented transport protocol and send ACKs confirming whether or not the segments arrived. On the other hand, if the user is streaming a video over the World Wide Web, it would be useless to use a connection-oriented protocol because the time sensitivity involved with video streaming would not accommodate the transmission of ACKs.

 Test Tip: Connection-oriented = Guaranteed, reliable delivery; Connectionless = Nonguaranteed, unreliable, best-effort delivery.

1.8 THE UPPER LAYERS (LAYERS 5, 6, AND 7)

The three upper layers transmit and receive data to the transport layer as one single stream of data. The data can contain error-correction information, specific formatting, and support for network applications. In this section, we take a look at each of the three upper layers, first the session layer, then the presentation layer, and finally the application layer.

SESSION LAYER (LAYER 5)

The session layer of the OSI model is responsible for establishing a session between two nodes. The session opened at this layer is available for communication that occurs between networked applications in addition to the session established at the transport layer. The session layer offers three types of communication modes:

- **Simplex.** Provides one-way communication. For example, a television operates in simplex communication mode.

- **Half-duplex.** Provides two-way communication; however, only one device can communicate at a time. For example, walkie-talkies operate in half-duplex mode.

- **Full-duplex.** Provides two-way communication, and both entities can transmit at the same time. For example, telephones operate in full-duplex mode.

PRESENTATION LAYER (LAYER 6)

The presentation layer of the OSI model is responsible for presenting the data to the receiving machine in a readable format. The presentation layer deals with how the data will be read when they get to the other machine. For example, some microprocessors read bits (1s and 0s) from left to right, whereas others read them from right to left.

The presentation layer provides translation services for these nodes, ensuring that the data are properly formatted for the application layer protocol. Also, data compression, decompression, encryption, and decryption take place in this layer.

APPLICATION LAYER (LAYER 7)

The application layer does not refer to applications such as word-processing programs or spreadsheet programs. It is primarily involved with services and interfaces that support applications that require network resources. Such services include, but are not limited to, file transfer services, send and receive message services, database services, printing services, and networked application services. For example, when a user is writing an e-mail message to another user, the process of writing the message in the application provided by a vendor is not part of the network transmission procedure. However, when the user clicks on the Send Message button, the message is handed to the application layer of the OSI model to process it.

Test Tip: Session layer = Host-to-host session; Presentation layer = Formatting data; Application layer = Network applications.

1.9 NETWORK COMPONENTS AND A LAYERED MODEL

The OSI model acts as a guide for developing network communication standards. As stated earlier, it guides vendors and manufacturers in the development of both hardware and software components that allow network communication to occur. Hardware components include, but are not limited to, hubs, layer 2 switches, bridges, and routers. Software components are made up of protocols that work at various layers of the model.

HARDWARE (CONNECTIVITY DEVICES)

Hardware devices map to specific layers of the OSI model based on their functionality. The CCNA Exam is geared toward the hardware components at the physical, data-link, and network layers.

Physical Layer

Many hardware components are mapped directly to one layer of the OSI model. However, a component can map to several layers in some instances. The hardware components that map to the physical layer are considered the least intelligent and consist of wire, wire connectors, hubs, repeaters, channel service units (CSUs)/digital service units (DSUs), and so on.

The *data terminal equipment (DTE)/data circuit equipment (DCE)* communication standard is defined at the physical layer. DTE and DCE are governed by the RS232c standard, stating that one component must send a signal and another must receive it. For example, Cisco routers are all DTE, or sending devices. The router itself is not mapped to the physical layer, but the serial interface (DTE) that is actually placing signals on a wire is. The receiving device, or DCE, is normally a CSU/DSU. The purpose of a CSU/DSU is to convert a LAN signal into a WAN signal and vice versa. The types of serial connectors (DTE/DCE interface standards) used between the router and CSU/DSU are listed in Table 1.1.

TABLE 1.1   PHYSICAL LAYER CONNECTION DEVICES

P	Hub
H	Repeater
Y	CSU/DSU
S	V. 24
I	X. 21
C	EIA/TIA 232/449
A	V. 35
L	HSSI

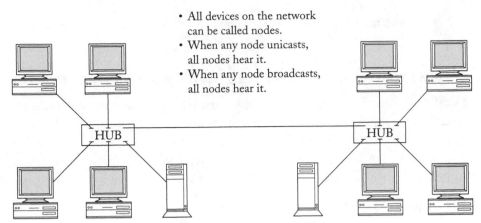

- All devices on the network can be called nodes.
- When any node unicasts, all nodes hear it.
- When any node broadcasts, all nodes hear it.

Figure 1.12 *Hub network with the same collision and broadcast domains*

Repeaters and *hubs* operate at the physical layer. Repeaters regenerate signals and retransmit them in an attempt to increase the distance of communication. Hubs act as central points for connecting multiple nodes on a network. They come in two types: passive and active. A *passive hub* can only perform the role of wire management. It does not have any repeating capabilities and does not need power. Throughout this book and the CCNA Exam, the word "hub" implies "active hub" unless otherwise stated. *Active hubs* need power to operate and perform the functions of a repeater. An active hub performs the role of a *multiport repeater*. When a hub hears a signal on one of its ports, it repeats that signal to every port (see Figure 1.12).

A hub operates in its own *collision domain* and *broadcast domain*. A collision domain is a segment of the network where all devices compete for access to the wire and all transmissions are forwarded to all cable segments of the network. In a broadcast domain, when one node on a segment broadcasts a signal, all nodes will receive it. Nodes of the same collision domain or the same broadcast domain use each other's MAC address to communicate. One broadcast domain can contain several collision domains, but one collision domain cannot span multiple broadcast domains.

Data-Link Layer

There are three hardware components at the data-link layer of the OSI model. First and foremost is the *network adapter board* or *network interface card (NIC)*. The NIC controls how data are placed on the wire and is directly related to the media access method discussed earlier. Therefore, the NIC operates at the data-link layer of the OSI model.

The next data-link layer device is the *bridge*. The bridge's main purpose is to physically divide an overpopulated network to free up bandwidth. Bridges create separate collision domains for each segment of wire that is attached to the bridge. However, they still operate under one broadcast domain. Bridges do not filter out broadcast messages. Broadcast messages are forwarded to all segments of the wire attached to the bridge.

Step 1   Node 1 sends message to Node 3.
Step 2   All nodes and bridge hear it.
Step 3   Bridge opens the frame and reads the source
          and destination address; forwards to Port B.
          Source = Node 1
          Destination = Node 3
Step 4   Bridge learns Node 1 is connected to Port A,
          and adds an entry to its bridge table.

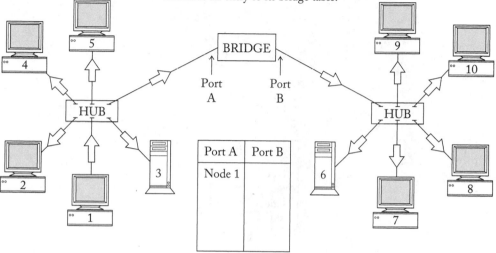

Port A	Port B
Node 1	

Bridge Table

Figure 1.13 *Node 1 sending data to node 3 in a bridged network*

 Test Tip: Bridges create multiple, smaller collision domains and are used for LAN segmentation.

Bridges operate at the data-link layer because they filter data based on MAC addresses. Bridges maintain a table sometimes called a MAC table, a forwarding table, or even a bridge table. This table records all addresses read in the source and destination portion of all frames that enter the bridge. When a bridge reads the source address of node 1 in a frame that came from segment A, it records the information and then forwards frames destined for node 1 to segment A (see Figure 1.13).

If the source MAC address and destination MAC address of a frame are both located on the same segment of the bridged network, the bridge will not forward the frame to the other segment (see Figure 1.14).

Switches generally work at layer 2 as well. Although there are switches that work at additional layers of the OSI model, the CCNA Exam focuses on layer 2 switches. Switches use a technology similar to bridges. They filter packets using the MAC addresses of nodes. They create multiple smaller collision domains but maintain one

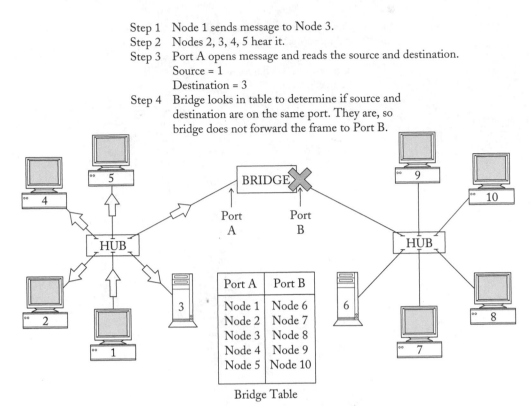

Step 1   Node 1 sends message to Node 3.

Step 2   Nodes 2, 3, 4, 5 hear it.

Step 3   Port A opens message and reads the source and destination.
           Source = 1
           Destination = 3

Step 4   Bridge looks in table to determine if source and
           destination are on the same port. They are, so
           bridge does not forward the frame to Port B.

Port A	Port B
Node 1	Node 6
Node 2	Node 7
Node 3	Node 8
Node 4	Node 9
Node 5	Node 10

Bridge Table

Figure 1.14 *Bridge restricting data flow by using the bridge table*

broadcast domain. Switches are a popular replacement for active hubs when trying to increase throughput in a network. Each switch interface (port) can be connected to a different node in the network. Collision domains are created at each switch interface. This reduces collisions dramatically between nodes connected to the switch. Nodes connected to the switch get the full amount of bandwidth allocated to them. Switches provide full-duplex media access. Both switches and bridges must use the same frame type on all segments connected.

Network Layer

At the network layer, there is one device to be aware of for the CCNA Exam: the router. Routers have the functionality available to segment networks, yet more accurately, routers connect separate independent networks, which, in turn, means they segment internetworks. Routers create separate broadcast domains because they do not forward broadcast messages by default. Because routers operate at the third layer of the OSI model, they are not concerned with the protocol used at the data-link layer. Therefore, they can connect dissimilar layer 2 frame types. When a packet arrives at a router, the router de-encapsulates the packet up to the network layer. It then re-encapsulates the packet and forwards it out of the destined interface. Routers can support multiple layer 2 interfaces. For example, one router can contain an Ethernet interface and a Token Ring interface. A packet can be received on the Ethernet interface and forwarded out of the Token Ring interface.

When a router receives a packet, it determines which network it should send the packet to next to get the packet one hop closer to its final destination. Each router the packet crosses can make its own intelligent decision about where to forward the packet next. All this functionality comes with a price, however. Routers are traditionally slower than bridges and switches due to the increased processor use associated with calculating the best path available.

SOFTWARE (PROTOCOLS)

Protocols can map directly to a single layer of the OSI model or they can combine the functionality of multiple layers. This allows for modularity of the *protocol suite* or *protocol stack,* which is a group of protocols that work together under the same set of rules to provide network connectivity. For example, to create a new transport layer protocol to be implemented in an existing protocol suite, a vendor does not have to design an entirely new protocol suite; instead, the vendor concentrates on determining how to get the new transport layer protocol to communicate with the network layer and the upper layers of the existing protocol suite.

See Table 1.2 to examine and compare protocols with their respective layers of the OSI model. At this point, an in-depth discussion of each protocol is not necessary.

TABLE 1.2 PROTOCOLS MAPPED TO THE OSI MODEL

A	SMTP SNMP DNS IMAP FTP TFTP POP HTTP	*Network Support Applications*
P	**Text:** ASCII EBCDIC HTML **Sound:** MIDI MPEG WAV **Graphic:** JPEG GIF TIFF **Video:** AVI QuickTime	*Presentation Standards*
S	NFS SQL RPC X Windows	*Session Services*
T	TCP UDP SPX	*Transport Protocols*
N	IP IPX ICMP ARP RARP	*Addressing and Routed Protocols*
D	ATM Frame Relay ISDN PPP SLIP Ethernet Token Ring ArcNet FDDI 802.3, 802.5	*Lower Layer and Routing Protocols*
P		

Test Tip: Be prepared to know what layer of the OSI model the pictorials in Table 1.2 are associated with.

CHAPTER SUMMARY

This chapter covered the seven layers of the OSI model and Cisco's three-layered hierarchical model. It also examined why the industry uses a layered model. Many of the topics covered here were directly related to the OSI model such as the functions of each layer, the hardware devices that map to each layer, and protocol standards for each layer. The chapter covered physical addressing and introduced logical addressing. Complete the knowledge test before going on to the next chapter.

KNOWLEDGE TEST

Choose one answer for all questions unless directed to do otherwise.

1. Name the five steps of encapsulation in the correct order.
    a. Data, frame, segment, bits, packets
    b. Bits, frame, packet, segment, data
    c. Frame, bits, packet, segment, data
    d. Data, segment, packet, frame, bits

2. De-encapsulation is the process of:
    a. Adding control information to a PDU
    b. Stripping control information off a PDU
    c. Forwarding a frame to the appropriate network
    d. Running a mathematical algorithm through a segment

3. Choose the correct services provided by the session layer.
    a. NFS, RPC, X Windows
    b. SQL, DNA, DOC
    c. X Windows, NFS, TIFF
    d. Session establishment, CRC, DDNS

4. What is the network layer of the OSI model responsible for?
    a. Routing packets
    b. Encapsulating frames
    c. Physical addressing
    d. Session establishment

5. Flow control, acknowledgments, and windowing occur at what layer of the OSI model?
    a. Session
    b. Transport

   c. Data-link
   d. Network
   e. Presentation

6. The session layer of the OSI model is responsible for which of the following? (Choose all that apply.)
   a. Adding sequence numbers to segments
   b. Formatting data for application layer protocols
   c. Placing checkpoints in the data stream for error correction
   d. Establishing virtual circuits between two nodes
   e. Establishing and terminating sessions between applications

7. A connection-oriented session has which of the following characteristics? (Choose all that apply.)
   a. It takes place at the session layer.
   b. It takes place at the transport layer.
   c. Frames are sequenced and put back in order at the destination PC.
   d. Segments are sequenced and put back in order at the destination PC.
   e. Multiple acknowledgments are sent for one segment.

8. The physical address is the address associated with the network cable.
   a. True
   b. False

9. What are bridges used for? (Choose all that apply.)
   a. To break up the broadcast domain
   b. To create multiple smaller collision domains.
   c. To connect a Token Ring and an Ethernet network.
   d. To segment a network.

10. Repeaters break up the collision domain.
   a. True
   b. False

11. A SAP or SNAP is:
   a. Defined at the MAC layer of the data-link layer
   b. What defines how data are transmitted onto the wire
   c. What defines how data travel to upper-layer protocols
   d. A control mechanism that sends an acknowledgment for every segment that is received

12. The "base" in 10BaseT stands for:
   a. 10 Mbps
   b. Ethernet transfer
   c. Bandbase transmission
   d. Baseband transmission

13. Full-duplex transmission is described as:
   a. Sending or receiving transmissions only
   b. Sending and receiving transmissions in one direction at a time
   c. Sending and receiving transmissions in both directions at the same time

knowledge TEST

14. What are characteristics of a switch? (Choose all that apply.)
    a. Decreasing collisions on a network
    b. Adding broadcast domains to a network
    c. Half-duplex transmission only
    d. Switching frames based on MAC addresses

15. A physical network topology in which all nodes connect to a central device is:
    a. Bus
    b. Star
    c. Ring
    d. Mesh

16. What are the three general types of access methods?
    a. Bus, mesh, polling
    b. Polling, contention, token passing
    c. Contention, bus, polling
    d. Contention, token passing, ring

17. What network devices operate at the data-link layer of the OSI model?
    a. NIC, bridge, router
    b. Switch, bridge, router
    c. Switch, NIC, CSU/DSU
    d. Router, CSU/DSU, switch
    e. NIC, bridge, switch

18. Select the appropriate IEEE standards and the network standard they map to. (Choose all that apply.)
    a. 802.3 = Token Ring
    b. 802.3 = Ethernet
    c. 802.3 = Arcnet
    d. 802.5 = Token Ring
    e. 802.5 = Ethernet
    f. 802.5 = Arcnet

19. Which of the following are presentation layer standards? (Choose all that apply.)
    a. LW1
    b. JPEG
    c. DOC
    d. TIFF
    e. PICT
    f. EBCDIC to ASCII
    g. MIDI
    h. MPEG
    i. EXE

20. What are the characteristics of a physical address? (Choose all that apply.)
    a. It is 48 bits long represented by 48 binary digits.
    b. It is 48 bits long represented by 12 hexadecimal digits.
    c. The number is assigned by the board manufacturer.
    d. The number is assigned by the IEEE.
    e. The number is assigned by a combination of the IEEE and the manufacturer.

knowledge TEST

CHAPTER 2

Transmission Control Protocol/ Internet Protocol (TCP/IP)

OBJECTIVES

The following topics are discussed in Chapter 2:

- Design an IP addressing scheme to meet design requirements.
- Configure IP addresses, subnet masks, and gateway addresses on routers and hosts.
- Implement a LAN.
- Troubleshoot IP addressing and host configuration.
- Troubleshoot a device as part of a working network.
- Evaluate the TCP/IP communication process and its associated protocols.

INTRODUCTION

Transmission Control Protocol/Internet Protocol (TCP/IP) is the most popular protocol suite or protocol stack in the world. It is the universal language of the Internet. A *protocol* is a set of rules or instructions that work together to ensure that communication between multiple computers can take place. A protocol *suite* or protocol *stack* is a group of protocols that operate together. Protocol suites are normally mapped to the OSI model. The layers of the TCP/IP suite generally, not directly, correspond to the layers of the OSI model (Figure 2.1). The protocols of the TCP/IP suite as well as some of its features are discussed in this chapter.

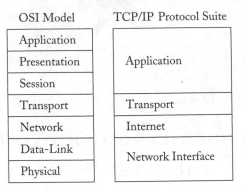

Figure 2.1 *TCP/IP suite mapped to the OSI model*

2.1 A BRIEF HISTORY OF TCP/IP

The roots of the TCP/IP suite actually go further back than the seven-layered OSI model used today.

THE DEPARTMENT OF DEFENSE (DOD) PROTOCOL SUITE

In the 1970s, the Defense Advanced Research Projects Agency (DARPA) had a set of protocols created to forward data in a packet-switched network. The protocol had four layers (Figure 2.2). The Department of Defense (DOD) protocol suite evolved into the TCP/IP suite used today.

 Test Tip: It may be helpful to use an acronym to remember the four layers of the DOD model.
PHIN
P = Process/Application, H = Host-to-Host, I = Internet, N = Network

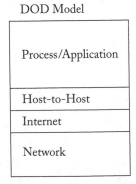

Figure 2.2 *DOD reference model*

2.2 THE TCP/IP MODEL AND THE OSI MODEL

The **TCP/IP model** consists of *four layers*. It can be mapped to the OSI model as seen next (Figure 2.3).

 Test Tip: It may be helpful to use an acronym to remember the four layers of the TCP/IP model.
ATIN
A = Application, T = Transport, I = Internet, N = Network Interface

NETWORK INTERFACE LAYER

The *network interface layer* of the TCP/IP model is closely related to the two lower layers of the OSI model. The standards that are covered in the network interface layer include wiring standards such as 10BaseT, 10Base2, and so on. Protocols that map the first layer of the TCP/IP suite include Ethernet (IEEE 802.3), Token Ring (IEEE 802.5), and all other data-link layer standards. The MAC and LLC sublayers of the OSI model are also included in the network interface layer.

INTERNET LAYER

The *internet layer* maps to layer 3 of the OSI model, the network layer, where routing and network addressing occur. Several protocols reside at this layer in the TCP/IP model. Some of these are the *Internet Protocol (IP)*, the *Internet Control Message Protocol (ICMP)*, the *Address Resolution Protocol (ARP)*, and the *Reverse Address Resolution Protocol (RARP)*.

Internet Protocol (IP)

IP deals with the delivery (and routing) of packets. It is a connectionless, unreliable protocol that gets its error correction from upper layer protocols. The IP header

OSI Model	TCP/IP Protocol Suite	DOD Model
Application	Application	Process/Application
Presentation		
Session		
Transport	Transport	Host-to-Host
Network	Internet	Internet
Data-Link	Network Interface	Network
Physical		

Figure 2.3 *TCP/IP suite mapped to the OSI model and DOD model*

contains the destination and source addresses of a packet. IP uses a hierarchical addressing scheme rather than a flat addressing scheme, which is used for physical (MAC) addressing. Hierarchical addressing consists of a logical grouping of addresses that share a commonality: all nodes using IP addresses on the same network share the same network number but have different node numbers. With a flat addressing scheme, every address is different with no relation to each other.

Internet Control Message Protocol (ICMP)

ICMP sends error and control messages between networked devices. The protocol sends several types of messages. Five of the most popular are

- **Echo request.** Message requesting ICMP at a receiving node to send a reply to test connectivity.

- **Echo reply.** Reply to an echo request.

- **Destination unreachable.** Message sent stating that a router is unable to deliver a packet.

- **Time exceeded.** Message sent stating that a specific packet has exceeded its hop limit.

- **Source quench.** A receiving node will send an ICMP message to a node that is sending data too fast for its memory buffers and processor to handle (a form of flow control).

ICMP sends the replies when using the *PING* command, which tests a network connection, and the *TRACE* command, which follows the path of a packet to determine if all routers in the path are operational.

Address Resolution Protocol (ARP)

ARP performs address resolution so nodes can successfully communicate in a TCP/IP network. For example, when two nodes communicate, they are using the physical addresses of one another to send data back and forth. However, when TCP/IP is implemented in a network, the nodes prefer to use IP addresses to communicate. ARP allows nodes to use IP addresses to communicate by resolving an IP address into a MAC address. When node 1 attempts to contact node 2, in most cases, node 1 sends an ARP request to determine the MAC address of node 2. Node 2 responds with its MAC address, allowing them to continue communicating (Figure 2.4).

Reverse Address Resolution Protocol (RARP)

RARP operates similar to ARP; however, it is the reverse process. RARP allows for MAC-to-IP address resolution. It is possible to use diskless workstations with a

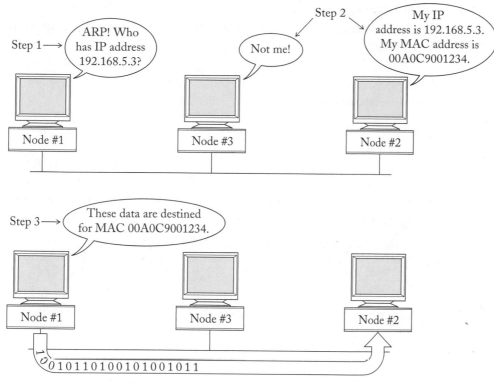

Figure 2.4 *Nodes sending ARP messages and data*

RARP server. When a diskless workstation boots up, the only address it knows is its MAC address. During the boot process, it sends a RARP request to receive an IP address. After it receives its IP address, the workstation can then request an operating system from the RARP server. The dynamic host configuration protocol (DHCP) and the bootstrap protocol (BOOTP) are similar to RARP.

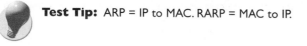 **Test Tip:** ARP = IP to MAC. RARP = MAC to IP.

TRANSPORT LAYER

The *transport layer* of the TCP/IP model maps directly to the transport layer of the OSI model. It does, however, contain some session layer functionality. It consists of two protocols: one offering connection-oriented communication and another offering connectionless communication. The connection-oriented protocol is TCP. The connectionless protocol is the *User Datagram Protocol (UDP)*.

Transmission Control Protocol (TCP)

TCP meets the connection-oriented standards of the transport layer because it provides several features:

- Sequencing
- Acknowledgments
- Windowing
- Flow control

TCP uses a *three-way handshake* to establish a session. The three-way handshake consists of a series of segments sent as session requests and acknowledgments between nodes. It is used to determine whether or not a session can be established. If so, a session between the nodes called a *virtual circuit* is established. For example, when PC A wants to establish a session with file server 1, it sends one segment requesting a session; this is the first handshake. File server 1 responds with an acknowledgment to the first handshake and requests to establish a session with PC A. PC A then sends an acknowledgment back to file server 1 confirming that it received the last segment and that a session has been established (Figure 2.5).

User Datagram Protocol (UDP)

UDP is a connectionless protocol that operates at the transport layer. It does not offer sequencing, acknowledgments, windowing, flow control, or the three-way handshake. Because UDP does not offer any of these features, it adds much less header information, reducing the overhead on the network's bandwidth. UDP is used for application layer protocols that do not require a connection-oriented transport. Application layer protocols that do not require a connection-oriented transport normally have error-correction mechanisms built into the protocol.

 Test Tip: TCP = connection-oriented, guaranteed delivery; UDP = connectionless, nonguaranteed delivery

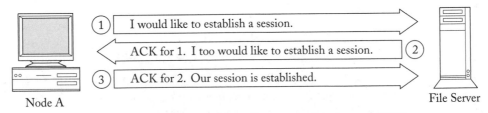

Figure 2.5 *Three-way handshake between two nodes using TCP/IP*

SOCKETS AND PORTS

When two nodes using TCP/IP communicate, there must be a means for the sending node's transport protocol to tell the receiving node's transport protocol where to deliver the application layer data. TCP/IP uses a socket to create the connection and a port to deliver the application layer data.

Sockets

A *socket* is a combination of the destination node's IP address, transport protocol (TCP or UDP), and port number. A socket is equivalent to a virtual pipe, which is established to give the sending node the capability to send data reliably.

Ports

A *port* represents the address assigned to the application layer protocol, in the TCP/IP suite, that is ultimately responsible for receiving data. When a node receives data, they must travel up the protocol stack. The data receive directions from the LLC of the data-link layer on how to go up the stack. Once the data make it as high as the transport layer, however, the transport protocol must know which application layer protocol to give the data to. Both TCP and UDP use port numbers to determine the application layer protocol that the data are destined for. Ports are represented by a value between 0 and 65534. This information is placed in the header of the TCP or UDP segment during encapsulation and must be read during de-encapsulation.

Although there are tens of thousands of ports, only 0 to 1023 are used on a regular basis. These port numbers are considered well-known port numbers. Ports 1024 and above are either randomly assigned ports or privately registered ports (for vendor-specific applications). Table 2.1 lists popular well-known ports and the respective application layer protocols that use them.

 Test Tip: Well-known Ports: 0 to 1023; Random/Dynamic Ports: 1024-65534

In some cases, port numbers are shared by both TCP and UDP. However, in most implementations, the application layer protocol only uses a TCP or UDP port. TCP and UDP are also given port numbers, considered protocol numbers. TCP uses port 6 and UDP uses port 17. These ports are used to identify the destination of the data coming from the internet layer in an IP packet going to the transport layer.

 Test Tip: TCP Port = 6; UDP Port = 17.

TABLE 2.1   PORT NUMBERS FOR POPULAR APPLICATION LAYER PROTOCOLS

Protocol		TCP Port	UDP Port
FTP	Program	20	
	Data	21	
Telnet		23	
SMTP		25	
DNS		53	53
TFTP			69
SNMP			161
RIP			520

APPLICATION LAYER

The *application layer* of the TCP/IP model is the equivalent to the application, presentation, and session layers of the OSI model. This means that all protocols developed at the application layer of the TCP/IP model have presentation and session layer codes written into them. Application layer protocols are assigned port numbers. There are several application layer protocols to be aware of for the CCNA Exam.

- **File Transfer Protocol (FTP).** Transfers files between two nodes. TCP port 20 and TCP port 21.

- **Telnet.** Terminal emulation used to configure routers. TCP port 23.

- **Simple Message Transport Protocol (SMTP).** E-mail sending protocol. TCP port 25.

- **Trivial File Transfer Protocol (TFTP).** A smaller version of FTP used to transfer router configurations. UDP port 69.

- **Domain Name System (DNS).** Provides domain name resolution. TCP port 53 for zone transfers; UDP port 53 for name resolution.

- **Dynamic Host Configuration Protocol (DHCP).** Provides automatic and dynamic IP address assignments to nodes on a network. UDP port 67.

- **Simple Network Management Protocol (SNMP).** Monitors network components. UDP port 161.

 Test Tip: The CCNA Exam may ask you questions related to the OSI model or the TCP/IP model in reference to where protocols belong in the suite. Be aware of the wording of the questions and which model is being referred to before answering the questions.

2.3   IP ADDRESSING

In the TCP/IP suite, addressing occurs at two levels: the network interface layer, which deals with physical (MAC) addressing, and the internet layer, which deals with logical (hierarchical) addressing. IP is responsible for addressing networks and hosts.

BINARY TO DECIMAL CONVERSION

An IP address is 32 bits long divided into 4 octets in a dotted decimal notation. For example, 192.19.43.29 is an IP address that has 4 octets each separated by a dot. The word *octet* means a group of eight. In this context it is referring to 8 bits, also known as a byte. Although the IP address is 192.19.43.29, when a computer processes the number, it reads:

11000000.00010011.00101011.00011101

This is because computers only know two states: electrical voltage ON and electrical voltage OFF. The ON state is equivalent to a 1 or an electrical signal that is there. The OFF state is equivalent to a 0 or an electrical signal that is not there. To further understand what a computer sees when an address is typed in with the decimal notation, a discussion on binary to decimal conversions is necessary.

The decimal numbering system has 10 possible digits to choose from—0, 1, 2, 3, 4, 5, 6, 7, 8, 9—and is known as base 10. The binary numbering system has two—1 and 0—and is known as base 2. For example, the decimal numbers **9 7 3** represent a total value of 973 when grouped together. It is easy to figure this out because placeholders are assumed for each digit. For example, in the ones column there is a 3, so it has a value of 3; in the tens column there is a 7, so it has a value of 70; and in the hundreds column there is a 9, therefore representing 900. When added together from left to right, a value of 973 is reached. The placeholders are part of the base 10 system, so each placeholder has a value equivalent to 10 times (10×) the holder before it. For example, start with the 1s column × 10 = 10; the 10s column × 10 = 100; the 100s column × 10 = 1,000; the 1000s column × 10 = 10,000, and so on. See the following example:

etc. | 1,000,000s | 100,000s | 10,000s | 1,000s | 100s | 10s | 1s

9 | 7 | 3

The number in the example is 973. If the numbers 9, 7, and 3 are placed under the chart beginning with the 3 in the ones column, the 7 in the 10s column, and the 9 in the 100s column, the value is 900 + 70 + 3 = 973.

As stated, binary is a base 2 system and works in a similar fashion. However, all the placeholders are powers of 2 rather than 10. For example, $1 \times 2 = 2$; $2 \times 2 = 4$; $4 \times 2 = 8$; $8 \times 2 = 16$; and so on. IP addressing uses octets so the number of bits in a single octet cannot exceed 8. See the following:

etc. | 128s | 64s | 32s | 16s | 8s | 4s | 2s | 1s

If the number 11001010 needed to be converted into decimal, it could be placed into its respective placeholders: where there is a one (1), add it; and where there is a zero (0), ignore it. See the following:

128 | 64 | 32 | 16 | 8 | 4 | 2 | 1

1 | 1 | 0 | 0 | 1 | 0 | 1 | 0

128 + 64 + 0 + 0 + 8 + 0 + 2 + 0 = 202

The highest value possible in an octet is 255, and this is a combination of all binary 1s as shown in the following example:

128 | 64 | 32 | 16 | 8 | 4 | 2 | 1

1 | 1 | 1 | 1 | 1 | 1 | 1 | 1

128 + 64 + 32 + 16 + 8 + 4 + 2 + 1 = 255

There are, however, 256 possible combinations within an octet. The 256th combination is all 0s. Because the highest decimal value is 255, each octet can only have a value between 0 and 255.

DECIMAL TO BINARY CONVERSION

To convert a decimal number to binary, simply divide the decimal number by the values of the base 2 placeholders, starting with 128 and working down to 1. If the decimal number can be divided by the base 2 placeholder, that placeholder gets a value of 1; if not, it gets a value of 0. See the following example to convert the number 233 into binary.

128 | 64 | 32 | 16 | 8 | 4 | 2 | 1

233 divided by 128 = 1 with a remainder of 105

105 divided by 64 = 1 with a remainder of 41

41 divided by 32 = 1 with a remainder of 9

9 divided by 16 = 0 with a remainder of 9

9 divided by 8 = 1 with a remainder of 1

1 divided by 4 = 0 with a remainder of 1

1 divided by 2 = 0 with a remainder of 1

1 divided by 1 = 1 with a remainder of 0

$$128 \mid 64 \mid 32 \mid 16 \mid 8 \mid 4 \mid 2 \mid 1$$
$$233 = 1 \mid 1 \mid 1 \mid 0 \mid 1 \mid 0 \mid 0 \mid 1$$

IP ADDRESS CLASSES

There are five IP address classes: class A, class B, class C, class D, and class E. The address classes are based on the value of the first octet (Table 2.2). In IP addressing, class A addresses use the first octet for networks and the last three octets for hosts. Class B addresses use the first two octets for networks and two octets for hosts. Class C addresses use three octets for networks and the last octet for hosts. This is considered classful addressing. It is a good place to start learning about IP addresses, but is no longer the rule. Many private networks still follow these rules, however, due to its simplicity. Refer to Table 2.2 to see possible combinations and total networks and hosts available for each class of addresses.

NETWORKS AND HOSTS

IP addresses are divided into two parts: the network and the host. The network and host method of addressing can be compared with the addressing of a street with houses

TABLE 2.2   IP ADDRESS CLASSES

Class	First Octet	Network #s	Networks Available	Hosts per Network
A	1–127	1–126.0.0.0	126	16,777,214
B	128–191	128–191.1–254.0.0	16,384	65,534
C	192–223	192–223.1–255.1–254.0	2,097,152	254
D	224–239	NA	NA	NA
E	240–255	NA	NA	NA

Address Structure		First Octet in Binary
*Class A	NNN.HHH.HHH.HHH	00000001†
Class B	NNN.NNN.HHH.HHH	10000000
Class C	NNN.NNN.NNN.HHH	11000000

*NNN = Network portion of address

HHH = Host portion of address

†Underlined bits in the first octet will always be set to the value shown

NA = Not applicable

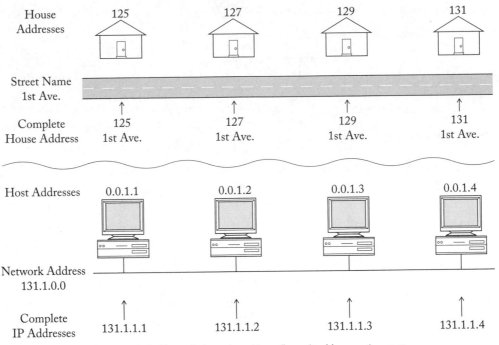

Figure 2.6 *Network (street) and host (house) address assignment*

on it. The network address is equivalent to the street name and the host addresses are equivalent to the houses on the street (Figure 2.6).

Although a node normally has a MAC address assigned to it already, IP has to assign an address to it as well. During communication, the IP node address is then resolved down to the MAC address using the ARP. All nodes on the same network must have the same address in the network portion of the IP address. Each host portion of the IP address must be unique on that network.

A limited amount of IP addresses are allocated for networks and a limited number of hosts can be on those networks based on what address class the network falls into. A network address of 15.0.0.0 is a class A address. A class A address can have 16,777,214 hosts. This is because three octets are dedicated to hosts. Because each octet has 8 binary digits within it, 24 binary bits are available for hosts. 2 to the 24th power equals 16,777,216 minus 2 for all 1s and all 0s, and the total amount of hosts available is 16,777,214 (all 1s and all 0s are illegal addresses, which is explained in the Special IP Addresses section). So in this example more than 16 million hosts are available. See possible hosts in Table 2.3.

Subnet Masks

When an IP address is assigned to a node, the node only reads a series of 32 bits. It has no way to distinguish between the host and network portions of the address

TABLE 2.3   EXAMPLES OF HOST ADDRESSES FOR THE 15.0.0.0 NETWORK

15.0.0.1–15.0.0.254
15.0.1.0–15.0.255.254
15.1.0.0–15.255.255.254

without an additional entry. The *subnet mask* is the entry responsible for telling the computer which part of the IP address is allocated for networks and which part is allocated for hosts. The subnet mask must be assigned to the node at the same time that the IP address is assigned. The subnet mask is a series of 1s starting from left to right with no breaks in it.

In classful addressing, each IP address class has a default subnet mask. Because we only use class A, class B, and class C for IP address assignment, that is what we will concentrate on. The default subnet mask for a class A network is 255.0.0.0. This subnet mask uses 8 bits and looks like this in binary:

11111111.00000000.00000000.00000000

The class B default subnet mask is 255.255.0.0 and looks like this in binary:

1111111.11111111.00000000.00000000

The class C default subnet mask is 255.255.255.0 and in binary is represented as:

11111111.11111111.11111111.00000000

When assigning an IP address and a subnet mask, it is easy to look at it all in binary to determine which portion of the address is assigned for the network and which portion is assigned for hosts. For example, the decimal IP address assignment and subnet mask would look like this:

> IP address   163.100.1.50
> Subnet mask   255.255.0.0

In binary, it looks like this:

> IP address   10100011.01100100.00000001.00110010
> Subnet mask   11111111.11111111.00000000.00000000

In the binary example, it is clear to see that where the 1s stop in the subnet mask, the hosts begin in the IP address. In the preceding example, 16 bits are used in the subnet mask. Cisco represents the subnet mask and the IP address in one statement like this:

> IP address and subnet mask   163.100.1.50/16

The "/16" means 16 bits are used, counting from left to right, forming the subnet mask. So if all bits were on (set to 1) in both octets, that would give a subnet mask of 255.255.0.0 because the highest value you can have in each octet is 255.

Special IP Addresses

Class D addresses are preassigned multicast addresses. A *multicast* is when a group of nodes are sent data but not the entire network. Class E addresses are used for experimental purposes and should not be a concern when addressing a network. There are more special addresses in addition to the class D and E addresses. For example, 127.0.0.1 is considered the loopback address and is used in conjunction with the *PING* command. *PING* tests the TCP/IP connection between two nodes using ICMP. If you *PING* the address 127.0.0.1, it will self-test the node's TCP/IP configuration that the *PING* command was generated from.

Another special address is 255.255.255.255. This is an "all networks broadcast" address that sends data to all nodes on all networks. There also is a "directed broadcast," which consists of all 1s in the host portion (for example, 15.255.255.255). By default, routers filter all networks broadcasts, but will forward directed broadcasts. All bits ON or OFF in either the network or host portion of an IP address are not used to address a node. There also are three private networks to be aware of. Packets containing private network addresses are filtered by routers on the public Internet. However, private IP addresses can be used by companies that plan on using IP on their private network without registering their IP address with the Internet authorities. These special addresses and others are identified in Table 2.4.

TABLE 2.4   SPECIAL IP ADDRESSES

Class D	223–239
Class E	240–255
All Networks Broadcast	255.255.255.255
Directed Broadcast	131.1.255.255 (example)
Default Route	0.0.0.0
Loopback Address	127.0.0.0
This Network Only	131.1.0.0 (example)
Private Network	10.0.0.0
Private Network	172.16–31.0.0
Private Network	192.168.1–255.0

All binary 1s or 0s in the host portion of the address are illegal.
All binary 1s or 0s in the network portion of the address are illegal.

2.4 IP SUBNETTING

There are two ways to prepare for the subnetting questions on the CCNA Exam: Memorize a lot of different numbers or *learn* how to subnet. This section focuses on learning how to subnet and includes a few tables to remember. However, memorization is not the goal.

One of the drawbacks of classful IP addressing is that when one company is given a class A address, the company has one network address with more than 16 million hosts, which is very wasteful. If a company got a class B address, it would have one network available with more than 65,000 hosts. Because of the Internet's growth in popularity thus depleting IP addresses, the Internet authorities began conserving addresses. One means of conserving addresses is to use a Variable Length Subnet Mask (VLSM), which allows you to subnet one network address into several network addresses by manipulating the subnet mask. Another method of conserving IP addresses is by Classless Inter Domain Routing (CIDR). The rules that apply to classful addressing do not apply to CIDR.

Here is an example of how a class B address could be manipulated to have several networks with less than 65,000 hosts per network. Company X applies for and receives a class B address. It is given the following address:

150.16.0.0/16

The network administrator realizes that the company needs five networks, but the Internet authority turns down the request for four more network addresses. Company X must now generate five networks out of the single address it was issued. The company can do this by using the third octet as a network octet rather than a host octet. If Company X uses all 8 bits of the third octet for networks rather than hosts, its subnet mask would become 255.255.255.0. In binary, the IP address and the subnet mask would look like this:

IP address   10010110.00010000.00000000.00000000

Subnet mask   11111111.11111111.11111111.00000000

Remember, where the 1s stop in a subnet mask, the hosts begin in the IP address. Therefore, the fourth octet in the IP address is reserved for hosts. Based on this subnet mask, the network administrator for Company X will have 254 legal network combinations with a possible 254 hosts on each network. The address is represented as 150.16.0.0/24. Table 2.5 shows examples of the network and host address combinations available to Company X.

In IP address subnetting, it is possible to borrow half of an octet or only a couple of bits. If Company X only needs five additional networks, it is not necessary to use all 8 bits of the third octet for networks. For example, what would happen if

TABLE 2.5   COMPANY X'S NETWORK AND HOST COMBINATIONS

Networks	Hosts
150.16.1.0	150.16.1.1 – 150.16.1.254
150.16.2.0	150.16.2.1 – 150.16.2.254
150.16.3.0	150.16.3.1 – 150.16.3.254
150.16.4.0	150.16.4.1 – 150.16.4.254
150.16.5.0	150.16.5.1 – 150.16.5.254
150.16.6.0	150.16.6.1 – 150.16.6.254
150.16.7.0	150.16.7.1 – 150.16.7.254
150.16.8.0	150.16.8.1 – 150.16.8.254
150.16.9.0	150.16.9.1 – 150.16.9.254
150.16.10.0	150.16.10.1 – 150.16.10.254

Networks will increase by 1 up to 254. 255 is an illegal network address.

Hosts will increase from 1 to 254 on each network. 255 is an illegal host address.

Subnet 150.16.1.0 and Hosts in Binary

Network ID	Subnet	Hosts	
10010110.00010000	.00000001	.00000001	
10010110.00010000	.00000001	.00000010	
10010110.00010000	.00000001	.00000011	
11111111.11111111	.11111111	.00000000	**Subnet Mask**

Company X required more than 254 hosts on each of the five networks? Using subnetting can make both of those requests possible. Refer to Tables 2.6 and 2.7 throughout the example.

In the example, if Company X needs five networks, you can determine the subnet mask in several ways. First, take the number of networks needed (5) and round up to the next higher number in the Number of Networks column (see Table 2.6). Follow the column up to the Subnet Mask row to find the value that must be placed in Company X's third subnet mask octet. The subnet mask that will allow Company X to have at least five networks is 255.255.224.0. After the subnet mask is determined, the networks will be numbered beginning with the number 32 because this is the low-end bit in the subnet mask. The networks will increase by 32 for a total of six legal networks (Table 2.8).

Subnetting using Table 2.6 works well but is not ideal for every situation. The next method is more accurate and consists of less steps. Company X still needs five networks. To determine what the subnet mask will be, refer to Table 2.7 to find which power of 2 number, minus 2 will get five networks. Remember, all 1s and all 0s are not valid network addresses so it is important to subtract 2 from the value. Therefore, 2^3 will

TABLE 2.6   BINARY CONVERSION CHART WITH SUBNET MASKS AND NUMBER OF NETWORKS

Binary to Decimal Conversion	128	64	32	16	8	4	2	1
Subnet Mask	128	192	224	240	248	252	254	255
Number of Networks Needed	NA	2	6	14	30	62	126	254
Possible Combinations of 1s and 0s	2	4	8	16	32	64	128	256

NA = Not applicable

TABLE 2.7   POWERS OF 2 CHART −2 FOR SPECIAL ADDRESSES

2^0 = 1	2^8 = 256
2^1 = 2	2^9 = 512
2^2 = 4	2^{10} = 1,024
2^3 = 8	2^{11} = 2,048
2^4 = 16	2^{12} = 4,096
2^5 = 32	2^{13} = 8,192
2^6 = 64	2^{14} = 16,384
2^7 = 128	2^{15} = 32,768
	2^{16} = 65,536

−2 from total for special addresses

TABLE 2.8   EXAMPLE OF COMPANY X'S NETWORKS IN BINARY AND DECIMAL

	Networks in Decimal	*Networks in Binary*
	150.16.32.0	10010010.00010000.00**1**00000.00000000
	150.16.64.0	10010010.00010000.0**1**000000.00000000
	150.16.96.0	10010010.00010000.0**11**00000.00000000
	150.16.128.0	10010010.00010000.**1**0000000.00000000
	150.16.160.0	10010010.00010000.**1**0**1**00000.00000000
	150.16.192.0	10010010.00010000.**11**000000.00000000
Subnet Mask	255.255.224.0	11111111.11111111.**111**0000.00000000

224 is an illegal network address because it contains all 1s and will be considered a broadcast. All network IDs fall within the same 3 bits of the third octet in the subnet mask.

TABLE 2.9   COMPANY X'S NETWORK AND HOST IDS

Networks in Decimal	Hosts in Decimal
150.16.32.0	150.16.32.1 − 150.16.63.254
150.16.64.0	150.16.64.1 − 150.16.95.254
150.16.96.0	150.16.96.1 − 150.16.127.254
150.16.128.0	150.16.128.1 − 150.16.159.254
150.16.160.0	150.16.160.1 − 150.16.191.254
150.16.192.0	150.16.192.1 − 150.16.223.254

Examination of the 32 Subnet

Networks and Hosts for the 32 Subnet

	Networks	Hosts			
Example 1 In this example, each host ID is in a different octet than the network ID.	10010010.00010000.001	00000.00000001			
	150.16.32	.1			
	10010010.00010000.001	00000.00000010			
	150.16.32	.2			
	10010010.00010000.001	00000.00000011			
	150.16.32	.3			
	10010010.00010000.001	00000.00000100			
	150.16.32	.4			
	10010010.00010000.001	00000.00000101			
	150.16.32	.5			
	10010010.00010000.001	00000.00000110			
	150.16.32	.6			

	Networks	Hosts			
Example 2 In this example, the networks and hosts are in the same octet. The network ID is 32. The host ID is added to the network ID to give a decimal number higher than 32 because they share the same octet. In binary, you can clearly see the distinction between the network and host IDs.	10010010.00010000.001	00001.00000001			
	150.16.32	+	1.1	=	150.16.33.1
	10010010.00010000.001	00001.00000010			
	150.16.32	+	1.2	=	150.16.33.2
	10010010.00010000.001	**11110.11111110**			
	150.16.32	+	31. 254	=	150.16.63.254

Subnet Mask   **11111111.11111111.111**   00000.00000000

allow for 8 networks minus 2 (all 1s and all 0s), which equals 6 networks. Because it is 2^3, that means 3 bits out of the third octet will be used for the subnet mask. After the first 3 bits of the third octet are converted to decimal, the value will be 224 and the subnet mask will be 255.255.224.0.

In the example, Company X needed 300 hosts per network. To determine whether or not the administrator can accommodate that number, just look at the number of bits set to 0 in the subnet mask and determine their power. See the following:

IP Address	10010110.00010000.00000000.00000000
Subnetted Mask	11111111.11111111.11100000.00000000

In this example, the decimal subnet mask is 255.255.224.0, which leaves a total of 13 remaining 0s. 2^{13} equals 8192 minus 2, which allows for 8190 hosts per network. Table 2.9 shows the host and network addresses for Company X.

The additional benefits to subnetting a network include reducing network traffic and optimizing your bandwidth. Subnetting also provides a method to simplify administration because only a certain number of hosts per network is allowed.

 Test Tip: Benefits to subnetting = preserves IP addresses, reduces network traffic, optimizes bandwidth, and simplifies administration.

CHAPTER SUMMARY

This chapter covered the TCP/IP suite, the protocols that reside at different layers of the TCP/IP suite, and how those layers map to the OSI model. We also looked in-depth at IP addressing, as well as converting decimal numbers to binary and vice versa. The benefits of subnetting were also covered. The knowledge test will challenge you and allow you to practice subnetting. Use Tables 2.6 and 2.7 for assistance.

KNOWLEDGE TEST

Choose one answer for all questions unless directed to do otherwise.

1. The TCP/IP model's application layer maps to which OSI model layers?
   a. Physical, data-link, network
   b. Data-link, network, transport
   c. Network, transport, session
   d. Session, presentation, application

2. Which protocol sends echo, echo reply, and source quench packets?
   a. IP
   b. TCP
   c. ICMP
   d. ARP
   e. IPMC

3. Which transport layer protocol of the TCP/IP suite is connection oriented?
   a. UDP
   b. IP
   c. ICMP
   d. TCP

4. TFTP uses port 21 over a UDP connection.
   a. True
   b. False

5. SMTP uses what TCP port?
   a. 21
   b. 25
   c. 53
   d. 69

6. DNS uses UDP port 53 for zone transfers.
   a. True
   b. False

7. The binary value of 197 is:
   a. 11000101
   b. 11001001
   c. 11011011
   d. 11100001

8. The decimal value of 11100010.10001011.00010101.10100101 is:
   a. 226.137.21.165
   b. 220.141.15.165
   c. 228.238.41.155
   d. 226.139.21.165

9. Which IP address class allows for the most network addresses and the least amount of host addresses?
   a. Class A
   b. Class B
   c. Class C
   d. Class D
   e. Class E

10. CIDR stands for:
    a. Classless Inter Domain Routing
    b. Classful Inter Domain Routing
    c. Classful Intra Domain Routing
    d. Classless Intra Domain Routing

11. The subnet mask for the IP address 191.13.34.15/19 would be:
    a. 255.255.240.0
    b. 255.254.224.0
    c. 255.255.255.0
    d. 255.255.224.0

12. What statements are true about the IP address 85.1.66.245/20? (Choose all that apply.)
    a. The subnet mask is 255.255.224.0.
    b. The subnet mask is 255.255.240.0.
    c. The host address is 0.0.2.245.
    d. The network address is 85.1.0.0.
    e. The host address is 0.0.0.245.
    f. The network address is 85.1.64.0.

13. The "/18" in the IP address 131.1.71.0/18 means:
    a. There are 18 bits reserved for the subnet mask.
    b. There are 18 bits reserved for hosts.
    c. There are 18 network addresses available.
    d. There are 18 host addresses available.

14. Your company is issued a class C address of 193.160.18.0. However, your company has three locations that need three separate network addresses. Each network is required to have at least 50 node addresses. Is it possible to accomplish this with one class C address?
    a. Yes
    b. No

15. Your company is given a class B address of 150.5.0.0. You are responsible for creating 32 subnets with 500 hosts per subnet. What is your subnet mask going to be?
    a. 255.255.240.0
    b. 255.255.248.0
    c. 255.255.255.0
    d. 255.255.252.0

16. You have an IP address of 165.100.32.44/19. What are the valid host addresses for the network?
    a. 165.100.17.1 – 165.100.63.254
    b. 165.100.32.1 – 165.100.63.254
    c. 165.100.32.1 – 165.100.95.254
    d. 165.100.33.1 – 165.100.96.254

17. You have an IP address of 165.100.32.35/27. What are the valid host addresses for the network?
    a. 165.100.32.32 – 165.100.32.47
    b. 165.100.32.33 – 165.100.32.47
    c. 165.100.32.33 – 165.100.32.62
    d. 165.100.32.33 – 165.100.32.63

knowledge TEST

18. The default subnet mask for a class B address is:
    a. 255.255.0.0
    b. 255.255.255.0
    c. 255.0.0.0

19. If your network address has 9 bits left over for hosts, how many valid host IDs can you have?
    a. 512
    b. 510
    c. 256
    d. 254

20. Suppose computer A has the IP address of computer B. Computer A must get the MAC address of computer B to initiate communication. What process does computer A go through to get the address?
    a. ARP
    b. RARP
    c. Bridge table lookup
    d. Routing table lookup

CHAPTER 3

Configuring and Managing a Cisco Router

OBJECTIVES

The following topics are discussed in Chapter 3:

- Configure IP addresses, subnet masks, and gateway addresses on routers and hosts.

- Configure a router for additional administrative functionality.

- Manage system image and device configuration files.

- Perform an initial configuration on a router.

- Troubleshoot a device as part of a working network.

INTRODUCTION

This chapter provides an introduction to the procedures used to conduct basic management and configuration of a Cisco router. Types of router configurations, the hardware components of a router, and a router's boot-up procedure are among the topics covered. This chapter also introduces the command line interface (CLI) and the most common router commands used to configure the router.

3.1 COMPONENTS OF A CISCO ROUTER

Several types of Cisco routers are available to support networks of different sizes. Cisco categorizes routers by using a number. For example, the 700/800 and the 1600/1700 routers are suitable for home offices; the 2500 and 2600 routers are available for small offices; the 3600 and 5000 routers are used for branch offices; and the 4000, 7000, and 12000 routers are used to support IP backbones. The screen shots in this chapter were taken from a 2600 series router. Although the physical size and shape of the different routers may vary, there are commonalities among them such as the hardware (for example, interfaces and storage devices) and the software (Internetwork Operating System [IOS] and configuration files).

INTERFACES

An interface is a type of hardware connector also known as a port; the terms are interchangeable. Interfaces provide the router with the capability to connect to and communicate with other devices. The number of interfaces on a router may vary, depending on the router's series.

Three interfaces allow for configuration of the router: the *auxiliary interface,* the *network interface,* and the *console interface.* Each interface has a different means of logging in to the router. For example, to configure the router over the auxiliary interface, the administrator would dial in to the router over a modem. The administrator could use the Telnet program over a TCP/IP connection, to configure the router through the network interface. Finally, an administrator can log in to the console interface using the rollover cable (console cable) provided by Cisco. A rollover cable is an RJ-45 to RJ-45 cable and should not be confused with a crossover cable. It may be necessary to place a serial to RJ-45 adapter on the workstation's serial interface (com port) to connect using this method. A terminal emulation program on the workstation will provide the login capability.

Routers can also have DB60 (60-pin connector) serial interfaces. Serial interfaces are normally used to connect to a WAN service provider's network. When using the serial interface of a router, it is treated as either DTE or DCE. DTE/DCE is an RS232c standard that defines two ends of a communication channel—a DTE is a sending device and a DCE a receiving device. The connection between the router and the WAN service provider is classified as DTE/DCE. The cable connector that links the DTE to the DCE is where the responsibility of the data changes hands from the private network to the public network. The DCE is responsible for providing a clocking mechanism for the transfer of data. It is normally the service provider's CSU/DSU that provides the timing. However, if two routers are being connected together through their serial ports, one must act as the DCE and the other as the DTE. The type of physical connector (V.35, X.21, and so on) used to connect the router's serial interface with the DCE is determined by the line speed of the service provider.

Other router interfaces available on Cisco routers include

- Ethernet and Fast Ethernet
- Token Ring

- Asynchronous Transfer Mode (ATM)
- Fiber Distributed Data Interface (FDDI)
- Integrated Services Digital Network (ISDN)

These interfaces are used for routing packets. However, you can log in to any active interface provided it is using TCP/IP. The mode of connection is with a virtual terminal (VTY) program such as Telnet.

STORAGE

Routers use four types of storage to maintain the IOS, the configuration of the IOS, and the routing tables they operate with. They do not use hard disks for storage. All four types of storage are some form of chip-based memory and include *random-access memory (RAM), nonvolatile RAM (NVRAM), read-only memory (ROM),* and *flash RAM (flash memory)*. Although each type of memory serves a different purpose, they work together in several ways.

RAM

RAM is the physical location where the IOS and the running configuration file are loaded into during boot-up and where they run from while the router is powered on. When the router is powered off, all information residing in RAM (that has not yet been saved elsewhere) is lost because RAM is volatile. Routing tables are also run from RAM.

NVRAM

NVRAM is the physical location where the router's configuration file is stored when the router is powered off. It is nonvolatile and can maintain its state when the router is powered off through the use of a battery.

ROM

ROM is where the POST information is located. During the boot-up sequence, the POST checks the CPU, the RAM, and the interface circuitry before activating the bootstrap code to load the IOS into RAM. ROM also contains the ROM monitor, which is available for manufacturer testing and troubleshooting, as well as the RXBOOT code, which is a mini IOS software file available for maintenance operations.

Flash RAM (Flash Memory)
Flash RAM stores the IOS software image. Some routers can run the IOS software directly from flash RAM and do not need to transfer the image to the physical RAM.

3.2 BOOTING UP A ROUTER

When a Cisco router boots up, it goes through a series of steps before it becomes operational. It is important to understand the boot-up process to assist in troubleshooting.

BOOT SEQUENCE

During the boot sequence, ROM starts the POST and then loads the bootstrap program, which finds the IOS and its configuration file and loads it into memory. The bootstrap program sequence can be broken down into four steps for simplicity: (1) POST, (2) load and run the bootstrap code, (3) find and load the Cisco IOS software, and (4) find and load the configuration.

Step 1. Power-On Self-Test (POST)
POST is the process of checking and verifying that all hardware components are operational. POST is executed from microcode stored in the ROM.

Step 2. Load and Run the Bootstrap Code
The bootstrap code is stored in ROM and at bootup is responsible for locating and running the Cisco IOS software.

Step 3. Find and Load the Cisco IOS Software
The bootstrap code is responsible for finding the IOS software and is normally located in flash memory. The *configuration register* determines where the IOS software is. The configuration register is a 16-bit value represented in hexadecimal notation, the lowest 4 bits of which determine where the IOS is located. Hexadecimal values are preceded by a "0x," and each hexadecimal value of 0-F represents four bits. (Hexadecimal is base 16 with the values being 0-9 and A-F, A = 10, B = 11, and so on.) So a configuration register value of 0x2102 converted to binary would look like 0010 0001 0000 0010. The rightmost set of 4 bits represents the boot field and tells the bootstrap loader where the IOS software is located. Following are the values to be aware of for the CCNA Exam. The boldfaced letter represents the boot field of the configuration register.

- 0x210**0** Boot with mini IOS stored in ROM monitor.

- 0x210**1** Boot from IOS image stored in ROM.

- 0x210**2** - 0x210**F** Get boot instructions from the configuration file stored in NVRAM. If none are available, use the first file found in flash RAM (default).

- 0x21**42** Bypass configuration settings in NVRAM during a password recovery procedure.

If the configuration register is set to the default, the bootstrap code looks for instructions in NVRAM to find the IOS. The administrator can dictate where the IOS should be loaded from by using the *boot system* command that specifies the name and location of the IOS image to be loaded. The boot system options are to load a specific IOS image stored in flash RAM, load an IOS image from ROM, and load an IOS image from a TFTP server. If these settings are not configured in the router's startup-configuration file, the bootstrap code initializes the first IOS image found in flash RAM. The boot system commands are shown in Table 3.1. After the bootstrap code finds the IOS software, it loads it into RAM or runs it from flash memory.

Step 4. Find and Load the Configuration File

The configuration file of a router records any changes made to the IOS, including IP address assignment, interface configuration, protocols installed, and all other settings. The configuration of the router is normally executed from NVRAM where the startup-configuration file is stored. It can also be loaded from a TFTP server. When found, the configuration of the router is loaded into RAM. But if the router's configuration is not found in NVRAM or on a TFTP server, the IOS will go into *setup mode* and allow the administrator to configure a basic configuration.

Configuration files are referenced differently in the Cisco IOS command line, based on their current location. For example, when the router is functioning properly and the configuration file has been loaded into RAM, it is the *running-configuration* file. The configuration file located in NVRAM is the *startup configuration* file and acts as a backup to the running-configuration file. It is possible to copy the configuration file from RAM to NVRAM and vice versa. It is even possible to copy the configuration file (either startup or running) to a TFTP server as a backup for additional fault tolerance.

3.3 COMMAND LINE INTERFACE (CLI)

Cisco uses a CLI to configure and manage its routers. Some features of the CLI include assisting in completing command-line syntax, having the ability to execute abbreviated (shortcut) commands, maintaining a history of commands, and providing error messages when a command is typed incorrectly. The commands available at the CLI vary, depending on which mode the router is in.

MODES OF CONFIGURATION

Several different modes of configuration are available in the Cisco IOS. To administer a router, it is essential to be able to switch between different modes so the configuration file can be modified. The level of access and available commands change based on the configuration mode that the router is in. The modes available are

- Setup Mode
- User EXEC Mode

- Privileged EXEC Mode
- RXBOOT Mode
- Global Configuration Mode
- Additional Configuration Modes

Setup Mode

If the router has not been configured or if the configuration file is missing from NVRAM, the router enters the setup mode on initialization. The setup mode asks several questions with an interactive prompt that assists in setting up the router's initial configuration file. See the following to view the screen presented when a router is booted for the first time.

```
—System Configuration Dialog—
Would you like to enter the initial
    configuration dialog? [yes/no]: y

At any point you may enter a question mark '?'
    for help.

Use ctrl-c to abort configuration dialog at
    any prompt.

Default settings are in square brackets '[]'.

Basic management setup configures only enough
    connectivity for management of the system,
    extended setup will ask you to configure
    each interface on the system

Would you like to enter basic management
    setup? [yes/no]: y

Configuring global parameters:

Enter host name [Router]: EastRouter

The enable secret is a password used to
    protect access to privileged EXEC and
    configuration modes. This password, after
    entered, becomes encrypted in the
    configuration.

Enter enable secret: MyEncryptedPassword

The enable password is used when you do not
    specify an enable secret password, with
    some older software versions, and some
    boot images.
```

```
Enter enable password:

The virtual terminal password is used to
    protect access to the router over a
    network interface.

Enter virtual terminal password:
    MyTelnetPassword

Configure SNMP Network Management? [yes]: n

Current interface summary

Any interface listed with OK? value "NO" does
    not have a valid configuration

Interface          IP-Address   OK? Method Status   Protocol

FastEthernet0/0    unassigned   NO unset up         down

Serial0/0          unassigned   NO unset down       down

FastEthernet0/1    unassigned   NO unset up         down

Serial0/1          unassigned   NO unset down       down

Enter interface name used to connect to the
    management network from the above interface
    summary: fastethernet0/0

Configuring interface FastEthernet0/0:

Use the 100 Base-TX (RJ-45) connector?
    [yes]: y

Operate in full-duplex mode? [no]: n

Configure IP on this interface? [yes]: y

IP address for this interface: 10.0.0.1

Subnet mask for this interface [255.0.0.0] :
    255.0.0.0

Class A network is 10.0.0.0, 8 subnet bits;
    mask is /8
```

The router gives a summary of the configuration file created after all the preceding questions have been answered. Following is the summary:

```
The following configuration command script was
    created:

hostname EastRouter

enable secret 5 $1$eKV1$J2KkZkgdRLVbRXW/f0e43/
```

```
enable password
line vty 0 4
password MyTelnetPassword
no snmp-server
!
no ip routing
!
interface FastEthernet0/0
no shutdown
media-type 100BaseX
half-duplex
ip address 10.0.0.1 255.0.0.0
!
interface Serial0/0
shutdown
no ip address
end

[0] Go to the IOS command prompt without
    saving this config.
[1] Return back to the setup without saving
    this config.
[2] Save this configuration to nvram and exit.
    Enter your selection [2]:
```

The setup mode is only used to set up a router with a basic configuration. Additional configuration will be needed after running through the setup configuration. It is possible to cancel out of the setup mode by selecting "no" at the system configuration dialog prompt or by pressing Ctrl+C.

User EXEC Mode

The router enters the user EXEC mode when a user logs in. The user EXEC mode offers a subset of commands available in the privileged EXEC mode. No router configuration commands are available while in the user EXEC mode because it is a view-only mode. It allows a user to see the configuration of the router but not change any settings. The CLI prompt changes, depending on which mode you are in. When in the user EXEC mode, the CLI prompt will appear as:

```
Router>
```

The word "Router" preceding the ">" is the default host name of the router, which can be changed.

Privileged EXEC Mode

When the router is in the privileged EXEC mode, the ability to make simple configuration changes is available. To enter the privileged EXEC mode, use the *enable* command at the user EXEC mode prompt. If a password has been set up to enter the privileged mode, a password prompt appears. The command is

```
Router>enable
Password:
```

If the correct password is entered, the CLI prompt will then change to

```
Router#
```

The router can enter the global configuration mode and additional configuration modes from the privileged EXEC mode. To return to the user EXEC mode from the privileged EXEC mode, use the *disable* or *exit* command:

```
Router#disable
Router>
```

RXBOOT Mode

RXBOOT mode, also known as ROM Monitor, is a diagnostic mode. Enter RXBOOT mode by pressing the Break key during the router's boot-up sequence from the console interface or by changing the configuration register to 0x2000. The CLI prompt for RXBOOT mode is

```
rommon>
```

This mode is useful in the event that the password to enter the router has been lost or the IOS image is corrupt.

Global Configuration Mode

Global configuration mode allows you to make changes to the entire router, not a specific interface. From this mode, it is possible to change the host name of the router, change and create privileged EXEC mode passwords, and enter additional configuration modes. To enter the terminal configuration mode, enter *configure terminal*. For example:

```
Router#configure terminal
```

or

```
Router#config t
```

The CLI prompt will then appear as

```
Router(config)#
```

Once in the terminal global configuration mode, any changes will be made to the running-configuration file. However, to ensure these changes are not lost if the router is reloaded, copy the running-configuration file to the startup-configuration file with the *copy* command. If the command *configure memory* is used, it will load the startup-configuration file from NVRAM and that will become the active running-configuration file. The *Config network* command loads a configuration file from a TFTP server. Entering *configure* without the terminal or memory argument returns a prompt option to select either terminal, memory, or network as shown:

```
Router#configure
Configuring from terminal, memory, or network
    [terminal]?
```

To configure interfaces, protocols, routing protocols, subinterfaces, terminal lines, and controllers, it is necessary to enter the global configuration mode first, and then specify the additional configuration mode that must be configured.

Test Tip: Three ways to make changes to the running-config (config in RAM) are (1) config terminal, (2) config memory, and (3) config network.

Additional Configuration Modes

To enter additional configuration modes, use *major commands* that point to a specific interface or process. Major commands work in conjunction with *subcommands*. The major command points to the interface and the subcommand tells the interface what to do. For example, the *interface configuration* mode is the mode available to configure a specific interface. To go into the interface configuration mode from the global configuration mode, type the major command:

```
Router(config)#interface serial0
```

or

```
Router(config)#int s0
```

The command shown points to the first serial interface on the router. Cisco starts the numbering of interfaces with "0." The CLI prompt will change to

```
Router(config-if)#
```

After the router is pointing to serial interface 0, it is possible to use a subcommand to change the interface's configuration. For example:

```
Router(config-if)#shutdown
```

The subcommand *shutdown* administratively disables the first serial interface on the router.

The additional configuration modes that may be seen on the CCNA Exam are

Mode	CLI
• Subinterface (Virtual Interface)	• Router(config-subif)#
• Console Line	• Router(config-line)#
• Terminal Line	• Router(config-line)#
• Controller	• Router(config-controller)#
• IP Routing Protocol	• Router(config-router)#

To return to any prior mode, use the *exit* command until the router is back to privileged EXEC mode. Ctrl+Z will also end a configuration session and return the CLI to the privileged EXEC mode from any additional configuration mode the router is in.

 Test Tip: Be sure to have a good understanding of the different configuration modes and the type of commands that can be entered at each mode.

CLI UTILITIES

Four IOS features are available to help you identify the commands available and facilitate use of the CLI: the *context-sensitive help*, the *command history buffer, enhanced editing commands,* and *console error messages.*

Context-Sensitive Help

To view the commands available while configuring a router, simply enter a question mark at the prompt. The router returns a list of commands available for execution in the current mode of configuration. The commands available in the user EXEC mode are displayed in the following example:

```
Router>?
```

If a portion of a command is entered followed by a question mark, the router will return all the commands available that start with the syntax you typed. For example, the following command returns the commands available in the user EXEC mode that begin with the letter "s":

```
Router>s?
set show slip systat
```

If the command name, such as *show*, is known but the complete command syntax is unknown, use the question mark in place of a keyword or argument. For example:

```
Router>show ?
```

This returns all the possible arguments that can be entered with the *show* command.

Command History Buffer

The command history buffer allows the router to maintain a history of commands that are typed during the session. The command history buffer is on by default and its default setting remembers up to 10 commands. It can be configured to remember more with the *terminal history size* command. The maximum number of lines the buffer can hold is 256. The next example shows the size of the command history buffer being increased to 25:

```
Router#terminal history size 25
```

To navigate through the command history buffer, use the up arrow or the Ctrl+P key sequence to recall older commands. To get back to the most recent commands used, use the down arrow or Ctrl+N. To view all the commands in the command history buffer use:

```
Router>show history
```

Enhanced Editing Commands

The CLI has enhanced editing features available that help with editing long commands as well as automatically completing the syntax of a command. If a command is too long to fit on the CLI, the Cisco router shifts the command string of characters 10 spaces to the left to allow more space to type the command. When the characters are shifted, a "$" appears at the beginning of the CLI denoting that the line has been shifted. For example, the *banner motd* message will appear as

```
Before = Router(config)#banner motd # This
        banner shows how the command line ha
After =  Router(config)#$d # This banner shows
        how the command line has shifted. #
```

This command has shifted to the left to allow more space for the current command being typed in.

To assist in moving the cursor from one end of the command line to the other, an additional enhanced editing feature specifies "editor hot keys" consisting of specific keystroke combinations:

Ctrl + A = Move cursor back to beginning of line*.

Ctrl + B = Move cursor back one character*.

Ctrl + D = Delete one character to the left of cursor.

Ctrl + E = Move cursor to end of line*.

Ctrl + F = Move cursor forward one character*.

Ctrl + R = Redisplay current line.

Ctrl + U = Erase one line.

Ctrl + W = Erase one word to left of cursor.

Ctrl + Z = End configuration mode.

Esc + B = Move cursor back one word*.

Esc + F = Move cursor forward one word*.

Tab = Complete partially entered command if enough characters have been entered to make it unique. For example:

```
Router>en <Tab>
Router>enable
```

The *en* in the command will be interpreted as *enable* when the Tab key is pressed.

Test Tip: Be aware of keystrokes with * for the CCNA Exam.

If a command is partially typed on a Cisco router and there are enough letters to make the command unique, it is not necessary to complete the command or press the Tab key to complete the command. Cisco routers anticipate the command and return the desired results if there are enough characters to make the command unique. However, for the CCNA Exam it is necessary to know both the full syntax and the shortened syntax for some commands. A list of abbreviated commands is available in Appendix A.

Console Error Messages

Console error messages identify when a command has been entered incorrectly at the CLI. There are three messages to be aware of for the CCNA Exam:

- `% Invalid input detected at the '^' marker`
  The command was entered incorrectly. The ^ under the specific letter of the command shows where the error occurred.

- `% Incomplete command`
  All the necessary arguments were not entered with the command.

- `% Ambiguous Command: "s"`
  There were not enough characters entered to make the command unique. In this example, the command could be *set*, *show*, and so on.

If any of the listed errors occur, use the context sensitive help (?) utility to learn the correct syntax of the command being typed.

CLI COMMANDS AVAILABLE

There are many commands available in the EXEC modes and in the configuration modes of a Cisco router. Each mode has a different set of commands.

Show Command

The *show* command is the one used at the CLI to see configuration information on a router. The command *show* is followed by another argument. For example:

```
Router#show running-config
Building configuration...

Current configuration:
!
version 12.0
service timestamps debug uptime
service timestamps log uptime
no service password-encryption
!
hostname Router
!
enable password password
!
ip subnet-zero
!
interface FastEthernet0/0
ip address 10.0.0.1 255.0.0.0
no ip directed-broadcast
duplex auto
```

```
speed auto
!
interface Serial0/0
description line
ip address 11.0.0.1 255.0.0.0
no ip directed-broadcast
no ip mroute-cache
shutdown
no fair-queue
!
ip classless
no ip http server
!
line con 0
transport input none
line aux 0
line vty 0 4
login
!
no scheduler allocate
end
```

The *show running-config* command returns the configuration information that is currently loaded into RAM. To view the configuration file that is loaded into RAM from NVRAM during the boot process, use the following command (only a partial output is given):

```
Router#show startup-config
Using 721 out of 29688 bytes
!
version 12.0
service timestamps debug uptime
service timestamps log uptime
no service password-encryption
!
```

```
hostname Router
(PARTIAL OUTPUT)
```

The output from both the *show running-config* and the *show startup-config* are just about identical. Notice in the *show running-config* output that the words *current configuration* appear on the third line of the output. This explains that the information on the screen is what the router is currently using.

Another valuable *show* command is the *show version* command. Following is the output from the *show version* command of a Cisco 2600 series router:

```
Router#show version
Cisco Internetwork Operating System Software
IOS (tm) C2600 Software (C2600-I-M), Version
    12.0(7)T, RELEASE SOFTWARE (fc2)
Copyright (c) 1986-1999 by Cisco Systems, Inc.
Compiled Tue 07-Dec-99 02:12 by phanguye
Image text-base: 0x80008088, data-base:
    0x807AAF70
ROM: System Bootstrap, Version 12.1(3r)T2,
    RELEASE SOFTWARE (fc1)
Router uptime is 2 hours, 9 minutes
System returned to ROM by power-on
System image file is "flash:c2600-i-mz.
    120-7.T"
cisco 2621 (MPC860) processor (revision 0x200)
    with 26624K/6144K bytes of memory
    .
M860 processor: part number 0, mask 49
Bridging software.
X.25 software, Version 3.0.0.
2 FastEthernet/IEEE 802.3 interface(s)
2 Serial network interface(s)
32K bytes of non-volatile configuration
    memory.
8192K bytes of processor board System flash
    (Read/Write)
Configuration register is 0x2102
```

The *show version* command displays information about system hardware, software versions, the boot image, and the configuration register (the last entry shown).

The *show* command is a valuable command with many arguments. To determine what arguments are available while working on a router, use the context-sensitive help. The CCNA Exam requires a strong understanding of the *show* command. Table 3.1 has a list of *show* commands that are useful in studying for the CCNA Exam.

Copy Command

The *copy* command is commonly used for copying the running-configuration (the working configuration in RAM) to the startup-configuration (configuration stored in NVRAM) or to a TFTP server. The configuration file stored in NVRAM or on the TFTP server acts as a backup to the running-configuration.

When making changes to the current configuration the changes take place immediately. Because the current configuration is located in RAM and RAM is volatile, all the configuration changes made are lost when the router is shut down or rebooted. To avoid losing these data, copy the running-configuration to the startup-configuration using the following command:

```
Router#copy running-config startup-config
Destination filename [startup-config]? <enter>
Building configuration...
[OK]
```

or

```
Router#copy ru st
```

To copy the startup-configuration file from NVRAM to RAM, use this command:

```
Router#copy startup-config running-config
```

or

```
Router#copy st ru
```

With Cisco, you can also copy configuration files to TFTP servers for fault tolerance. To copy a running configuration file to a TFTP server, use this command:

```
Router#copy running-config tftp
```

After typing this command, the CLI poses several questions to determine the address or host name of the TFTP server. It will also prompt you for a file name. To recall the TFTP configuration file and place it into RAM as the running configuration file, use the following command:

```
Router#copy tftp running-config
```

Password Command

You can set passwords on a router to increase security. Passwords can be set so users have to know and enter the correct password to get from the user EXEC mode to the privileged EXEC mode. Passwords can also be set on the console line, auxiliary line, and VTY lines to ensure that only authorized users are accessing and configuring the router. To set a privileged EXEC password of Delmar on a router type, use the following command from the global configuration mode:

```
Router(config)#enable password Delmar
```

To set Delmar as an encrypted password, use the following command:

```
Router(config)#enable secret Delmar
```

The *enable password* and *enable secret* commands are not used in conjunction with one another. They are used in an either/or instance.

To set a password on the console line, enter the console line interface configuration mode, then type **login,** and finally type **password** with the password. See the following:

```
Router(config)#line console 0
Router(config-line)#login
Router(config-line)#password Thomson
```

This command sequence points to the line console and then changes the password of the console line to Thomson. The command sequence is generally the same to set the password on the aux line and the VTY line. See Table 3.1 to see the command sequence to set the passwords on aux and VTY lines.

A series of commands is available that allows for encryption of all passwords: *service password-encryption* and *no service password-encryption*. The commands are typed (in the global configuration mode) before and after the *password* command sequence. For example:

```
Router(config)#service password-encryption
Router(config)#enable password Anthony
Router(config)#line console 0
Router(config-line)#login
Router(config-line)#password Anthony1
Router(config-line)#exit
Router(config)#no service password-encryption
```

This command sequence encrypted the privileged EXEC mode password of Anthony as well as the line console password of Anthony1. To disable passwords, use the *no* argument before the *password* command.

Banner Command

A *banner* is a string of characters that are shown at the CLI during login. Four banner commands are available: *EXEC Banner, incoming banner, login banner,* and *MOTD banner.* The banner command that may be seen on the CCNA Exam is the *MOTD banner.* Use context-sensitive help to learn how to configure the additional banners.

The *MOTD banner* displays a message to any user connecting to a router whether they are dialing in, using Telnet, or simply connecting through the console port. The command to set the message of the day banner uses a delimiting character before and after the message is typed. For example:

```
Router(config)#banner motd # This is a secured
    Router. #
```

The text between the two # signs is displayed when users connect. The delimiting character does not have to be a symbol; it can be a letter or a number as well. It must, however, be the same at the beginning and at the end of the message.

 Test Tip: Familiarize yourself with the syntax of the banner MOTD command.

DNS Configuration

Cisco routers are set up to be DNS clients by default. If a router does not understand a command, it tries to have the command resolved by a DNS server with an IP address of 255.255.255.255. The DNS request must time out before any other configuration can be done. This function can be disabled using the *no ip domain lookup* command from the global configuration mode. To enable the router as a DNS client, use the *ip domain-lookup* command.

To give a DNS host name to a router, use the *ip host* command. In the next example, *EastRouter* is the host name of the router and its IP address is *10.0.0.1*:

```
Router(config)#ip host EastRouter 10.0.0.1
```

The router can use up to six different name servers for name resolution. To configure the router with the correct DNS server's address, use the following:

```
Router(config)#ip name-server 10.0.0.25
```

Additional Commands

See Table 3.1 for a list of router management and configuration commands.

TABLE 3.1 CISCO ROUTER COMMANDS

Commands	Command Sequence	Remarks
	User EXEC Mode	
	Router>login asmith	Log in as user asmith.
	Router>enable or Router>en	Enter privileged EXEC mode from user EXEC mode.
	Router>?	Lists commands available; can be done in any mode.
	Router>show history	Shows commands in the command history buffer.
	Privileged EXEC Mode	
Show Interface Information	Router#show interfaces	Shows you all interfaces in alphabetical order.
	Router#show interfaces Ethernet 0	Shows interfaces Ethernet 0's configuration.
	Router#show IPX interface	Shows the IPX configuration on all interfaces.
	Router#show CDP interface	Shows administrative and protocol statistics for the CDP interfaces.
	Router#show line	Shows external interfaces that are being accessed.
	Router#show users	Shows who is logged into any external interfaces.
Show Configurations	Router#show startup-config	Shows the startup configuration that is stored in NVRAM for the router.
	Router#show running-config	Shows the running configuration that is currently in RAM for the router.
Show Protocols	Router#show protocols	Shows all routed protocols running on all interfaces.
	Router#show IP protocols	Shows TCP/IP routing protocols running on the router.
Show Routing Tables	Router#show IP route	Shows routing tables for TCP/IP.
	Router#show IPX route	Shows routing tables for IPX.
	Router#show AppleTalk route	Shows routing tables for AppleTalk protocol.
Show CDP Information	Router#show CDP	Shows CDP information.
	Router#show CDP neighbors	Shows directly connected CDP neighbors.
	Router#show CDP neighbor details	Shows detailed CDP information about all neighbors.
	Router#show CDP entry	Shows additional information about the interface type.
	Router#show CDP entry*	Shows detailed CDP information about all neighbors.
	Router#show CDP entry 100.5.0.1	Shows information specific to neighbor 100.5.0.1.
	Router#show CDP traffic	Shows CDP traffic and the status of packets sent.
Show Version	Router#show version	Shows IOS version, name, and source of configuration files and hardware.

Commands	Command Sequence	Remarks
Show Flash RAM	*Router#show flash*	Shows the files stored in flash RAM.
Show Controllers	*Router#show controller serial 0*	Displays information about the physical interface connected to serial 0.
Show ISDN Configuration	*Router#show dialer*	Shows current connection, idle timer, number of successful connections made.
	Router#show isdn active	Shows in-progress calls.
	Router#show isdn status	Displays statistics of an ISDN connection; confirms validity of SPIDs.
Copy	*Router#copy startup-config running-config*	Copies the startup configuration file stored in NVRAM to RAM.
	Router#copy running-config startup-config	Copies the running configuration file from RAM to NVRAM.
	Router#copy running-config tftp	Copies the running configuration file from RAM to a TFTP server.
	Router#copy tftp flash	Copies files stored on a TFTP server to flash RAM.
	Router#copy flash tftp	Copies IOS to TFTP server, creating a backup of the IOS image.
Telnet Configuration	*Router#telnet 10.0.0.1*	Opens a Telnet connection with host 10.0.0.1 (the word *telnet* is optional).
	Router#show session	Displays a list of hosts with established Telnet connection.
	Router#show user	Displays a list of hosts with an established Telnet session on the local router.
	Router#resume [session number]	Resumes a suspended Telnet session; session number is needed only if router has more than one established Telnet session.
	Router#exit or Router#logout	Closes a Telnet session from the remote device.
	Router#disconnect [session number]	Closes a Telnet session from the local device; session number is needed only if router has more than one established Telnet session.
	Router#clear line [line number]	Closes a Telnet session opened by another user on the local device.
Miscellaneous Commands	*Router#ping 100.5.0.1*	Tests the connectivity between the router and host 100.5.0.1.
	Router#trace 10.10.0.1	Sees the path a packet takes to get to host 100.5.0.1.
	Router#show hosts	Displays Host Names table.
	Router#Setup	Starts interactive prompt to configure the router's configuration file.
	Router#disable	Returns to user EXEC mode from privileged EXEC mode.

continues

TABLE 3.1 continued

Commands	Command Sequence	Remarks
Miscellaneous Commands *continued*	*Router#configure terminal*	Enters global configuration mode and configures the startup configuration.
	Router#configure memory	Loads the startup configuration into memory.
	Router#clock set [hh:mm:ss:dd:month:year]	Sets the internal clock and calendar.
	Router#terminal editing	Turns on enhanced editing features.
	Router#no terminal editing	Turns off enhanced editing features.
	Router#terminal history size [1–256]	Sets the command history to a value between 1 and 256 for the current session.
	Router# history size [1–256]	Sets the command history to a value between 1 and 256 permanently.
	Router#erase startup-configuration	Erases the saved configuration file in NVRAM.
	Router#ip classless	Allows the router to send packets with unknown destination to default gateway.
Verify Access Lists	*Router#show access–list*	Displays all access lists and their parameters.
	Router#show access–list 100	Displays access list 100 and its parameters.
	Router#show ip access–list	Displays only the IP access lists.
	Router#show ipx access–list	Displays only the IPX access lists.
	Router#show ip interface	Shows what IP interfaces have access lists applied to them.
	Router#show ipx interface	Shows what IPX interfaces have access lists applied to them.
	Router#show running–config	Shows access lists and which interface they are applied to.

Global / Additional Configuration Modes

Commands	Command Sequence	Remarks
Password Configuration **Enable Password**	*Router(config)#enable password Learning*	Restricts access to the privileged EXEC mode from the user EXEC mode.
Enable Secret Password	*Router(config)#enable secret cisco*	Used instead of enabling password. Encrypts the password.
Encrypt Passwords	*Router(config)#service password-encryption*	Encrypts passwords typed before the *no service password-encryption* command.
Disable Passwords	*Router(config)#no…*	Uses the *no* command with any password syntax to disable the specific password.
Boot System Commands	*Router(config)#boot system flash R1*	Bootstrap code loads the IOS image R1 from flash RAM at bootup.
	Router(config)#boot system ROM	Bootstrap code loads the IOS image stored in ROM at bootup.
	Router(config)#boot system tftp R1 10.0.0.2	Bootstrap code loads the IOS image R1 from the TFTP server 10.0.0.2.

Commands	Command Sequence	Remarks
Enter Interface Modes	*Router(config)#config-register [value]*	Manually configures configuration register. Value must be 0x2100-0x210F.
	Router(config)#interface serial 0	Enters serial 0 configuration mode.
	Router(config)#interface ethernet 1	Enters Ethernet 1 configuration mode.
	Router(config)#interface ethernet 1/0	Enters Ethernet 0 on slot number 1 (series 2600, 3600, 4000, 7000, 7200).
	Router(config)#interface ethernet 1/0/0	Enters Ethernet 0 on port adapter 0 in slot number 1 (series 7000, 7500).
Miscellaneous		
Change Router's Name	*Router(config)#hostname [name]*	Changes the router's name and the CLI prompt to the value specified.
Set Message of the Day	*Router(config)#banner motd #...#*	Sets the MOTD banner. Places syntax between two delimiting characters.
Shuts CDP Off	*Router(config)#no cdp run*	Shuts CDP off globally.
	Router(config)#cdp run	Enables CDP globally.
ACCESS LISTS Type @ Router(config)#		
TCP/IP Access-List	*access-list 1 permit 144.10.10.0 0.0.0.255*	Permits network 144.10.10.0 into your network with a standard access list.
	access-list 101 permit any any	Extended access list to permit any source address to any destination access.
	access-list 102 deny 131.107.16.0 0.0.15.255 any eq 23	Denies access to the 131.107.16.0 network to Telnet to any network.
	access-list 102 deny 0.0.0.0 255.255.255.255	Implicit *deny* at the end of all access list.
	Router(config-if)#ip access-group 1 [in | out]	Applies access list to an interface.
IPX/SPX Access-List	*access-list 800 deny 4b2c*	Standard access list to deny network 4b2c.
	access-list 901 permit 2d1d –1	Extended access list to permit network 2d1d to all networks.
	access-list 1020 permit ab3 4	SAP access list to allow servers from network ab3.
Line Configuration		
VTY Lines	*Router(config)#vty 0 4*	Enters VTY line configuration mode (virtual terminal/Telnet).
	Router(config-line)#login	Logs in to a line interface.
	Router(config-line)#password Delmar	Applies a log-in password of Delmar for all VTY ports.
	Router(config-line)#access-class 10 in	Applies security to all your VTY ports from access list 10.

continues

TABLE 3.1 continued

Commands	Command Sequence	Remarks
Console Line	Router(config)#console 0	Enters console line configuration mode.
	Router(config-line)#login	Logs in to a line interface.
	Router(config-line)#password password	Applies a login password for the console.
	Router(config-line)#exec-timeout 0 0	Sets the timeout session for the console to never time out.
	Router(config-line)#logging synchronous	Prevents console messages from popping up as you are typing commands.
Auxiliary Line	Router(config)#aux 0	Enters AUX line configuration mode.
	Router(config-line)#login	Logs in to a line interface.
	Router(config-line)#password password	Applies a login password of auxpassword for the AUX port.
Line Password Configuration Sequence		
Console Session	Router(config)#line console 0	Sets the console password to ensure that when a session is
	Router(config-line)#login	established over the console interface, the user must log in to
	Router(config-line)#password Delmar	the console interface.
Virtual Terminal Session	Router(config)#line vty 0 4	Sets the vty password to ensure that when a session is started
	Router(config-line)#login	over Telnet (virtual terminal), the user must log in to the
	Router(config-line)#password Thomson	interface.
Auxiliary Session	Router(config)#line aux 0	Sets the aux password to ensure that when a session is started
	Router(config-line)#login	over the modem (dial-in), the user must log in to the interface.
	Router(config-line)#password CCNA	
Interface Configuration		
Serial Interface	Router(config)#serial 0	Enters serial interface 0.
	Router(config-if)#no shutdown	Enables the interface that has been administratively shut down.
	Router(config-if)#shutdown	Administratively shuts down the interface.
	Router(config-if)#clock rate 64000	Sets the DCE cable clock rate to 64000 bps (only in router to router config).
	Router(config-if)#bandwidth 64	Sets the serial interface bandwidth to 64 Kbps (default is 1.544 Mbps).
	Router(config-if)#no cdp enable	Shuts CDP off on serial 0 only (overrides global configuration setting).
	Router(config-if)#cdp enable	Enables CDP on serial 0 only (overrides global configuration setting).
	Router(config-if)#exit	Returns to global configuration mode.

Commands	Command Sequence	Remarks
Ethernet Interface	Router(config)#ethernet 1	Enters Ethernet interface 1.
	Router(config-if)#no shutdown	Enables the interface that has been administratively shut down.
	Router(config-if)#shutdown	Administratively shuts down the interface.
	Router(config-if)#media-type 10baset	Selects the physical connector the router will use as Ethernet 1.
	Router(config-if)#no cdp enable	Shuts CDP off on Ethernet 1 only (overrides global configuration setting).
	Router(config-if)#cdp enable	Enables CDP on Ethernet 1 only (overrides global configuration setting).
	Router(config-if)#exit	Returns to global configuration mode.
	Router(config-if)#ip address [address][mask]	Sets the IP address and subnet mask for the interface.

DNS Configuration

	Router(config)#no ip domain-lookup	Turns off the DNS lookup.
	Router(config)#ip domain-lookup	Turns on the DNS lookup.
	Router(config)#ip host R1 address 10.0.0.6	Sets router's DNS host name.
	Router(config)#ip name-server 10.0.0.25	Sets DNS lookup.
	Router#show hosts	Shows list of cached host names.

RIP Configuration

	Router(config)#Router RIP	Enables RIP on the router.
	Router(config-router)#network 10.0.0.0	Configures RIP to route network 10.0.0.0.
	Router#debug ip rip	Displays RIP routing updates.

IGRP Configuration

	Router(config)#Router IGRP 200	Starts IGRP for AS 200.
	Router(config-router)#network 131.107.0.0	Adds network 131.107.0.0 to IGRP for routing.
	Router#debug igrp events	Displays summary of IGRP routing updates.
	Router#debug igrp transactions	Displays IGRP transactions.

OSPF Configuration

	Router(config)#Router OSPF 1	Starts OSPF with a process-id of 1 (local to this router only).
	Router(config-router)#network 192.168.1.0 0.0.0.255 area 0	Configures OSPF for a single network and a single area.
	Router(config-router)#ip ospf cost 100	Sets the cost of the route to 100.
	Router(config-router)#ip ospf hello-interval 15	Sets the hello timer.
	Router(config)#show ip ospf interface	Shows all OSPF interfaces on the router.
	Router(config)#show ip ospf neighbor address	Shows the details of the neighbor with the address you specify.

continues

TABLE 3.1 *concluded*

Commands	Command Sequence	Remarks
Ethernet Interface		
continued	**EIGRP Configuration**	
	Router(config)#router eigrp 150	Starts EIGRP routing for AS 150.
	Router(config–router)#network 168.1.0.0	Enables EIGRP for the interface associated with 168.1.0.0.
	Router(config)#show ip eigrp topology	Shows the topological database of the router.
	Router(config)#show ip eigrp neighbors	Lists the neighbors that the router knows about.
	Frame Relay Configuration	
	Router(config-if)#encapsulation frame-relay	Starts Frame Relay on interface with either Cisco or IETF encapsulation.
	Router(config–if)#frame-relay lmi type	Sets the LMI type.
	Router(config–if)#frame-relay inverse-arp	Enables inverse arp. Add the protocol and DLCI being used to the command.
	Router(config–if)#frame-relay map	Sets a static DLCI.
	Router(config–if)#interface serial0.0	Establishes a subinterface. You must define multipoint or point-to-point.
	Router(config–subif)#frame-relay interface–dlci	Sets the DLCI on a subinterface.
	Router#show frame-relay map	Shows current DLCI to IP address mappings.

3.4   CONFIGURING ROUTER INTERFACES

A router's interface is the data port that forwards packets to destination networks. A single router can have several interfaces, for example, Ethernet, serial, and Token Ring, but can also have several interfaces of the same type. When configuring the interfaces, the interface type and number must be identified. All interfaces of a specific type are numbered, beginning with zero (0).

IDENTIFYING AN INTERFACE

To configure an interface, the router must first be in the global configuration mode. Next, specify the interface to configure with a major command. For example:

```
Router(config)#interface ethernet0
```

or

```
Router(config)#int e0
```

Either command will enter the interface configuration mode, returning a CLI prompt of

```
Router(config-if)#
```

When entering the interface mode, the CLI will not define which interface is being configured. It will only give the generic prompt of (*config-if*). However, any changes made at this point will only pertain to the interface specified. In the previous example, all changes will pertain to *ethernet0*.

The command is similar to configure a serial interface:

```
Router(config)#interface serial0
```

To enter the configuration mode for an interface on a Cisco series 2600, 3600, 4000, 7000, or 7200 router, you must define which physical slot the interface is connected to as well as the port number. For example:

```
Router(config)#interface serial0/0
```

This command points to slot number one (1) of the router and serial interface zero (0) on the module in that slot. While using a 7000 or 7500 series router with a versatile interface processor (VIP), it is necessary to identify the slot, adapter, and port number.

A Fast Ethernet interface on a 2600 series router would be identified as *interface fastethernet0/0* or *interface f0/0*.

DISABLING AND ENABLING AN INTERFACE

By default a router's interfaces are down. In other words, they are not configured to send or receive packets. The *no shutdown* command is used to turn the interfaces on. The sequence to turn on an Ethernet interface that is shut down follows:

```
Router>enable
Router#config terminal
Router(config)#interface ethernet0
Router(config-if)#no shutdown
```

The changes to the interface will occur immediately and must be saved to NVRAM so they will not be erased if the router is shut down. To make this configuration part of the startup configuration file in NVRAM, use the *copy running-config startup-config* command.

There are several reasons why an interface must be shut down, including performing maintenance on the router or the network itself. Cisco routers provide the *shutdown* command, which allows an interface to be administratively shut down. The following series of commands administratively shuts down the serial0/0 interface:

```
Router>enable
Router#config t
Router(config)#interface Serial0/0
Router(config-if)#shutdown
```

CONFIGURATION COMMANDS

Interface configuration includes, but is not limited to, specifying which type of connector the interface is using, configuring clock speeds and bandwidth, and setting IP addresses.

If the interface has an option to use different media types (for example, 10BaseT or AUI for an Ethernet interface), set the connector of choice with the *media-type* command. To set an IP address on an interface, use the *ip address* followed by the address and subnet mask of the interface. The router will then be able to route packets to that network. To configure an IP Fast Ethernet interface to be on the 10.0.0.0 network, use the following command:

```
Router(config)#interface f0/0
Router(config-if)#ip address 10.0.0.2
     255.0.0.0
```

If a router is used as a DCE in a router-to-router configuration, the clock rate for the DCE serial interface must be set. To determine if the interface is using a DTE or DCE type of physical connector, use the following command:

```
Router#show controller serial 0/0
```

If the interface is DCE, set the clock rate. The following clock rate is set to 64,000 bps.

```
Router(config)#interface serial0/0
Router(config-if)#clock rate 64000
```

To set the bandwidth of a serial interface to 64 Kbps, use the following command:

```
Router(config)#interface serial0/0
Router(config-if)#bandwidth 64
```

Test Tip: Clock rate for a serial interface is set in bits per second (64,000 bps). Bandwidth for a serial interface is set in kilobits per second (64 kbps).

SHOW INTERFACE COMMAND

Use the *show interface* command to determine whether an interface is operational or to verify changes made to the interface. This command can be given from the privileged EXEC mode.

```
Router#show interface serial0/0
```

When entering this command, the CLI returns information on the interface. For the CCNA Exam, it is important to understand the four possible states of the line and the protocol status for an interface. After typing the preceding command, the router checks the status of the physical cable and the layer 2 keepalives. The results will be reported as one of following four possible conditions:

- *Serial0 is up, line protocol is up.* The line and protocol on the interface are both operational.

- *Serial0 is up, line protocol is down.* A problem exists with the layer 2 protocol. There may be a problem with the encapsulation type or keepalives.

- *Serial0 is down, line protocol is down.* The interface is having a problem. Because the interface is down, the cable could be missing or may have never been attached. This message may also be caused by a missing cable on the other end of the router's connection.

- *Serial0 is administratively down, line protocol is down.* The interface has been manually shut down or disabled in the current configuration.

To see the status of all interfaces, use the following command:

```
Router#show interfaces
FastEthernet0/0 is up, line protocol is down
 Hardware is AmdFE, address is 0003.280b.ab61
   (bia 0003.280b.ab61)
 Internet address is 10.0.0.1/8
 MTU 1500 bytes, BW 100000 Kbit, DLY 100 usec,
   reliability 255/255, txload 1/255, rxload
   1/255
 Encapsulation ARPA, loopback not set
 Keepalive set (10 sec)
 Auto-duplex, Auto Speed, 100BaseTX/FX
 ARP type: ARPA, ARP Timeout 04:00:00
 Last input never, output 00:00:08, output
   hang never
 Last clearing of "show interface" counters
   never
 Queueing strategy: fifo
 Output queue 0/40, 0 drops; input queue 0/75,
   0 drops
 5 minute input rate 0 bits/sec, 0 packets/sec
 5 minute output rate 0 bits/sec, 0
   packets/sec
  0 packets input, 0 bytes
  Received 0 broadcasts, 0 runts, 0 giants, 0
   throttles
  0 input errors, 0 CRC, 0 frame, 0 overrun,
   0 ignored
  0 watchdog, 0 multicast
  0 input packets with dribble condition
   detected
  18 packets output, 1893 bytes, 0 underruns
  0 output errors, 0 collisions, 1 interface
   resets
  0 babbles, 0 late collision, 0 deferred
  0 lost carrier, 0 no carrier
```

0 output buffer failures, 0 output buffers swapped out

Serial0/0 is administratively down, line protocol is down

Hardware is PowerQUICC Serial

Description: line

Internet address is 11.0.0.1/8

MTU 1500 bytes, BW 1544 Kbit, DLY 20000 usec, reliabiliy 255/255, txload 1/255, rxload 1/255

Encapsulation HDLC, loopback not set

Keepalive set (10 sec)

Last input never, output never, output hang never

Last clearing of "show interface" counters never

Queueing strategy: fifo

Output queue 0/40, 0 drops; input queue 0/75, 0 drops

5 minute input rate 0 bits/sec, 0 packets/sec

5 minute output rate 0 bits/sec, 0 packets/sec

0 packets input, 0 bytes, 0 no buffer

Received 0 broadcasts, 0 runts, 0 giants, 0 throttles

0 input errors, 0 CRC, 0 frame, 0 overrun, 0 ignored, 0 abort

0 packets output, 0 bytes, 0 underruns

0 output errors, 0 collisions, 3 interface resets

0 output buffer failures, 0 output buffers swapped out

0 carrier transitions

DCD=down DSR=down DTR=down RTS=down CTS=down

(PARTIAL OUTPUT)

3.5 CISCO DISCOVERY PROTOCOL (CDP)

CDP is a proprietary Cisco protocol that operates at the data-link layer. A router has CDP enabled on its interfaces by default, and it is used to identify any other Cisco devices that may be directly connected. A router running CDP will broadcast its information every 60 seconds. Routers that hear the CDP broadcast will retain the CDP data for 3 minutes. This duration is called the *CDP holdtime*. If a new broadcast is not heard before that point, the receiving router will drop the CDP information of its neighbor.

CONFIGURING CDP

CDP is turned on by default. To see CDP interface configuration at the privileged EXEC mode, type the following:

```
Router#show cdp interface
```

If CDP is enabled, this command generates statistics such as the administrative and protocol conditions of the line, the encapsulation type for the interfaces, the frequency that the CDP packets are sent, and the holdtime of the CDP packets. If nothing is returned at the command prompt after typing this command, CDP is not enabled.

To see the neighbors that are connected to a router, use the command:

```
Router#show cdp neighbors
```

The information that will be reported for connected CDP neighbors includes

- **Device ID.** The neighboring device's host name, domain name, and MAC address.
- **Local Interface.** The local device's interface that is connected to the same network as its neighbor.
- **Holdtime.** The amount of time the receiving device will hold the CDP information before discarding it.
- **Capacity.** The neighboring device's function: R = Router, T = Transparent Bridge, B = Source Route Bridge, S = Switch, I = IGMP, and r = Repeater.
- **Platform.** The series of the neighboring router or switch.
- **Port ID.** The interface the neighboring device is communicating through.

The command to turn CDP off at the global configuration mode is

```
Router(config)#no cdp run
```

To enable it, use

```
Router(config)#cdp run
```

If you want to shut it off on only one interface, you can enter that interface and turn it off while allowing it to run on all other interfaces. Use this series of commands to turn CDP off on the *Ethernet0* interface only:

```
Router>enable
Router#configure terminal
Router(config)#interface ethernet0
Router(config-if)#no cdp enable
```

Additional CDP Commands

See Table 3.1 for additional commands.

3.6   TELNET

Telnet is a TCP/IP virtual terminal program that allows users to connect to remote devices using TCP/IP. You can use the Telnet program to connect to and remotely administer routers and switches. Telnet can support multiple remote sessions at a time. Unlike CDP, Telnet can retrieve information about routers that are not directly connected to each other.

CONNECTING VIA TELNET

To open a Telnet connection from one router to another, simply type the TCP/IP address of the remote router and press Enter. For example:

```
Router#10.0.0.100
```

Or to open a connection with a switch:

```
Router#telnet 10.0.0.100
```

The device you are telnetting from will attempt to make a Telnet connection with the remote TCP/IP address.

For Telnet to be successful, the VTY password on the remote device must be set. To avoid setting the VTY password on the router, use the *no login* command. This could lead to a security breach and should not be considered. Once authenticated, the prompt will appear as

```
RemoteRouter>
```

Successfully entering the VTY password only allows a connection to the user EXEC mode of the remote router. To access the privileged EXEC mode, enter the privileged EXEC password after the *enable* command.

VIEWING TELNET SESSIONS

To view the current Telnet sessions established from the local router, use the *show sessions* command as shown:

```
Router#show sessions
```

This command returns information such as a list of remote devices with established sessions, host name and IP address of the remote devices, as well as the amount of time the sessions have been idle. A "*" symbol in the session output represents the last session the router was using. The *show user* command gives statistics on the console lines and VTY lines of the remote devices.

SUSPENDING AND CLOSING A TELNET SESSION

Using the Ctrl+Shift+6 keystroke followed by the letter x suspends a Telnet session and returns the router to its local CLI. To close a Telnet session, use the *exit* or *logout* command from the remote device's CLI type:

```
RemoteRouter#logout
```

To close the session from the local device's CLI, type the following:

```
Router#disconnect [session number]
```

CHAPTER SUMMARY

This chapter covered the basic configuration of a router. The chapter recognized the hardware components of a router and how they were used during the boot process. We also covered the commands that are expected to be on the CCNA Exam. Table 3.1 summarizes all other commands in the chapter. You should have a strong understanding of the commands in Table 3.1 before taking the CCNA Exam. It also is a handy tool when configuring a router outside of the classroom. In the following chapters, we will look at the core responsibilities of a router and how to configure routing protocols, but first complete the knowledge test.

KNOWLEDGE TEST

Choose one answer for all questions unless directed to do otherwise.

1. Which router component stores the startup-configuration file?
   a. RAM
   b. ROM
   c. Flash RAM
   d. NVRAM

2. What is the correct command sequence to change the console password to Delmar?
   a. *Router#line con 0*
      Router#password Delmar
   b. *Router#line console 0*
      Router(config-line)#login
      Router(config-line)#password Delmar
   c. *Router(config)#line console 0*
      Router(config-line)#login
      Router(config-line)#password Delmar

3. What command will configure serial interface 0 with a bandwidth setting of 64 Kbps?
   a. *Router(config-if)#bandwidth 64000*
   b. *Router(config-if)#bandwidth 64*
   c. *Router(config)#bandwidth 64*
   d. *Router(config-if)#bandwidth 64kbps*

4. What is the command to back up the running configuration?
   a. *Copy running-startup tftp-startup*
   b. *Copy running-config startup-config*
   c. *Copy running-config tftp-config*
   d. *Copy active-config startup-config*

5. What are the commands that will enter privileged EXEC mode? (Choose two.)
   a. *Router>en*
   b. *Router>enabling*
   c. *Router>enter*
   d. *Router>enable*

6. What command would allow you to see the possible arguments available with the show command?
   a. *show ?*
   b. *show help*
   c. *show?*
   d. *? show*

7. What command would you use to show the IOS version, hardware information, and configuration register?
   a. *show version*
   b. *version*
   c. *s version*
   d. *see version*

8. What command would you use to copy the running configuration to a TFTP server in your network?
   a. *copy startup-config tftp*
   b. *copy running-config tftp*
   c. *copy tftp startup-config*
   d. *copy running config tftp*

9. What would the configuration register setting be if you used the *boot system rom* command?
   a. 0x2100
   b. 0x2102
   c. 0x210A
   d. 0x2101

10. What is the command to determine if interface Ethernet 0 is active?
    a. *Router#Show Ethernet0*
    b. *Router#Show E0*
    c. *Router#sh e0*
    d. *Router#sh int e0*

11. What is the correct command to display a login message that reads "This is a secured router"?
    a. *Router#banner motd @This is a secured router.@*
    b. *Router(config-if)#banner motd @This is a secured router.@*
    c. *Router.banner motd @This is a secured router.@*
    d. *Router(config)#banner motd @This is a secured router.@*

12. What is the command to enable the interface serial 0?
    a. *Router(config-if)#Enable interfaces*
    b. *Router(config-if)#no shutdown*
    c. *Router(config-if)#enable*
    d. *Router(config-if)#enable serial 0*

13. How do you set an encrypted, privileged EXEC password of Thomson?
    a. *Router(config)#enable encrypted Thomson*
    b. *Router#enable secret Thomson*
    c. *Router(config)#enable secret Thomson*
    d. *Router(config)#enable password Thomson*

14. Which command is used to load the IOS from a location other than the default location?
    a. *boot system*
    b. *load system boot*
    c. *load boot*
    d. *system boot*

15. The default command history buffer remembers 10 commands. What is the command that will increase the command history buffer to remember 25 commands?
    a. *terminal history + 15*
    b. *terminal history size + 15*
    c. *terminal history size 25*
    d. *terminal history 25*

16. Which command would you use to view all directly connected routers and switches?
    a. *show cdp interface*
    b. *Show cdp neighbors*
    c. *Show cdp adjacencies*
    d. *Show cdp traffic*

17. Which keystroke will move the cursor to the beginning of the CLI?
    a. Ctrl+A
    b. Ctrl+P
    c. Ctrl+B
    d. Ctrl+C

18. What is the proper command to view detailed information about CDP neighbor 10.0.0.1?
    a. *show cdp neighbor 10.0.0.1*
    b. *show cdp neighbor*
    c. *show cdp entry 10.0.0.1*
    d. *show cdp entry*

19. What is the command to load the IOS image named IOS1 from a TFTP server with a TCP/IP address of 192.168.1.25?
    a. *boot tftp IOS1 192.168.1.25*
    b. *bootsystem tftp IOS1 192.168.1.25*
    c. *boot system tftp 192.168.1.25*
    d. *boot system tftp IOS1 192.168.1.25*

20. Which command sequence will encrypt all passwords entered between the two commands?
    a. *enable secret*
        no enable secret
    b. *password encryption*
        no password encryption
    c. *enable password*
        no enable password
    d. *service password-encryption*
        no service password-encryption

CHAPTER 4

IP Routing (RIP and IGRP)

OBJECTIVES

The following topics are discussed in Chapter 4:

- Select an appropriate routing protocol based on user requirements.
- Design a simple internetwork using Cisco technology.
- Configure routing protocols given user requirements.
- Troubleshoot routing protocols.
- Troubleshoot a device as part of a working network.
- Evaluate the characteristics of routing protocols.

INTRODUCTION

This chapter focuses on how to integrate a router into a network operating with the TCP/IP suite of protocols. The chapter begins with an overview of routing and then describes the difference between routing protocols and routed protocols. Finally, it describes route configuration methods and how to configure two routing protocols: RIP and IGRP. Chapter 5 will introduce two additional IP Routing protocols: OSPF and EIGRP.

4.1 AN OVERVIEW OF ROUTING

In computer networking terms, *routing* is the process of sending data packets from one network to another. The separate networks can belong to a small, private internetwork or can be members of the global Internet. Routers know where to send packets because they maintain a table called a *routing table*. A routing table lists known networks and routes (paths) available to those networks.

Routers operate based on a set of rules known as *routing algorithms*. A routing algorithm defines how a router learns about the internetwork, how it builds its routing table, and how it communicates with other routers. Routing protocols implement routing algorithms and provide the communications mechanism.

ROUTED VS. ROUTING PROTOCOLS

A *routed protocol* is a protocol, such as IP, that can be routed by a router. Routed protocols encapsulate packets of data and send them to their destination via the router's interfaces. The *routing protocol* enables the routing process by learning routes and preparing routing tables to be sent to other routers in the internetwork.

Routing Protocols

The two major types of routing protocols are *Interior Gateway Protocols (IGP)* and *Exterior Gateway Protocols (EGP)*. These are broken down into routing protocol classes that actually implement the routing algorithms. IGPs are used within an autonomous system. An *autonomous system (AS)* is a group of networks given an administrative number by the Internet Assigned Numbers Authority (IANA). All autonomous systems with the same number are normally under the same administration. It is possible to operate within a private AS, which would not be assigned a number by IANA. EGPs, such as the *Border Gateway Protocol (BGP)*, are used to connect autonomous systems together. Examples of IGPs are the *Interior Gateway Routing Protocol (IGRP)*, *Routing Information Protocol (RIP)*, *Open Shortest Path First (OSPF)*, and the *Enhanced Interior Gateway Routing Protocol (EIGRP)*. The CCNA Exam covers IGPs only.

ROUTING ALGORITHMS

Routing protocols must have rules that specify how information will be passed on to other routers in the network. These rules are defined by routing algorithms, which are associated with routing protocols used in the internetwork. The IGP uses three routing algorithms: *distance-vector routing*, *link-state routing*, and *hybrid routing*. Hybrid routing is a combination of both distance-vector and link-state routing. Each routing protocol is associated with a type of routing algorithm:

- Distance-vector routing = RIP (version 1) and IGRP
- Link-state routing = OSPF
- Hybrid routing = EIGRP

The CCNA Exam focuses on RIP, IGRP, OSPF, and EIGRP. Therefore, a detailed description of the distance-vector routing algorithm is provided in this chapter.

Link-state routing and hybrid routing are discussed in detail in Chapter 5. Some of the rules defined by routing algorithms include metrics, administrative distances, and convergence.

Metrics

Routers examine their routing table when they need to forward packets to a destination network. The routing table maintains a listing of all networks and known routes to them. Each network is associated with a *metric* that determines the *cost* of the network path. Normally, routers will send the data to the next router with the lowest cost in the routing table. Several metrics routers are used to determine the cost. Some of the more common metrics are

- **Hop count.** The number of routers the packet must pass through to get to its destination.

- **Tick count.** Timing mechanism to determine how long it will take to get the packet from one router to the next. A tick is approximately 55 milliseconds.

- **Cost.** An arbitrary value assigned by an administrator that can be based on monetary cost, bandwidth, or other calculation.

- **Bandwidth.** Data capacity of the line.

- **Delay.** Timing mechanism.

- **Reliability.** Reliability of the line.

- **Maximum transmission unit (MTU).** Defines the size of the packets allowed on all links in the path.

Administrative Distance

Each routing algorithm uses a different means of calculating the cost to a network. If two different routes have the same cost, the router reverts to the *administrative distance* of the network. The administrative distance is the trustworthiness of the routing information received by a neighboring router. It carries a value between 0 and 255, with 0 being the most trusted and 255 not being trusted. There are several default administrative distances to be aware of:

- A connected interface has a default distance of 0. This interface is always used to send data to a network that is directly connected to a router.

- A static route has a default distance of 1.

- If a route is learned by EIGRP, the distance is 90.

- If a route is learned by IGRP, the distance is 100.

- If a route is learned by OSPF, the distance is 110.

- If a route is learned by RIP, the distance is 120.

- If a route is learned by an external EIGRP source, the distance is 170.

- If the route source is unknown, it has a distance of 255 and is never used.

Route Source	Default Distance	
Connected interface	0	
Static route address	1	
EIGRP	90	
IGRP	100	
OSPF	110	
RIP	120	
External EIGRP	170	
Unknown or unbelievable	255	(Not used to pass data)

 Test Tip: You should memorize the previous administrative distance values.

Convergence

Convergence is the process of all routers updating neighboring routers (also known as *adjacencies*) with their current routing information. The network is fully converged when all routers know about every network in an internetwork. The time it takes to converge with adjacent routers is one means of evaluating a routing algorithm—the less time it takes to converge, the more efficient the algorithm. Each algorithm converges a different way.

DISTANCE-VECTOR ROUTING ALGORITHM

The word *vector* means direction. The distance-vector algorithm bases its routing information on the distance and direction (vector) to other networks. One of the metrics used in the distance-vector algorithm is the hop count. A network that is two routers away from the current router is two hops away. Therefore, if the only metric being used is the hop count, then the metric in the sending router's routing table is 2.

In a distance-vector–based internetwork, the routers initially seed their own routing tables by adding their directly connected networks (as configured). The initial routing tables that are sent out to other routers are small, but many exchanges are made as the routers converge. This method of convergence causes a lot of congestion on the network links. This, however, is the only way that distance-vector routers converge. Distance-vector routing has a slow convergence time because each router only sends updates every 30 or 90 seconds.

| 12.0.0.0 | Router A | 13.0.0.0 | Router B | 10.0.0.0 | Router C | 11.0.0.0 |

Network	Metric	Next Node
12.0.0.0	0 hop	–
13.0.0.0	0 hop	–

Network	Metric	Next Node
13.0.0.0	0 hop	–
10.0.0.0	0 hop	–

Network	Metric	Next Node
10.0.0.0	0 hop	–
11.0.0.0	0 hop	–

Routing Tables before Convergence

| 12.0.0.0 | Router A | 13.0.0.0 | Router B | 10.0.0.0 | Router C | 11.0.0.0 |

Network	Metric	Next Node
12.0.0.0	0 hop	–
13.0.0.0	0 hop	–
10.0.0.0	1 hop	B
11.0.0.0	2 hops	B

Network	Metric	Next Node
13.0.0.0	0 hop	–
10.0.0.0	0 hop	–
12.0.0.0	1 hop	A
11.0.0.0	1 hop	C

Network	Metric	Next Node
10.0.0.0	0 hop	–
11.0.0.0	0 hop	–
13.0.0.0	1 hop	B
12.0.0.0	2 hops	B

Routing Tables after Convergence

Figure 4.1 *Convergence with a distance-vector algorithm*

Distance-vector algorithms use secondhand information when creating their routing tables. All the routes that are learned through update packets are based on information given by other routers in the internetwork. Therefore, if one router is giving out inaccurate route information, all the other routers in the internetwork are prone to using it. See Figure 4.1 for an example of an accurate and successful convergence.

In Figure 4.1, Router B is directly connected to network 13.0.0.0 and network 10.0.0.0. Router C is directly connected to network 10.0.0.0 and 11.0.0.0. Router B will learn about network 11.0.0.0 from Router C during convergence. If the information in Router C's routing table is inaccurate, then Router B's routing table will be inaccurate as well. When Router B converges with Router A, Router A's routing table will also be inaccurate.

When Router A sends data to Router C, it bases its metric on the one given to it by Router B. Because Router B says network 11.0.0.0 is one hop away, Router A assumes network 11.0.0.0 must be two hops away. When the topology of a network using the distance-vector algorithm changes, convergence must take place again. However, distance-vector protocols do not send the changes immediately. They hold them until it is time to send the next update packet, which occurs every 30 or 90 seconds. Changes flow through the network iteratively until convergence is achieved. Each adjacent router examines the route table, updates its table, and then forwards it to its neighbors if there are any differences between its current table and the new table.

Problems in a distance-vector-algorithm–based internetwork may occur because of the slow convergence time of the algorithm. *Routing loops* are one of the problems encountered and are the cause of routers in an internetwork getting caught in a continuous loop of sending falsely advertised routes to one another.

The following example shows four networks and three fully converged routers.

| 15.0.0.0 | Router A | 20.0.0.0 | Router B | 145.10.0.0 | Router C | 35.0.0.0 |

Network	Metric	Next Node		Network	Metric	Next Node		Network	Metric	Next Node
15.0.0.0	0 hop	–		20.0.0.0	0 hop	–		145.10.0.0	0 hop	–
20.0.0.0	0 hop	–		145.10.0.0	0 hop	–		35.0.0.0	0 hop	–
145.10.0.0	1 hop	B		15.0.0.0	1 hop	A		20.0.0.0	1 hop	B
35.0.0.0	2 hops	B		35.0.0.0	1 hop	C		15.0.0.0	2 hops	B

Converged network

Network 35.0.0.0 goes down and the only router that knows about the problem is Router C, which advertises the route as down to Router B.

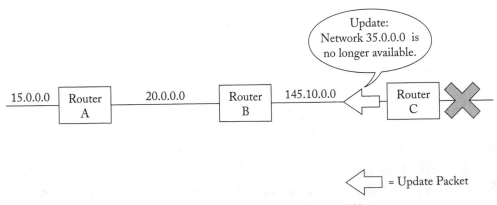

35.0.0.0 network advertised as no longer available

Before Router A gets the new information, it advertises 35.0.0.0 as two hops away. Router B updates its own table (which is currently accurate) with the inaccurate information learned from Router A. Router B assumes that the information is valid and places the cost in its own routing table, adding a metric of one hop to it. Now Router B believes network 35.0.0.0 is three hops away and advertises it that way. When Router A gets this update, it assumes Router B learned a new route to network 35.0.0.0 and increases its hop count to four. Router A advertises this route and Router B increases the value of the cost to five.

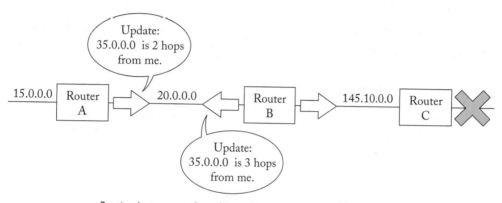

Routing loop occurs from false information advertised by Router A.

This loop continues until a mechanism is in place to stop it.

This continuous looping is called *count to infinity*. Several mechanisms are in place to keep it to a minimum. The four methods of avoiding the count to infinity are

- **Defining a maximum hop count.** The *maximum hop count* for the RIP distance-vector algorithm is 15. Anything above 15 hops is considered unreachable. Even with the maximum hop count in place, routing loops can still occur, but they will never loop more than 15 times. The maximum hop count for IGRP is 100 by default, but can be extended to 255.

- **Split horizon.** *Split horizon* does not allow any router to advertise information about a route on the interface from which the information was learned. In the example given earlier, Router A would have never sent the wrong information back to Router B because it learned about the 35.0.0.0 network from Router B.

- **Route poisoning (poison reverse).** *Route poisoning* is the process of advertising the downed route with an infinite cost, such as 16, for RIP. If route poisoning were used in the example when the 35.0.0.0 network was taken off-line, Router C would have changed its metric to the 35.0.0.0 network to 16, which is unreachable. The update would have been sent to Router B and subsequently to Router A.

- **Holddown timers and triggered updates.** A *holddown timer* is a timer set in a router that begins counting after a router receives an update packet. After the router receives an update packet, the holddown timer will not allow the router to accept any route changes unless the change has a better metric to a specified route. *Triggered updates* are used in conjunction with holddown timers. A triggered update allows a router to send its routing table without having to wait for its specified interval, which is 30 seconds for RIP and 90 seconds for IGRP. The routing table is sent immediately when using triggered updates. Triggered updates and holddown timers can speed up the convergence time of a distance-vector–based internetwork.

 Test Tip: The four methods of loop avoidance with a distance-vector algorithm are maximum hop count, split horizon, poison reverse, and holddown timers and triggered updates.

LINK-STATE ROUTING ALGORITHM

Link-state routing algorithms operate differently from distance-vector algorithms. The most common routing protocol that uses the link-state routing algorithm today is OSPF. Link-state algorithms are more complex than distance-vector algorithms and are more efficient when dealing with larger internetworks.

Link-state algorithms overcome some of the shortcomings of distance-vector algorithms. Although OSPF is covered in Chapter 5, here are some of the differences between link-state routing and distance-vector routing:

- Link-state routing maintains the topology of the entire network in a separate database.

- Link-state algorithms use firsthand information about routes to send data.

- Link-state algorithms only forward updates or changes to the routing tables after the initial convergence.

- Link-state algorithms can use classless IP addressing because the subnet mask is forwarded with routing table updates. With the exception of RIP version 2, most distance-vector algorithms do not support classless IP addressing.

- Link-state algorithm routing metrics are more complex, requiring more processor overhead on the router.

- Link-state algorithms have a faster convergence time.

- Link-state algorithms are not prone to the count to infinity problem.

HYBRID ROUTING ALGORITHM

Hybrid routing combines features of the distance-vector algorithms and the link-state algorithms. An example of a hybrid routing algorithm is the EIGRP. EIGRP uses the routing update mechanisms associated with link-state protocols with the metric system of the distance-vector algorithms. This provides for the fast convergence associated with link-state algorithms and the low processor overhead metric used by distance-vector algorithms. EIGRP is covered in Chapter 5.

4.2 CONFIGURING ROUTES

Routers and their routing tables must be configured properly by the network administrator. The administrator must ensure that the routing of data from one network to another is seamless to the end user. Three methods are used to configure the routes of a router: *static routing, default routing,* and *dynamic routing.*

STATIC ROUTING

Static routing is the process whereby the network administrator manually places all routes that the router can send packets to in the routing table. This should include all networks in the internetwork. The command used to configure static routing in an IP network is *ip route* from the global configuration mode. To remove a static route from a routing table, use the *no ip* route command from the global configuration mode. Following is an example of the *ip route* command:

```
Router(config)#ip route 10.0.0.0 255.0.0.0
   11.0.0.2
```

In the example, assume that the router being configured is on the 11.0.0.0 network and needs a route to the 10.0.0.0 network. Notice that the subnet mask of the destination network is placed in the command, as well as the interface of the router that can pass the packet to the 10.0.0.0 network (11.0.0.2 is the next hop). See the next diagram.

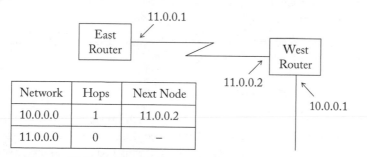

Routing Table for East Router

Example of statically configured route

The routing path is configured in only one direction. In the event the 10.0.0.0 network routers need to send data back to the 11.0.0.0 network, the administrator would have to statically configure the route in the 10.0.0.0 routers. The exact arguments that must be used with the *ip route* command are

- **Network address.** Defines the network address of the destination. This is a required parameter.

- **Subnet mask.** Defines the subnet mask of the destination network. This is a required parameter.

- **Next hop address.** This is the IP address of an interface on a router that is directly connected to the destination network. This parameter is used if the interface parameter is not used. If this argument is used, the router sends packets to the interface on another router, which should be connected directly or indirectly to the destination network.

- **Interface.** This parameter is used in place of the *next hop address* parameter. It refers to the interface that forwards the packet to the destination network.

- **Distance.** This is an optional parameter and describes the administrative distance to the network.

- **Permanent.** This is an optional parameter that keeps the route in the router even if the interface is shut down.

Use the *show ip route* command (seen later) to view the routing table after it has been configured with static routes type. To remove a static route from the router, use the following command:

```
Router(config)#no ip route 10.0.0.0 255.0.0.0
    11.0.0.2
```

The advantages of static routing are the following:

- It minimizes CPU use and the amount of bandwidth consumed during convergence.

- It secures the routes the router uses because it is not using a routing protocol to advertise itself on the network.

The disadvantages to static routing are the following:

- It can become very difficult to manage. Each time a network is added to the internetwork, an administrator must add the route to every router in the network, which can be time consuming and thus prone to human error.

- It is more suitable for small networks owing to the administrative overhead.

DEFAULT ROUTING

Default routing is the process of having a router send all packets destined for networks that do not appear in its routing table out of the same interface. Default routing ensures that if a router does not know about a route in its table, the packet can still make it to the network by using the default route. For example, assume that a private internetwork has several routers configured within it. Each router in the internetwork does not have to maintain all existing routes within the public Internet. Each router has to have the default route to the router connected to the public Internet. This allows all packets with an unknown destination to be forwarded to the public Internet. Without default routing, packets with unknown destinations are dropped. The command to configure default routing is

```
Router(config)#ip route 0.0.0.0 0.0.0.0
    11.0.0.2
```

In the command, the first 0.0.0.0 is typed in as a special network address. The second 0.0.0.0 is a special subnet mask, indicating that this is a default route. The 11.0.0.2 is the IP address of the next hop router, which will forward the packet to another default router or (if directly connected) to the destination.

When designing the network, consider using the IP classless command if a default route is configured. Because routers use classful addressing by default, they assume that all routes of a classful address are listed in their routing table. This is not always the case because the advent of Classless Inter Domain Routing (CIDR). With CIDR, address classes are broken up and two networks can have what seems to be the same network according to the router. To make the router aware of the CIDR notation, use the global configuration mode *ip classless* command in your configuration. This command ensures that a router will not drop a packet destined for the default route. For example, if a network has an address of 10.16.0.0/15 and a packet is destined for network 10.64.0.0/13, without the *ip classless* command, the router will assume that the 10.64.0.0 network should be in its routing table. However, the number of bits used in the subnet mask is different, which means the 10.64.0.0 network can be outside of the internetwork. The packet should then be forwarded to a default route. Without the *ip classless* command, the packet will be dropped when the router realizes the 10.64.0.0 network is not in its routing table.

DYNAMIC ROUTING

Dynamic routing gives the responsibility of creating and updating routes to the routing protocol implemented. There are advantages and disadvantages to dynamic routing. The advantages to dynamic routing are

- Less administrative overhead. Routers maintain routing tables and make changes to them without the immediate assistance of an administrator, thus reducing human error.

- More efficient in large intranetwork or internetwork.

The disadvantages of dynamic routing are

- CPU and memory use is increased while the router examines packets and determines the least cost route to the destination.
- Network bandwidth for data is limited while routers are sharing route information.

4.3 CONFIGURING ROUTING PROTOCOLS (RIP AND IGRP)

When the decision is made to use dynamic routing, first determine which routing protocol best suits the network. The choices available are distance-vector and link-state routing protocols. The decision should be based on the characteristics of the internetwork such as size, number of routers installed, speed of the links, and expected use. After the algorithm is decided, choose the routing protocol to configure. Here you will learn to configure RIP and IGRP, both of which use the distance-vector algorithm.

ROUTING INFORMATION PROTOCOL (RIP)

The Routing Information Protocol (RIP) is a distance-vector routing protocol available in two versions: RIP V1 and RIP V2. RIP V1 was the first version and only supported classful IP addresses, whereas RIP V2 supports classless IP addresses and sends the subnet mask along with route table updates. RIP for IP uses the hop count as its only routing metric (the maximum hop count for RIP is 15), sends its routing table updates every 30 seconds, and can load balance packets while sending them to the destination network. To accomplish load balancing, RIP can maintain up to six equal-cost paths (default is four) for each destination in the routing table.

CLI Configuration

Routing protocols are loaded from the global configuration mode. To install RIP, type the following:

```
Router(config)#router rip
Router(config-router)#
```

After the routing protocol is installed, use the *network* command (which is required), as shown next, to specify each directly connected network that will participate in sending and receiving routing information.

```
Router(config-router)#network 10.0.0.0
```

After configuring RIP, several commands are used to verify its configuration, verify its routing table, and view its updates. To verify the routing protocol being used on the router, use the *show ip protocols* command. The *show ip protocols* command shown next identifies what routing protocol is installed (RIP), how often RIP route table updates are being sent (30 seconds), the networks it is connected to (10.0.0.0 and 11.0.0.0), the administrative distance for RIP (120), as well as when the last update was received (00:00:19 and 00:00:28).

```
Router#show ip protocols
Routing Protocol is "rip"
  Sending updates every 30 seconds, next due in
    25 seconds
  Invalid after 180 seconds, hold down 180,
    flushed after 240
  Outgoing update filter list for all
    interfaces is
  Incoming update filter list for all
    interfaces is
  Redistributing: rip
  Default version control: send version 1,
    receive any version
    Interface        Send  Recv  Triggered RIP  Key-chain
    FastEthernet0/0   1    1 2
    Serial0/0         1    1 2
  Automatic network summarization is in effect
  Routing for Networks:
    10.0.0.0
    11.0.0.0
  Routing Information Sources:
    Gateway    Distance    Last Update
    10.0.0.1     120        00:00:19
    11.0.0.1     120        00:00:28
  Distance: (default is 120)
```

If a RIP router does not receive an update from a known router within 180 seconds, the router waiting for the update flags the missing router. When the holddown timer reaches 240 seconds for the flagged router, the router waiting for the update will drop the routes associated with the missing router from its routing table, assuming that the router is down.

The next command, *show ip route,* shows the routing table of a router. It identifies the routes the router knows about, the administrative distance and hop count (120/1) to each respective route, the interface to use to get to the route (serial0/0), the address of the next hop in the internetwork for each network specified in the table (11.0.0.2), and the time since the table was last updated. A "*C*" preceding a network address when viewing the routing table denotes that the network is directly connected to the router. An "*R*" preceding the network address means that the network was learned through RIP. See the following:

```
Router#show ip route
Codes: C - connected, S - static, I - IGRP,
    R - RIP, M - mobile, B - BGP
  D - EIGRP, EX - EIGRP external, O - OSPF,
    IA - OSPF inter area
  N1 - OSPF NSSA external type 1, N2 - OSPF
    NSSA external type 2
  E1 - OSPF external type 1, E2 - OSPF external
    type 2, E - EGP
  i - IS-IS, L1 - IS-IS level-1, L2 - IS-IS
    level-2, ia - IS-IS inter area
   * - candidate default, U - per-user static
    route, o - ODR
  P - periodic downloaded static route
Gateway of last resort is not set
R   129.5.0.0/16 [120/1] via 11.0.0.2,
    00:00:16, Serial0/0
C   10.0.0.0/8 is directly connected,
    FastEthernet0/0
C   11.0.0.0/8 is directly connected, Serial0/0
```

The last command described is the *debug ip rip* command, which allows the router to identify when routing updates occur. The CLI reports information when sending updates as well as when receiving them. Remember, RIP sends updates every 30 seconds, so a message shows up on the CLI stating that an update was sent at least every 30 seconds. This is not taking into account the number of updates received. The overhead associated with the *debug* command can adversely affect the performance of the router. Therefore, it should not be enabled for long durations. To disable the command, use the *no debug all* command to shut all debugging off. The syntax to enable and disable debugging is covered in Table 3.1 in Chapter 3.

INTERIOR GATEWAY ROUTING PROTOCOL (IGRP)

The Interior Gateway Routing Protocol (IGRP) uses the distance-vector routing algorithm. However, it is a much more sophisticated protocol than RIP. IGRP is a proprietary protocol developed by Cisco to overcome the shortfalls of RIP. All routers in the internetwork must be Cisco routers when using IGRP. IGRP is not limited to 15 hops as RIP is. It is limited to 100 hops by default, but can be configured to have a maximum hop count of 255.

IGRP does not base its routing metric on the hop count alone. It uses a *composite metric* that is based on two values by default, but can be configured to use up to five. The five values are

- **Bandwidth.** This is a default value and is based on the bandwidth capacity in kilobits of an interface.

- **Delay.** This is a default value and is based on the amount of microseconds it takes to send a packet to the destination.

- **Reliability.** This is based on keepalives, which are packets sent between routers to verify connectivity.

- **Load.** This value is based on the routing traffic of an interface.

- **Maximum transmission unit.** This value is based on the maximum size of packets allowed on all links in a path.

IGRP can maintain up to six paths for any given route in the routing table. It sends routing table updates every 90 seconds compared with RIP's 30-second interval. If IGRP does not receive an update from a known router within 630 seconds, it removes the route from its routing table, which is an increase from RIP's 270-second interval.

CLI Configuration

A few commands are necessary to successfully configure IGRP. Start the IGRP protocol by using the following command:

```
Router(config)#router igrp [autonomous system
    number]
Router(config-router)#network [network IP
    address]
```

In this command, the AS number is a mandatory argument for the *router IGRP* command. All IGRP routers in the internetwork must use the same AS number. The number does not have to be registered with IANA unless the network is accessible by public routers. The second command identifies the directly connected networks that will participate in IGRP routing.

To verify that the protocol has been started on the router, you can use the *show ip protocols* command. The output of the command gives the AS number, metrics being used, administrative distance, networks being advertised, and gateways.

To view the routing table of an IGRP router, use the *show ip route* command. The output is similar to the RIP table. However, if a route listed in the table is preceded by the letter *I*, it means the route was learned by IGRP. Each route also has a value like this: (*100/numeric value*). The 100 represents the administrative distance, whereas the numeric value represents the composite metric. The lower the composite metric, the better the route.

IGRP supports two debugging commands. The first one is the *debug ip igrp events* command, which displays a summary of routes requested and broadcasts sent. It only displays a summary because IGRP can support up to 255 hops, and if all the updates were shown on a router, it would drastically affect the router. The updates show the interface that broadcasts the table, the address of the router requesting the update, and the number of routes that have been updated. The syntax of the command is as follows:

```
Router#debug ip igrp events
```

To turn the debugging off, use the *no debug all* or the *no debug ip igrp events* command.

The second debugging command used with IGRP is the *debug ip igrp transactions* command. This command shows which router is requesting a route and the updated routes being sent. The command line syntax is

```
Router#debug ip igrp transactions
```

To turn off debugging, use the *no debug all* command or the *no debug ip igrp transactions* command.

CHAPTER SUMMARY

This chapter covered routing algorithms, routing protocols, and configuration methods. The routing algorithms that were discussed include the distance-vector routing algorithm, the link-state algorithm, and the hybrid routing algorithm. Also covered were the types of routing protocols such as the IGPs and BGPs. The chapter focused on two IGPs (RIP and IGRP), and how to configure the network to successfully use each of them. IPX routing will be discussed in the next chapter, but first complete the knowledge test.

KNOWLEDGE TEST

Choose one answer for all questions unless directed to do otherwise.

1. What network is considered unreachable when using RIP routing?
   a. The 14th network
   b. The 15th network
   c. The 16th network
   d. The 12th network

2. What link-state routing algorithm do Cisco routers use to route packets within an AS?
   a. RIP
   b. OSPF
   c. BGP
   d. IGRP

3. What are the disadvantages of RIP routing? (Choose two.)
   a. Slow convergence
   b. Fast convergence
   c. Low processor overhead
   d. High processor overhead
   e. Routing loops
   f. Holddown timers

4. What is the proper command sequence to enable RIP routing on the interfaces that are connected to the 129.5.0.0 network?
   a. *Router#Rip*
      Router(config)#network 129.5.0.0
   b. *Router(config)#rip 129.5.0.0*
      Router(config-router)#network 129.5.0.0
   c. *Router(config)#router rip*
      Router(config-router)#network 129.5.0.0
   d. *Router(config)#router rip*
      Router(config-router)#rip 129.5.0.0

5. What are some of the features of IGRP? (Choose all that apply.)
   a. It is a link-state routing algorithm.
   b. It was developed by Cisco.
   c. It has a maximum hop count of 15.
   d. It uses the hop count as its only metric.
   e. It must be configured with an AS number.
   f. Because of processor overhead it does not support debugging.

6. For a router to successfully route a packet to a network that is directly or indirectly connected to it, what must the router know?
   a. The source router address
   b. The destination address of the packet
   c. The packet's network source address
   d. The next hop address

7. What are the correct statements about dynamic routing? (Choose all that apply.)
   a. Dynamic routing has less processor overhead than static routing.
   b. Dynamic routing has less administrative overhead than static routing.
   c. Dynamic routing is best suited for large internetworks.
   d. Dynamic routing is best suited for small internetworks.
   e. Dynamic routing was Cisco's response to the shortcomings of RIP.

8. What is the proper command sequence to configure IGRP with an AS number of 100 on the 141.27.0.0 network?
   a. *Router#igrp*
      Router(config)#igrp 100
      Router(config-router)network 14.27.0.0
   b. *Router(config)#router igrp*
      Router(config-router)#as 100
      Router(config-router)network 14.27.0.0
   c. *Router(config)#router igrp 100*
      Router(config-router)#network 141.27.0.0
   d. *Router(config)#router igrp*
      Router(config-router)#as 100
      Router(config-router)network 14.27.0.0

9. What are true statements about RIP? (Choose all that apply.)
   a. RIP broadcasts its routing table every 90 seconds.
   b. RIP broadcasts its routing table every 60 seconds.
   c. RIP broadcasts its routing table every 30 seconds.
   d. RIP does not broadcast its routing table; it only sends changes to the routing table.
   e. RIP has a maximum hop count of 15.
   f. RIP uses split horizon to avoid routing loops.
   g. The administrative distance of a RIP learned route is 1 in a RIP internetwork.
   h. RIP uses a composite metric to determine the best path to a network.
   i. RIP is a distance-vector routing algorithm.

10. RIP is susceptible to routing loops. What mechanisms does RIP have in place to avoid the count-to-infinity problem? (Choose two.)
    a. Horizon adjust
    b. Route poisoning
    c. Split horizon

    d. Route adjust

    e. Link-state routing algorithm

11. What is the command to view routing updates in a RIP internetwork?

    a. *Router#debug ip rip*

    b. *Router#debug rip*

    c. *Router#ip rip debugging*

    d. *Router#rip debugging*

12. What command will display the current routing table of an IGRP router?

    a. *Router#show route*

    b. *Router#show ip route*

    c. *Router#show igrp route*

    d. *Router#show ip igrp route*

13. What must you know to enable RIP?

    a. The directly connected routers

    b. The indirectly connected routers

    c. The directly connected networks

    d. The indirectly connected networks

14. Which mechanism is used by RIP to avoid routing loops by not advertising the route to the interface where it learned it?

    a. Holddown timers

    b. Poison reverse

    c. Triggered updates

    d. Split horizon

15. What command can be used to determine the routing protocol that is being used on a router?

    a. *Router#show ip debugging*

    b. *Router#show ip route*

    c. *Router#show ip protocols*

    d. *Router#show protocols*

16. When a router is using IGRP, it has two debugging options available. What are they?

    a. Transactions and events

    b. Routes and metrics

    c. Transactions and metrics

    d. Transactions and routes

    e. Metrics and events

    f. Events and routes

17. Which mechanism does RIP use to avoid routing loops that falsely advertise routes as 16 or unreachable?

    a. Triggered updates

    b. Holddown timers

    c. Split horizon

    d. Route poisoning

18. Which statements are characteristics of the link-state routing algorithm? (Choose all that apply.)
    a. Routing tables are broadcast to all routers in the internetwork.
    b. Only changes to the route tables are sent to other routers in the internetwork.
    c. IGRP uses a link-state routing algorithm.
    d. Link-state routing has a maximum hop count of 255.
    e. Link-state routing has high processor overhead in comparison with static routing.

19. What command is used to ensure packets are not dropped when using a default route?
    a. *classless ip routing*
    b. *ip classless*
    c. *classless routing*
    d. *ip classless routing*

20. What does a holddown timer ensure?
    a. That a route with a worse metric is not added to the routing table within a specified amount of time
    b. That a router must send a routing table change to another router before the timer ends
    c. That a router ignore a route with a better metric than the route it just learned for a specified amount of time
    d. That a router broadcast its routing table every 30 seconds

CHAPTER 5

IP Routing (OSPF and EIGRP)

OBJECTIVES

The following topics are discussed in Chapter 5:

- Select an appropriate routing protocol based on user requirements.
- Design a simple internetwork using Cisco technology.
- Configure routing protocols given user requirements.
- Troubleshoot routing protocols.
- Troubleshoot a device as part of a working network.
- Evaluate the characteristics of routing protocols.

INTRODUCTION

Chapter 5 expands on the topics covered in Chapter 4. In Chapter 4, two popular IP routing protocols were discussed: RIP and IGRP. Chapter 5 discusses two additional IP routing protocols: Open Shortest Path First (OSPF) and Enhanced Interior Gateway Routing Protocol (EIGRP). This chapter covers the specifics of both protocols as well as how to configure them.

5.1 LINK-STATE ROUTING ALGORITHM

Link-state routing algorithms operate differently than distance-vector algorithms. Link-state algorithms are more complex than distance-vector algorithms and are more efficient when dealing with larger internetworks. Link-state routing handles route selection, convergence, and route metrics differently than distance-vector routing. In an internetwork, routers send updates to other routers when changes to the database occur, rather than at a predefined time limit. To communicate with one another, the routers make use of multicasting data to specific multicast addresses. Therefore, the only recipients of the data are the routers that are a part of that multicast address.

Link-state algorithms overcome many of the shortcomings of distance-vector algorithms. Some of the differences between link-state routing and distance-vector routing are addressed here:

- Link-state routing maintains the topology of the entire network in a separate database.

- Link-state algorithms use first-hand information about routes to send data.

- Link-state algorithms only forward updates or changes to the routing tables after the initial convergence.

- Link-state algorithms can use classless IP addressing because the subnet mask is forwarded with routing table updates.

- Link-state algorithm routing metrics are more complex, which requires more processor overhead on the router.

- Link-state algorithms have a faster convergence time.

- Link-state algorithms are not prone to the count to infinity.

 Test Tip: Distance-vector–based routing protocols forward the entire routing table.

OPEN SHORTEST PATH FIRST (OSPF)

Today, the most common routing protocol that uses the link-state routing algorithm is OSPF. OSPF was developed by the IETF, and is currently in its second version. Most medium to large IP internetworks are configured to use OSPF. Before discussing OSPF, there are several OSPF-related terms to be aware of. The terms are broken down into three categories: router roles, OSPF packets, and OSPF design.

Router Roles

The first category, OSPF router roles, consists of the roles in which the routers of an OSPF hierarchy operate. The roles to be aware of are the designated router, the backup designated router, and the DROTHER:

- **Designated Router (DR).** The DR is the OSPF router in the network that is responsible for sending route updates to all routers in the network. By default, the DR is elected by other routers in the network based on the router's priority. The first OSPF router in the internetwork will elect itself as the DR. A router can be configured to be the DR.

- **Backup Designated Router (BDR).** The BDR has an identical database as the DR but does not send route update packets to the other routers in the internetwork during normal operation. The BDR is prepared to take over as the DR if the DR fails.
- **DROTHER (Non-DR).** Any router in the OSPF design that is not a DR or a BDR.

OSPF Packets

The next category, OSPF packets, consists of different types of packets sent between routers in an OSPF network. OSPF routers send several types of packets between each other, including hello packets, database description packets, link-state request packets, and link-state update. They are described here:

- **Hello packets.** Hello packets are exchanged between routers to establish and maintain neighbor relationships with other routers. Neighbor relationships are an integral part of OSPF operations.
- **Database Description Packet (DDP).** During the formation of an adjacency, routers send DDPs to one another to learn the status of each other's current link-state database.
- **Link State Request (LSR).** If a receiving router's database is different from the sending router's database during the exchange of DDPs, the receiving router will send an LSR to the router with the new information.
- **Link State Announcements (LSA).** LSAs are used by OSPF routers to advertise the routes they know about, as well as the status of the routes. The five types of LSAs sent by Cisco OSPF routers are listed in Table 5.1. The LSA is not the actual packet; it is a subsection of other packets sent.
- **Link State Update (LSU).** An LSU is the packet that carries the actual LSA.

TABLE 5.1   FIVE TYPES OF LSAs

LSA Type	Sent By	Contains
1 Router Links	Routers in Area	Describes the state and cost of routers interfaces
2 Network Links	Designated Router	Describes all routers in the area
3 IP Summary	Area Border Router	Describes inter-area destination IP networks
4 ASBR Summary	Area Border Router	Describes inter-area ASBR destinations
5 AS-External	AS Boundary Router	Describes destinations that are external to the AS, to include the default route

Design Terms

The last category to be aware of is the OSPF-related design terms. OSPF uses several terms to describe the relationship between routers, as well as the topology it uses. This section describes the neighbor relationship, adjacency, and several other terms.

- **Neighbor relationship.** Neighbor relationships are formed between routers in the network. This is the first step a router takes in its attempt to build a route table and topological database. When a router receives a response to a hello packet it has issued, it places the address of the responding router in its neighbor database.

- **Adjacency.** The path between two routers. To become adjacent with one another, routers must first have formed a neighbor relationship. In most OSPF networks with more than one router, all routers form adjacencies with the DR and the BDR only. This reduces the overhead on the network.

- **Autonomous System Border Router (ASBR).** ASBRs sit at the edge of an AS. Remember, an AS is a group of networks under the same management domain using an IGP such as OSPF (see Figure 5.1). ASBRs can also be used within an AS to redistribute routes learned from IGPs other than OSPF.

- **Area.** A self-contained routing management domain that is part of the larger AS. An area consists of one or more IP networks (see Figure 5.1).

- **Backbone area.** Logical area (considered "Area 0") of the OSPF network to which all other areas must be connected (see Figure 5.1).

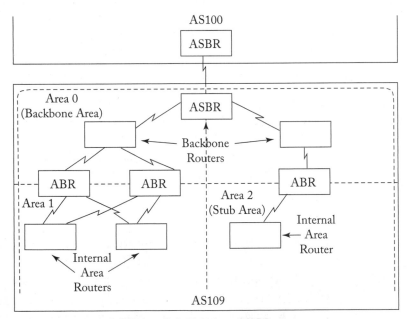

Figure 5.1 *Multi-Area OSPF Design*

- **Backbone router.** A backbone router is a router that has at least one interface in Area 0 (see Figure 5.1).

- **Area Border Router (ABR).** A router that has interfaces in multiple areas, including a connection to the backbone. An ABR can be considered a backbone router because it has at least one interface in Area 0 (see Figure 5.1). Because ABRs are required to route data for two or more areas, it is important for them to be extremely powerful.

- **Internal area router.** A router that has all interfaces within the same OSPF area (see Figure 5.1).

- **Stub area.** An area of the OSPF network that has one ABR acting as the default router for all packets leaving the area by preventing Type 4 and Type 5 LSAs into the stub area. A totally stubby area will even prevent Type 3 LSAs into the area. Neither a stub nor stubby area can contain an ASBR (see Figure 5.1).

OSPF OPERATIONS

The key to having an OSPF network operate successfully is the neighbor relationship. Without the neighbor relationship, adjacencies would never be formed and databases would never be exchanged. The first router that is turned on in the OSPF network becomes the designated router by electing itself as the DR. However, it is possible to configure a different router as the designated router after initial installation. When any other routers in the network are initialized they send *hello packets* that identify them as OSPF routers in the network. When a receiving router hears this hello packet, it responds with a response to the hello packet. In this response, the original hello packet's source address is listed as a neighbor and the two routers have formed a neighbor relationship. See Figure 5.2 for an example of how this works.

In Figure 5.2, Router 9 and Router 12 are in the same network. Router 9 is the DR. When Router 12 is initialized, it sends a hello packet to all router networks it is connected to. All OSPF routers send hello packets at the same interval. When Router 12 sees its IP address listed in Router 9's hello packet as a neighbor, Router 12 adds Router 9 to its neighbor database. After this occurs, the routers are free to exchange databases with DDPs.

After neighbor relationships are formed, adjacencies can be formed. An adjacency is the relationship between two routers that exchange databases and link updates. In most OSPF networks, each router has an adjacency with the DR and the BDR. Therefore, LSUs containing LSAs are sent only to those two routers on the multicast address of 224.0.0.6. The DR is then responsible to send the changes received to all routers in the network on the multicast address 224.0.0.5. This substantially cuts down the network

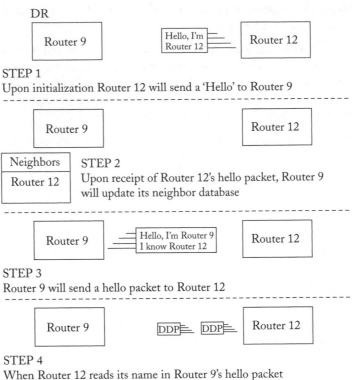

Figure 5.2 *Hello Packet Exchange*

traffic. The BDR only sends LSAs to all routers in the network if the DR goes down and the BDR becomes the new DR. If the failed DR is returned to a working state, it can become the new BDR by election. It will not return to the network as the DR.

OSPF Databases

The routers that use Cisco's implementation of OSPF use three databases to maintain the information needed to forward data. The first database used is the *neighbor database*. The neighbor database lists all the router's neighbors. Remember, the router cannot maintain an adjacency with another router unless it is a neighbor first. The next database is the *topology database*. Data stored in the topology database includes a listing of network links, the routers advertising the links, and the type of link being advertised, as well as other information. The third and final type of database is the *routing table*. The routing table for OSPF maintains four different types of routes:

- **Intra-area routes.** Intra-area routes are identified by an "O" in the routing table and consist of routes that are in the area the router belongs to.

- **Inter-area routes.** Inter-area routes are identified by an "IA" in the routing table. They are routes that were learned from areas the router does not belong to.

- **External Type 1 routes.** External Type 1 routes are identified by an "E1" in the routing table. These routes come from another AS and have two costs associated with them: an external cost, which is from the source, and an internal cost, which is from the internal router advertising the route.

- **External Type 2 routes.** External Type 2 routes are identified by an "E2" in the routing table. E2 routes consist of routes learned from another AS. However, the internal cost is not used. E2 routes are preferred over E1 routes.

OSPF Route Calculation

OSPF uses the shortest path first (SPF) algorithm, also known as the Dijkstra algorithm. Each router uses the topological database to view the network as a hierarchy or an inverted tree. Each router sees itself as the root of the tree or operating at the top of the hierarchy. The SPF algorithm is based on a complex mathematical algorithm that takes several factors into consideration when building the route table. After a router learns a route to a destination network, it attempts to place the newer route in its routing table. However, if it already knows a route to the learned destination, it compares the two known routes together. The route with the lowest cost to the destination is the route stored in the table. The route with the higher cost is maintained in the topological database and available for use if the current active route fails.

OSPF TOPOLOGIES

Generally speaking, OSPF recognizes four types of network topologies: *point-to-point, point-to-multipoint, broadcast,* and *nonbroadcast multiaccess (NBMA)* networks. Each of these topologies has characteristics that differ from the other topologies. When configuring OSPF, it is possible to treat the physical topologies differently from what they actually are. OSPF does, however, have default configurations based on the interface being configured. For example, an Ethernet interface configured with OSPF defaults to a broadcast network, and a serial interface defaults to point-to-point. Because OSPF is so flexible, it becomes much more complicated to configure.

Point-to-Point

The simplest OSPF configuration is that of the point-to-point link because only two routers are involved in the topology (see Figure 5.3).

Because only two routers are involved in this typology, there are no elections for the designated router and the backup designated router.

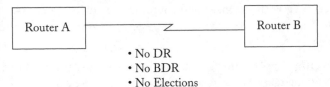

- No DR
- No BDR
- No Elections

Figure 5.3 *Point-to-Point Network with OSPF*

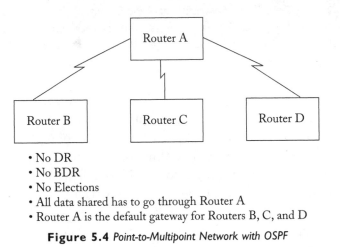

- No DR
- No BDR
- No Elections
- All data shared has to go through Router A
- Router A is the default gateway for Routers B, C, and D

Figure 5.4 *Point-to-Multipoint Network with OSPF*

Point-to-Multipoint

Point-to-multipoint topology is simply a collection of point-to-point networks with one router acting as a central location. This type of topology is often considered a hub and spoke. In this topology, as with the point-to-point, there is no need to have the DR and BDR elections (see Figure 5.4).

Broadcast

OSPF considers Ethernet, Fast Ethernet, Token Ring, and FDDI broadcast networks because every packet that is placed on the wire is forwarded to all nodes within the broadcast domain. If there were multiple OSPF routers on the network, the amount of traffic could become overwhelming. However, OSPF makes good use of the DR and the BDR in this type of network. All routers in the network form an adjacency with the DR and only send updates to the DR and the BDR. The DR, after updating its own table, sends LSAs to all the routers in the network so their topology tables are updated. DROTHERs, which are nondesignated and nonbackup designated routers, do not send updates to any other routers except the DR and the BDR. Figure 5.5 shows a broadcast topology and identifies the router roles.

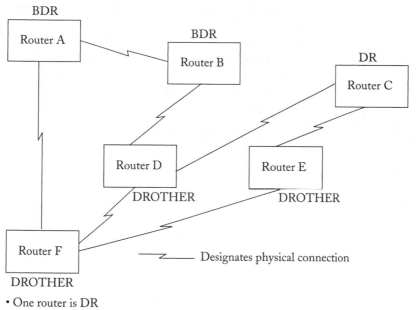

- One router is DR
- Several routers are set up as BDRs
- All others are DROTHER
- All routers will only send updates to Router A, B, or C
- Routers A, B, and C will then send LSAs to update link information in the network

Figure 5.5 *Broadcast Topology*

Nonbroadcast Multiaccess (NBMA)

NBMA networks work similarly to broadcast networks in a sense that multiple interfaces are on the same cable segment. However, NBMA networks are considered nonbroadcast because the interfaces do not have broadcast capability. In an NBMA topology, the DR and the BDR elections will take place. Configuring these network types with other than the default is covered in this text.

5.2 HYBRID ROUTING ALGORITHM

A hybrid routing algorithm combines features of both the distance-vector algorithm and the link-state algorithm. The routing protocol that implements a hybrid algorithm is the EIGRP. EIGRP is a routing protocol developed by Cisco as an enhancement to IGRP. EIGRP is truly a distance-vector protocol. However, after the enhancements to this protocol are revealed, it will be easy to understand why it is considered a hybrid-routing protocol. EIGRP combines the best features of both routing algorithms previously discussed, including the low bandwidth utilization associated with link-state algorithms and the low processor utilization associated with distance-vector algorithms.

Because EIGRP is, however, a proprietary protocol, all routers in the internetwork must be Cisco routers to implement it.

ENHANCED INTERIOR GATEWAY ROUTING PROTOCOL (EIGRP)

EIGRP is an IGP. Therefore, its primary purpose is to route data within an AS. EIGRP has many features that are beneficial to the operation of internetworks. EIGRP uses a composite metric for route calculation. It includes five variables that can be used in determining the metric. They are known as the K values:

> K1 = bandwidth
>
> K2 = load
>
> K3 = delay
>
> K4 = reliability
>
> K5 = MTU

The default configuration for EIGRP uses K1 and K3. These settings should not be changed unless you are fully aware of the consequences. Configuring the K values of EIGRP is not discussed in this text.

EIGRP Tables

Unlike traditional distance-vector routing protocols, EIGRP maintains three tables to ensure effective routing. The three tables are the neighbor table, the topology table, and of course, the routing table. Each table is described here:

- **Neighbor table.** The neighbor table in an EIGRP-based router contains a list of routers that the router exchanges data with.

- **Topology table.** The topology table is a topological view of all routers and networks the router knows about within the internetwork. The topology table maintains a list of alternative paths to networks in the internetwork.

- **Route table.** The route table or routing table of an EIGRP router maintains the paths the router must send data to in order to reach its destination. The best path to each known network in the internetwork will be kept active in the routing table. If an active route becomes unavailable, the EIGRP router looks to the topology table for an inactive route to the same destination. If an inactive route is available, it will become the active route to that destination. If there is no inactive route to the destination, the route to that particular destination will be flushed from the route table.

EIGRP Route Selection

To select a route to a destination network, an EIGRP router must first examine its routing table to determine which route to the destination network is the shortest path. EIGRP bases this on the composite metric discussed earlier. Neighbor routers send update packets to their neighboring routers. These update packets include the cost to known destination networks. When an EIGRP router receives an update packet, it must first compare the new route's cost to other route table entries that go to the same destination. If the update packet proves to be the shortest path to the destination network, the route is added to the EIGRP router's route table. An EIGRP cost can look similar to this: 258560 (of course, it can be a higher or lower value). This is based on the bandwidth and delay to the destination network. The bandwidth is the minimum bandwidth configured along the path to the destination network. The delay is the number of microseconds it takes to travel from the current router to the destination network. The path with the lowest cost (composite metric) will be the route selected for entry in the routing table.

EIGRP OPERATIONS

EIGRP is built primarily of two components: the *Protocol Engine* and *Protocol Dependent Modules* (see Figure 5.6). The protocol engine provides the functionality for the *Diffusing Update Algorithm (DUAL)*. It provides a reliable transport mechanism to ensure routing updates are successful, and also contains the neighbor discovery functionality. There are three protocol-dependent modules, one for IP, IPX, and AppleTalk routing. Each module maintains its own routing table, topology table, and neighbor table. Therefore, one EIGRP router can route data for all three protocols at the same time. Because of this functionality, it is not necessary to run multiple routing protocols in an environment that uses multiple protocol suites.

In an EIGRP network, routers exchange hello packets much like OSPF to establish neighbor relationships. When EIGRP is configured on a router, the router sends hello packets to its directly connected networks, as shown in Figure 5.7.

	Dual	Reliable Transport	Neighbor Discovery
Protocol Engine			
	Client Interface		
Protocol-Dependent Modules	IP Client: *Tables Supported* Routing Topology Neighbor	IPX Client: *Tables Supported* Routing Topology Neighbor SAP	Appletalk Client: *Tables Supported* Routing Topology Neighbor

Figure 5.6 *EIGRP Architecture*

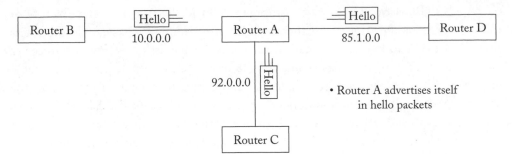

Figure 5.7 *EIGRP Hello Packets*

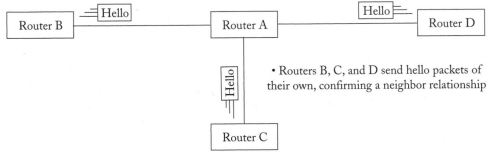

Figure 5.8 *EIGRP Operations*

When EIGRP routers receive the hello packets, they respond with their own hello packet. This hello response confirms that it is a neighbor of the original hello packet sending router, as seen in Figure 5.8.

The routers will both place an entry in their neighbor table for each other. After the relationship is established, the routers send routing updates using EIGRP's reliable multicast, which is a Cisco proprietary routing transport protocol (RTP). After the initial tables are built, EIGRP routers only send updates when topology changes occur in the internetwork. The type of packets sent in an EIGRP network include

- **Hello packets.** Hello packets are multicast packets that are sent at regular intervals to all routers listening.

- **Update packets.** Update packets contain route update information. These packets are only sent when the topology of the internetwork changes. For example, a new network coming on line or the loss of an existing network. All update packets require an ACK.

- **Query packets.** When a route becomes unavailable, DUAL looks to the topology table for a feasible successor. If no feasible successor is listed for a given destination network, a query packet is sent looking for a route to the destination network. These packets are sent reliably.

- **Reply packets.** Reply packets are sent by neighboring routers when they receive query packets. These packets are sent reliably.

- **ACK.** ACKs are acknowledgements to the packets in this list. If a router does not respond to a multicast message, unicasts will be sent directly to the nonresponding router. If the router does not respond with an ACK after 16 unicast packets are sent to it, then the neighbor router is considered dead.

Diffusing Update Algorithm (DUAL)

DUAL is a very important feature of the EIGRP routing process. It completes the route calculation and also provides the loop-avoidance schemes. In traditional distance-vector–based internetworks, split horizon and poison reverse are used to avoid loops. EIGRP does not use these mechanisms. It relies on DUAL to ensure that each time a new route is advertised it completes the route calculation, and if the composite metric is not lower than the current metric being used, the route table will not be updated. The topology database, however, can be updated. The topology database maintains a topological view of all neighbors in the network and their possibility of becoming the next hop router in the path to a destination network.

DUAL Terminology

In DUAL-based networks, routers are in one of two states: the active state or the passive state. Active state routers are those that are either in the route-learning mode or the route-advertising mode. Passive state routers are those that are in a stable, packet-forwarding condition. Routes of an EIGRP router are considered one of several terms. Terms to be aware of when considering the routes that an EIGRP router knows about follow:

- **Feasible distance (FD).** The route to a destination network that has the lowest metric among all known paths. This is the path to a destination network listed in the routing table.

- **Advertised distance (AD).** The router's feasible distance to any destination network also becomes the advertised distance. This is the path a router will share with its neighbors during convergence.

- **Feasibility condition (FC).** In EIGRP, the feasibility condition states that if a route learned from a neighbor has a lower metric than the current FD to the same destination network, the learned route then becomes the router's FD.

- **Feasible successor (FS).** List of routers that could possibly become the next hop router in the path to a destination network. Routers listed as feasible successors must have an AD that is lower than the local router's FD. FSs are listed in the topology database.

- **Successor.** The successor is a router that is selected as the next hop router to a destination network. In normal operations, the successor will have a lower cost metric to the destination network because it is one hop closer. The successor is chosen from the list of FSc in the topology database and is substantially listed in the routing table, becoming both the FD and the AD.

The topology database greatly enhances the speed of convergence in an EIGRP-based network. If a route went down in traditional distance-vector routing protocols, it would take up to several minutes for the new route to be advertised. For example, if a RIP router stops advertising a route for one reason or another, neighbor routers will keep the unadvertised route in their table for a given amount of time, normally 90 seconds. After the router discards the route, it must wait for the new route table from the network with the failed route to propagate through the network. In an EIGRP network, if there are multiple paths to a network, the EIGRP router maintains them all. However, except for the route with the lowest cost, all routes are considered inactive and are stored in the topology database as one of the roles mentioned earlier. If the route with the lowest cost becomes unavailable, the EIGRP router checks the topology database and activates another route to the destination network. If no other routes are available in the topology database, the router initiates a query packet to find a path to the destination from one of its neighbors. If none are available, the route is flushed from the table.

5.3 CONFIGURING OSPF

Configuring OSPF in a single area within a single AS is discussed here. Because it is one of the more complex routing protocols, there are countless commands to configure OSPF. The full spectrum of OSPF routing will not be covered in this text.

OSPF has many configurable options. The CCNA objectives focus on basic configuration that will help set up OSPF in a single area.

STARTING OSPF

The command to start the OSPF routing process is *router ospf*. This command is similar to the other routing protocols command. However, in this command, the process-id must be included. The process-id is a value between 1 and 65535, and uniquely advertises the OSPF process running on the router. It is possible to have more than one OSPF process running on the router. Shown here is a router being configured with OSPF and a process-id of 1.

```
Router(config)#router ospf 1
```

Network and Area Identification

After the OSPF process is started, it is time to configure the networks in which it will advertise. When configuring the networks, it is mandatory to configure the area that the interfaces will belong to. This command is unlike any other router configuration mode network command because with OSPF you use a wildcard mask to identify the network or networks that OSPF will route data for. The following command identifies a single network:

```
Router(config-router)#network 10.0.0.0
    0.255.255.255 area 0
```

In the preceding command, the wildcard mask is the inverted subnet mask (0.255.255.255). When determining the wildcard mask for a single network, simply convert the binary 1s in the network's subnet mask to binary 0s, and the binary 0s to binary 1s. Here's an example:

Network	Subnet Mask	Wildcard Mask
10.0.0.0	255.0.0.0	0.255.255.255
172.16.0.0	255.255.0.0	0.0.255.255
192.16.1.0	255.255.255.0	0.0.0.255

In wildcard masking, the 0s mean compare and the 1s mean ignore (conversely, in a subnet mask, the 1s mean compare and the 0s mean ignore). When a router in the configuration of OSPF checks its interfaces, it advertises the information to its neighbors if one of the interface addresses match the network address and wildcard mask.

You can identify a range of networks with a wildcard mask rather than a single network. In the next example, the routing process is going to be configured for any networks that fall within the 172.16.0.0/20. Remember, the /20 means that there are 20 ON bits in the subnet mask. Therefore, the third octet in the example is broken up and the subnet mask is 255.255.240.0. With a subnet mask of 240 in the third octet, the networks increment by 16 as seen here:

172.16.16.0

172.16.32.0

172.16.48.0

172.16.64.0

172.16.80.0

172.16.96.0, and so on

Assuming that all networks are to be in the same OSPF area, the network command would be

```
Router(config-router)#network 172.16.0.0
    0.0.0.255 area 0
```

Notice the 0s in the first three octets of the wildcard mask. This ensures that all networks match the OSPF criteria to advertise routes for area 0. Now, assume that network 172.16.64.0 had to be moved into area 1. This can be accomplished by using the following command:

```
Router(config-router)#network 172.16.64.0
    0.0.15.255 area 1
```

In this command, the 172.16.64.0 is the network statement. The subnet mask increments the networks by 16, so the wildcard mask will be 15, which is one digit lower than what the networks increment by. Therefore, only the single subnet (172.16.64.0) will be placed in the correct area. Wildcard masking is covered in depth later in the text. For now, though, the shortcut method to wildcard masking is to subtract the network ID from the network's broadcast address as shown here:

BROADCAST ADDRESS	172.16.79.255
NETWORK ADDRESS	172.16.64.0/20
WILDCARD MASK	0.0.15.255

Note: Wildcard masks are covered more in Chapter 6.

IP OSPF Cost

The *IP OSPF cost* command is used to change the default cost of sending a packet on an interface. The lower the cost of the interface, the better the route. It is normally used when trying to load balance traffic, reduce monetary costs associated with a link, or avoid a link altogether. When OSPF is configured on the router, it bases its metrics-to-destination routes on the cost of the link. The cost of the link is determined by the following equation:

$$Cost = 100,000,000/\text{Bandwidth in bits per second}$$

Using this equation to determine the cost of a 100 Mbps Ethernet link, divide 100,000,000 by 100,000,000, which equals 1. This, of course, is an extremely low cost in terms of routing metrics. If the same equation is used to determine a 512 Kbps connection, the cost would be much higher and more realistic. The equation would be

$$Cost = 100,000,000/512,000 = 195$$

For a T-1 line it would be

$$Cost = 100,000,000/1,544,000 = 64$$

To change the cost of the interface to 100, use this interface configuration command:

```
Router(config-if)#ip ospf cost 100
```

To reset the interface back to the default, use the *no* argument before the command.

IP OSPF Priority

The *ip ospf priority* command is used to increase or decrease a router's chance of becoming the designated or backup designated router. This command is not used on point-to-point links because there is no DR or BDR when there are only two routers. The value of this command is between 0 and 255. If a router has its priority set to 0, it will never become the DR, however, the highest priority is 1. To set the priority of a router to become the DR, use this interface configuration command:

```
Router(config-if)#ip ospf priority 1
```

OSPF TIMERS

An OSPF router has three timers: hello timer, dead timer, and wait timer.

Hello Timer

The hello timer is the amount of time a router waits before sending hello packets to its neighbors. The default hello timer interval for point-to-point and broadcast networks is 10 seconds. For point-to-multipoint and nonbroadcast multiaccess networks, the default value is 30 seconds. The hello timer is a configurable option; however, you should not change it unless there is a specific need to do so. If the hello timer is changed, it **must** be changed for all routers on the cable segment. To change the hello timer to 15 seconds, use this interface configuration command:

```
Router(config-if)#ip ospf hello-interval 15
```

Dead Timer

The dead interval is the amount of time a router waits before a route is declared dead. The default for this timer is set to four times the hello timer. The dead timer can be configured as well by using the *ip ospf dead-interval* interface configuration mode command as seen here:

```
Router(config-if)#ip ospf dead-interval 60
```

Wait Timer

This timer is a nonconfigurable timer that is equal to the dead timer. For example, if the dead timer is set to 120 seconds, then the wait timer is set to 120 seconds as well. The wait timer is used to determine how long the router waits after the dead timer expires before it flushes a dead router out of its database.

VERIFYING AND TROUBLESHOOTING OSPF

When working with OSPF, several OSPF-related show commands as well as OSPF-related debug commands are used to verify the configuration. The *show ip protocols* and the default *show ip route* commands were already discussed, and they work with all routing protocols so they will not be described here. However, *show ip route* will be described with an additional argument.

 Test Tip: OSPF learned routes are shown with an O preceding the route table entry.

Show IP Route [Network]

To see network-specific routing information, use the *show ip route* command and append the network address to the end of it. This provides specific information about a single link or a range of networks. To see a single link, include the entire address (for example, 192.12.9.1). To see a range of links, append the command with the network address (for example, 192.12.9.0).

Show IP OSPF

To see the OSPF processes running on a router, use the *show ip ospf* command:

```
Router#show ip ospf
```

Show IP OSPF Interface

This command shows all OSPF interfaces on the router. To see a single interface, append the interface description to the end of the command:

```
Router#show ip ospf interface
```

Show IP OSPF Neighbor

Use the *show ip ospf neighbor* command to explore the contents of the router's neighbor table. Append the address of a specific neighbor to see the details of a single neighbor. See the following example:

```
Router#show ip ospf neighbor
```

Neighbor ID	Pri	State	Dead Time	Address	Interface
191.10.64.1	1	FULL/	-00:00:33	191.10.48.2	Serial0/0

```
Router#show ip ospf neighbor 192.168.64.1
```

Neighbor 191.10.64.1, interface address 191.10.48.2

In the area 8 via interface Serial0/0

Neighbor priority is 1, State is FULL, 6 state changes

DR is 0.0.0.0 BDR is 0.0.0.0

Options is 0x42

Dead timer due in 00:00:36

Neighbor is up for 00:40:03

Index 1/1, retransmission queue length 0, number of retransmission 1

First 0x0(0)/0x0(0) Next 0x0(0)/0x0(0)

Last retransmission scan length is 1, maximum is 1

Last retransmission scan time is 0 msec, maximum is 0 msec

Additional Show Commands

There are too many show commands available with OSPF to explain them all in this book. To explore the different show commands, visit Cisco's website or use the context-sensitive help. Here is a list to explore further:

```
Router#show ip ospf border-routers
Router#show ip ospf databases
Router#show ip ospf flood-list
Router#show ip ospf request-list
Router#show ip ospf retransmission-list
Router#show ip ospf summary-address
Router#show ip ospf virtual-links
```

Debugging Commands

Usually you should not run debugging on production routers. However, if the show commands are not giving enough detail as to why a router is experiencing problems, use one of the following debug commands from the privileged exec mode:

```
Router#Debug ip ospf adj
Router#Debug ip ospf database-timer
Router#Debug ip ospf events
Router#Debug ip ospf flooding
```

```
Router#Debug ip ospf lsa-generation
Router#Debug ip ospf packets
Router#Debug ip ospf retransmission-events
```

The debugging operation puts additional stress on a router. Do not use it unless it is absolutely necessary. To turn off debugging, use the *no* argument before the command.

5.4 CONFIGURING EIGRP

There are primarily four major processes that allow for the functionality of EIGRP:

- **Protocol-dependent modules.** Provide support for routing IP, IPX, and AppleTalk.

- **Diffusing update algorithm.** Provides loop-free route computation and recomputation by effectively calculating the composite metric to routes and placing the best routes in the routing table of the router.

- **Neighbor discovery process.** EIGRP builds a neighbor database through the use of hello packets and maintains a topology of the entire network.

- **Reliable transport protocol (RTP).** EIGRP uses RTP to guarantee the delivery of routing updates.

STARTING EIGRP ROUTING

To start EIGRP routing, simply type *router eigrp* in the global configuration mode. However, remember that the AS must be configured at this time. For example, see how EIGRP is configured on a router using AS 900:

```
Router(config)#router eigrp 900
Router(config-router)#
```

After the routing protocol has been loaded and the routing process has begun, add the directly connected networks of the router that will be participating in the EIGRP routing process. Again, this process is similar to IGRP. Two networks are added to the EIGRP process here:

```
Router(config-router)#network 191.10.48.0
Router(config-router)#network 191.10.64.0
```

VERIFYING EIGRP

After EIGRP has been loaded on a router and the routing process is started, a few commands are available to verify that it is running.

Show IP Protocols

Use the *show ip protocols* command to verify that it is started. The *show ip protocols* command shows several configuration options of EIGRP. For example, when this command is used, the output shows what routing protocol is being used. In this example, the protocol is EIGRP; the AS the router is a member of; the K values that are being used to calculate the composite metric of the routes; and the maximum hop count, to name a few.

```
Router#show ip protocols
```

Routing Protocol is "eigrp 900"

 Outgoing update filter list for all interfaces is not set

 Incoming update filter list for all interfaces is not set

 Default networks flagged in outgoing updates

 Default networks accepted from incoming updates

 EIGRP metric weight K1=1, K2=0, K3=1, K4=0, K5=0

 EIGRP maximum hopcount 100

 EIGRP maximum metric variance 1

 Redistributing: eigrp 900

 Automatic network summarization is in effect

 Maximum path: 4

 Routing for Networks:

  191.10.0.0

 Routing Information Sources:

Gateway	Distance	Last Update
191.10.48.1	90	00:01:23
191.10.64.2	90	00:01:23

 Distance: internal 90 external 170

Show IP Route

The *show ip route* command lists the routing table. When viewing EIGRP-learned routes, notice that the letter that precedes the route is a "D." This command shows the administrative distance of the route and the composite metric together listed within the square brackets. Also shown is what network must be traversed to reach the destination, the age of the entry, and the interface it was learned on. This is all seen in the following example:

```
Router#show ip route
```

Codes: C—connected, S—static, I—IGRP, R—RIP, M—mobile, B—BGP

    D—EIGRP, EX—EIGRP external, O—OSPF, IA—OSPF inter area

    N1—OSPF NSSA external type 1, N2—OSPF NSSA external type 2

    E1—OSPF external type 1, E2—OSPF external type 2, E—EGP

    i—IS-IS, L1—IS-IS level-1, L2—IS-IS level-2, ia—IS-IS inter area

    *—candidate default, U—per-user static route, o—ODR

    P—periodic downloaded static route

Gateway of last resort is not set

    191.10.0.0/20 is subnetted, 5 subnets

C   191.10.48.0 is directly connected, Serial0/1

D   191.10.16.0 [90/2172416] via 191.10.48.1, 00:05:19, Serial0/1

D   191.10.96.0 [90/41024000] via 191.10.48.1, 00:03:44, Serial0/1

D   191.10.80.0 [90/41024000] via 191.10.64.2, 00:04:39, Serial0/0

C   191.10.64.0 is directly connected, Serial0/0

If the address of a destination is appended to the *show ip route* command, additional parameters are listed, as seen here:

```
Router#show ip route 191.10.16.0
```

Routing entry for 191.10.16.0/20

    Known via "eigrp 900," distance 90, metric 2172416, type internal

    Redistributing via eigrp 900

    Last update from 191.10.48.1 on Serial0/1, 00:06:42 ago

    Routing Descriptor Blocks:

    * 191.10.48.1, from 191.10.48.1, 00:06:42 ago, via Serial0/1

        Route metric is 2172416, traffic share count is 1

        Total delay is 20100 microseconds, minimum bandwidth is 1544 Kbit

        Reliability 255/255, minimum MTU 1500 bytes

        Loading 1/255, Hops 1

Show IP EIGRP Topology

To see the topological database entries, use the *show ip eigrp topology* command. This command produces output that shows the FSs to a given route.

Notice in the following output, the routes are listed as passive routes:

```
Router#show ip eigrp topology

IP-EIGRP Topology Table for AS(900)/ID(191.10.64.1)
Codes: P—Passive, A—Active, U—Update, Q—Query, R—Reply,
    r—reply Status, s—sia Status
P 191.10.48.0/20, 1 successors, FD is 2169856
    via Connected, Serial0/1
P 191.10.16.0/20, 1 successors, FD is 2172416
    via 191.10.48.1 (2172416/28160), Serial0/1
P 191.10.96.0/20, 1 successors, FD is 41024000
    via 191.10.48.1 (41024000/40512000), Serial0/1
P 191.10.80.0/20, 1 successors, FD is 41024000
    via 191.10.64.2 (41024000/40512000), Serial0/0
P 191.10.64.0/20, 1 successors, FD is 40512000
    via Connected, Serial0/0
```

Show IP EIGRP Neighbors

The *show ip eigrp neighbors* command lists the neighbors that the router knows about in the neighbor database. Remember, EIGRP routers send hello packets to one another to maintain their status as neighbors with the other routers in the internetwork. EIGRP uses two timers to ensure neighbor relationships are maintained:

- **Hello-interval.** The hello-interval is how often routers sends hello packets to maintain the neighbor relationship. The default setting is 5 seconds for high-speed links such as Ethernet or point-to-point serial links, and 60 seconds for slower media such as ISDN BRI, T-1 links, or slower lines. The hello-interval is a configurable option by using the *ip eigrp hello-interval* interface configuration mode command. In EIGRP routers, the routers can have different hello-intervals.

- **Holdtime interval.** The holdtime interval is the maximum time a router keeps a neighbor relationship alive without receiving a hello packet. The default holdtime is three times the hello-interval. This, too, can be configured manually by using the *ip eigrp hold-time* command from the interface configuration mode to change the interval.

```
Router#show ip eigrp neighbors
```

IP-EIGRP neighbors for process 900

H	Address	Interface	Hold (sec)	Uptime	SRTT (ms)	RTO Cnt	Q	Seq Num
1	191.10.64.2	Se0/0	14	00:07:51	28	2280	0	5
0	191.10.48.1	Se0/1	13	00:08:30	1061	5000	0	3

The preceding table lists the neighbor table information from left to right. The leftmost column denotes in which order the neighbors were learned. The Address column is the address of the neighbor, and the Interface column shows the interface in which the local router is receiving hello packets from the neighbor. The Hold column denotes the amount of time since a hello packet has been received by a neighbor. The Uptime column is the total time the relationship has been established. The SRTT column is the Smooth Round-Trip Time, which is the average time it takes to receive an ACK from a neighbor when an update packet is sent to it. RTO is the time between unicast transmissions if the router is forced into unicast mode after failed attempts to update a neighbor through multicast transmissions. The Q column represents the packets in the queue, and Seq is the sequence number used by the RTP.

MONITORING AND TROUBLESHOOTING EIGRP

Several show and debug commands are available to monitor the EIGRP process.

Show IP EIGRP Traffic
This command gathers statistics on the overall routing traffic of an EIGRP router. The output of the command includes hello packets, route updates, and ACKs, to name a few.

Show IP EIGRP Events
This command displays the last 500 events that occurred on the EIGRP router in reverse chronological order.

Show IP EIGRP Interfaces
This command shows what interfaces EIGRP is running on, the number of neighbors on each interface, the average SRTT, the packets waiting in the queue, and the maximum number of seconds the router will send multicast EIGRP packets. When using this command, it is possible to specify an individual interface and an AS. If neither of these options are used, all interfaces on the router are shown as well as all EIGRP processes.

```
Router#show ip eigrp interfaces
```

Debug EIGRP Packet

This command shows extremely detailed information being sent between EIGRP routers. Use this command sparingly because debugging processes put a heavy load on the router's processor.

Debug EIGRP Neighbor

This command displays the neighbors discovered by the EIGRP process. The information given in this output is more detailed than the information given in the *show ip eigrp neighbors* command.

Debug EIGRP FSM

This command helps you observe EIGRP-FS activity. It also helps determine whether or not route updates are being added and removed to the routing table. Be sure not to debug any of these services for an extended amount of time.

CHAPTER SUMMARY

This chapter discussed two popular IP routing protocols. OSPF is a link-state based routing algorithm and EIGRP was described as a hybrid routing protocol because it uses characteristics of both link-state and distance-vector–based algorithms. Both protocols are IGPs and operate within an AS. If you were to connect two autonomous systems together, you would use an EGP such as the BGP. Many configuration commands were described within the chapter as well. Now complete the knowledge test and move on to Chapter 6.

KNOWLEDGE TEST

Choose one answer for all questions unless directed to do otherwise.

1. Identify the features of a link-state routing protocol?
   a. Updates are sent every 30 seconds.
   b. The entire routing table is sent in every update.
   c. Updates are only sent when changes in the network take place.
   d. Update timers are utilized.

2. Which command will successfully identify the OSPF process?
   a. *Router#ospf process 1*
   b. *Router(configt)#router ospf 1*
   c. *Router#router ospf 1*
   d. *Router(configt)router process ospf 1*

3. Identify the mechanisms used by EIGRP to calculate routes (choose two).
   a. Adjacency
   b. Bandwidth
   c. Neighbor
   d. Vector
   e. Delay

4. Which EIGRP process allows for the support of multiple network layer protocols.
   a. Protocol-Dependent Modules
   b. Diffusing Update Algorithm (DUAL)
   c. Reliable Transport Protocol (RTP)
   d. Neighbor Database

5. Which command can be used to see the FSs to a given EIGRP-based route?
   a. *Show database*
   b. *Show ip topology*
   c. *Show eigrp topology*
   d. *Show ip eigrp topology*

6. You are given instructions to configure a router for EIGRP routing. The two networks the router will route for are the 129.41.20.0/24 network and the 11.98.0.0/16 network. The router should route for the 871 AS. Which set of commands will you use?
   a. *Router(config)#router eigrp*
      Router(config)#network 129.41.20.0
      Router(config)#network 11.98.0.0
   b. *Router#router eigrp 871*
      Router(config)#network 129.41.20.0
      Router(config)#network 11.98.0.0
   c. *Router(config)#router eigrp 871*
      Router(config-router)#network 129.41.20.1
      Router(config-router)#network 11.98.1.1
   d. *Router(config)#router eigrp 871*
      Router(config-router)#network 129.41.20.0
      Router(config-router)#network 11.98.0.0

7. Which command will list the interfaces EIGRP is running on and the number of neighbors on each interface?
   a. *Show ip eigrp events*
   b. *Show ip eigrp traffic*
   c. *Show ip eigrp interfaces*
   d. *Debug eigrp neighbors*

8. In OSPF configuration, it is common to use autonomous systems to divide areas.
   a. True
   b. False

9. The process ID in OSPF is a critical number that must be identical for all routers in the OSPF network.
   a. True
   b. False

10. How would you determine what the default cost of a 56 Kbps line would be in an OSPF routing table?
    a. Cost = 100,000,000 / 56
    b. Cost = 100,000,000 / 5600
    c. Cost = 100,000,000 / 56000
    d. Cost = 100,000,000 / 560000

11. Choose the statements that accurately depict link-state routing algorithms (choose three).
    a. Entire routing tables are forwarded from routers to update routes.
    b. First-hand information is used to update routes.
    c. Count-to-infinity is not an issue.
    d. The entire network topology is stored in a separate database.

12. Identify the three databases stored by OSPF (choose three).
    a. Routing Topology
    b. Neighbor Database
    c. Topology Network
    d. Routing Table
    e. Topology Database

13. Designated routers and backup designated routers are required in a point-to-point and a point-to-multipoint OSPF topology.
    a. True
    b. False

14. Match the term with its definition.
    a. Adjacency
    b. Backbone Area
    c. Area Border Router (ABR)
    d. Stub Area

    1. OSPF area in which all other areas are connected
    2. Path between two routers that formed a neighbor relationship
    3. OSPF area that has one ABR acting as the default router for all packets leaving the area
    4. Router with an interface in multiple areas to include the backbone area

15. What is the administrative distance for EIGRP?
    a. 80
    b. 90
    c. 100
    d. 110

16. What are the requirements to initiate OSPF routing in a single AS (choose three)?
    a. Configure the OSPF process ID
    b. Identify the AS
    c. Identify the OSPF network
    d. Configure the OSPF wildcard mask
    e. Manually configure the OSPF adjacencies

17. List the types of packets that are sent between OSPF routers.

    _____
    _____
    _____
    _____
    _____

18. List the types of packets that are sent between EIGRP routers.

    _____
    _____
    _____
    _____
    _____

19. Which command gathers statistics on the overall routing traffic of an EIGRP router?
    a. *Show ip eigrp traffic*
    b. *Show ip eigrp events*
    c. *Show ip eigrp packet*
    d. *Debug ip eigrp traffic*

20. Which command will show the contents of an OSPF router's neighbor table?
    a. *Show ip route*
    b. *Show ip ospf database*
    c. *Show ip neighbor*
    d. *Show ip ospf neighbor*

CHAPTER 6

Access Lists

OBJECTIVES

The following topics are discussed in Chapter 6:

- Develop an access list to meet user specifications.
- Implement an access list.
- Troubleshoot an access list.
- Evaluate rules for packet control.

INTRODUCTION

Access lists are a router's mechanism for defense. Organizations can configure their routers' access lists to permit or deny data packets from entering or exiting a particular interface. This chapter begins with an overview of access lists, followed by rules that apply to all access lists. It then covers IP standard access lists, IP extended access lists, and wildcard masks. Finally, named access lists are discussed.

6.1 AN OVERVIEW OF ACCESS LISTS

The access list control mechanisms are based on packet-filtering technology. When a packet arrives at a router's interface, the router examines it, and based on criteria set in the access list, allows the packet either to be forwarded through the router or be discarded. The router does this by analyzing the packet's header to determine criteria such as source address, destination address, protocol, port numbers, and additional information.

Think of a security guard guarding a secure facility as an analogy to access lists. When a visitor arrives at the gate, the guard asks the visitor for an identification badge, which normally has a name, number, or both. The guard checks the name against a list of names possibly called an access list. If the visitor's name is on the list that permits access to the facility, the guard lets the visitor through. But if the visitor's name is on the list denying access, the guard does not let the visitor through. If the list does not have an entry for the visitor, it is implied that the visitor is not welcome and is denied access.

ACCESS LIST RULES

The router has the capability to control packet access into and out of a specific interface. When access lists are created, they can be assigned to filter inbound or outbound traffic, or both. The following rules apply to access lists:

- After an access list is created, it is assigned as an inbound or outbound filter to a router's interface.
- Each interface can only have one access list per protocol, per direction, per interface. Based on this statement, each interface can have two access lists per protocol, one for inbound filtering and one for outbound filtering.
- Each packet arriving at the interface is compared with each line of the access list, starting at the top and working its way down. When there is a match between the packet and an access list entry, the packet is either forwarded or dropped (depending on the access list entry) and no further comparison is required. If there is no match in the access list, the packet is dropped. This is referred to as an *implicit deny all* entry.
- Due to the *implicit deny all* entry, access lists must have at least one permit statement to prevent all packets from being dropped.
- Data originating from the router are not filtered by any access lists.
- After an access list is created, it is not possible to selectively add or remove additional entries. The access list must be removed and re-created to do this.
- When adding entries to an access list, they are placed at the bottom of the list.
- Access lists must be given an identification number when they are created. The number assigned is based on the type of access list created. An abbreviated list of the ranges follows:

Range	Type of Access List
1–99	Standard IP
100–199	Extended IP
800–899	Standard IPX
900–999	Extended IPX
1000–1099	SAP filters

6.2 IP ACCESS LISTS

IP access lists can be *standard access lists* or *extended access lists*. Both filter IP packets, but extended IP access lists are more granular. Standard access lists only block packets based on the source (node sending the data) address portion of the TCP/IP packet. Extended access lists can block packets based on source address, destination address, UDP port, TCP port, and other criteria.

It is possible to create named IP access lists to overcome the limitation of numbers available. If creating named IP access lists, consider the following:

- The names must be unique between named IP access lists.
- They are not compatible with IOS releases before 11.2.
- You can selectively remove entries from the access list, but not selectively add them.

Named access lists will be discussed later in the chapter.

 Test Tip: IOS version 11.2 is the first IOS version that supported named IP access lists.

IP STANDARD ACCESS LISTS

IP standard access lists are used to restrict packets inbound to or outbound from a router's interface based on the source's IP address. This means that a standard access list uses the source address as filtering criteria. The addresses can be blocked individually or entire ranges of IP addresses can be blocked. In this section, CLI configuration and wildcard masks will be discussed. A *wildcard mask* is used to specify a range of IP addresses that are to be filtered with an access list.

CLI Configuration

Creating and applying access lists is a two-step process. First, the access list entries are typed using the *access-list* command in global configuration mode. There is no limit on the amount of entries in an access list. However, consider that the more access list entries there are, the higher the processing load on the router. The second step is to link the access list entries to an interface by using the *access-group* command in the interface configuration mode. Several parameters go along with these commands. For example, to create an access list entry with the identification number of 25, use the following command:

```
Router(config)#access-list 25 permit any
```

This command uses two arguments: the *permit* argument and the *any* argument. The *permit* argument is mandatory but can be replaced with the *deny* argument. The *any* argument specifies what IP addresses will be compared with the *permit* criterion. Using the *any* argument in an access list, essentially tells the router "all IP addresses." Although access list 25 has been created, it has not been applied to an interface and therefore will not perform any filtering. To activate an access list, use the following command from the interface configuration mode:

```
Router(config-if)#ip access-group 25 out
```

In this command, the access list with the identification number of 25 has been set to filter traffic on an outbound basis. The *out* argument states that the filter is placed on the outbound interface; the other available argument is *in*. If the *in* argument were used, it would filter all IP addresses that are entering the router's interface. Because access list 25 has already been created, it can be applied to multiple interfaces in multiple directions based on the needs of the network administrator.

If the network called for blocking an individual machine, the command argument to use in the access list is *host [ip address]*. The actual IP address of the machine to be filtered follows the *host* argument as shown next:

```
Router(config)#access-list 25 deny host
    192.168.1.10
```

This entry is specifically denying access to the host machine listed in the command. When using specific commands, it is very important to place the command in the access list before the *permit any* command entered earlier. If this command is placed in access list 25 after the *permit any* argument, this host will not be denied access because it would have already been permitted access by the *permit any* entry. When adding entries to access lists, they are appended to the end of the access list. Packets are compared with the access list from top to bottom. The last entry is always the implicit deny. After a packet matches an access list entry, the packet is processed based on the matching criteria. So to get the desired results of permitting any IP address except 192.168.1.10, the proper command sequence would be as follows:

```
Router(config)#access-list 25 deny host
    192.168.1.10
Router(config)#access-list 25 permit any
Router(config)#interface F0/0
Router(config-if)#ip access-group 25 out
```

This command sequence would ultimately configure interface Fast Ethernet 0/0 to allow all packets to be permitted out except the 192.168.1.10 host. View the diagram that follows to see the effects of the access list.

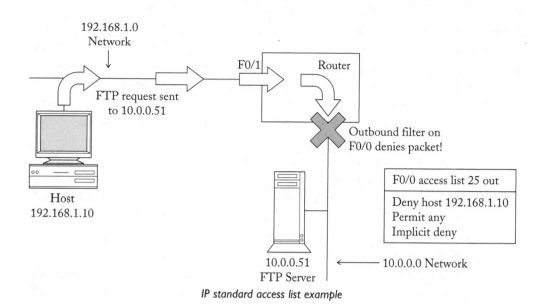

IP standard access list example

Wildcard Masks

A Cisco router uses a wildcard mask to identify multiple IP addresses in an access list entry. A wildcard mask used to represent a range of IP addresses is denoted in a dotted decimal notation. Wildcard masks in access lists serve a similar purpose to subnet masks in IP addressing. Whenever there is a binary 1 in a wildcard mask, it means the corresponding bit in the IP address will not be tested. Whenever there is a binary 0 in a wildcard mask, it means the corresponding bit in the IP address must match the specified bit. For example, the access list argument of 150.10.0.0 is the network address. A wildcard mask of 0.0.255.255 specifies that a packet entering a router with this access list entry must have come from the 150.10.0.0 network to use this access list entry. See the following:

```
Router(config)#access-list 10 permit
    150.10.0.0 0.0.255.255
```

To apply this access list to an interface, use the *ip access-group [in | out]* interface configuration command. Because there is an implicit deny entry in the access list, only packets from the 150.10.0.0 network will be compared with this access list and subsequently permitted access. All others will be dropped. Look at the IP address and wildcard mask in binary:

IP address in command: 10010110.00001010.00000000.00000000

Wildcard mask in command: 00000000.00000000.11111111.11111111

0 = compare; 1 = ignore

The address of the packet entering must be 150.10.0.0 in the source field.

Filtering Blocks of Addresses

Up to this point, we have used wildcard masks to filter whole octets only. If the network design calls for only a range of IP addresses within an octet to be filtered rather than an entire octet, access lists can become more complicated. For example, it is possible to block only eight networks or a certain number of hosts. Remember that the values of a subnet mask have to be a power of 2 such as 2, 4, 8, 16, 32, 64, 128. When working with wildcard masks and you need to specify a group of addresses rather than an entire octet, the group size must be a power of 2. For example, if the administrator needs to block out 26 addresses, he or she would have to round up to 32 and block all 32 addresses because 26 is not a power of 2 and because the next available number after 26 that is a power of 2 is 32. Because the administrator has to block out 32 addresses, the next rule to follow is that the wildcard mask must always be one less than the number of addresses grouped together. This type of access list entry would normally be used if the network you are working on has been subnetted. Consider the network address of 172.168.0.0/19. The subnet mask for this example is 255.255.224.0. With this subnetted network, six possible subnets are available:

172.168.32.0

172.168.64.0

172.168.96.0

172.168.128.0

172.168.160.0

172.168.192.0

The goal is to have an access list apply to a single subnet, which consists of 32 addresses in the third octet and 256 addresses in the fourth octet (including the 2 illegal addresses). Following is the command and an explanation:

```
Router(config)#access-list 10 deny
      172.168.32.0 0.0.31.255
```

The 172.168.32.0 network has been identified to be denied access in this access list. By specifying the address 172.168.32.0 and a wildcard mask of 0.0.31.255, the command states that the 32 in the IP address will be compared with the access list entry. Therefore, any host on the 32 network will have this access list entry applied to it. In binary it would look like this:

Address: 11001100.11001000.0010000.00000000

Wildcard mask: 00000000.00000000.00011111.11111111

Notice that the 32 bit in the third octet of the wildcard mask was set to 0. This means that any address with the 32 bit on will be compared with the access list entry. Because the entry is a deny entry, all hosts on the 32 subnet will be denied access to any router interface that this access list is applied to. Furthermore, the number 31 in the wildcard mask was derived from turning all the on bits in the third octet before the 32 bit. When added together in decimal, they equal 31 (1 less than the number of addresses blocked in the third octet).

A shortcut method for determining the wildcard mask consists of subtracting the network ID from the network broadcast address. Using the same network address of 172.168.32.0/19, see the following example to learn the shortcut method:

Network broadcast address: 172.168.63.255

Network ID of subnet: 172.168.32.0

Wildcard mask: 0.0.31.255

All addresses that begin with the 32 bit in the third octet will be compared with the access list. These addresses include

172.168.32.1-255

172.168.33.1-255

172.168.34.1-255

172.168.35.1-255

up to 172.168.63.255

The bits in the fourth octet are irrelevant at this point because if the network portion does not match, the source packet will not be compared any further.

 Test Tip: When wildcard masking, you must use a group that is a power of 2 and the wildcard mask will be 1 lower than the group number; for example, a group of 8 networks has a wildcard mask of 7; a group of 16 has a wildcard mask of 15, and so on.

Filtering VTY Access

Standard IP access lists can be used to secure your virtual terminal sessions on a router. To set this up, configure a standard IP access list as it would normally be done, filtering source addresses. Enter the line configuration mode that will have the access list applied to it. Assign the same access list to all VTYs because it is not possible to control which line a user will connect to. After entering the line configuration mode, use the *access-class* command to apply the access list to the terminal line. The command line sequence is

```
Router(config)#access-list 20 permit
    125.10.1.0 0.0.0.255
Router(config)#line vty 0-4
Router(config-line)#access-class 20 in
```

In the example, access-list 20, which permits all machines on the 125.10.1.0 network to initiate a connection with the VTY lines, has been applied. IP extended access lists can be used to control access over Telnet because it uses an upper layer TCP application port. However, at times it may be easier to filter where the packets are coming from. Do not forget that this access list has an implicit deny entry as well. So the only hosts allowed access will be those stated in the *permit* statement of the access list. Notice the big difference here is that we used the *access-class* command rather than the *access-group* command to apply the access list.

IP EXTENDED ACCESS LISTS

IP extended access lists give the network administrator much more control over packets that can be filtered with a router. Extended access lists can filter the destination address in a packet as well as the source address. They can also filter based on other criteria such as protocols (TCP, UDP, IP, ICMP, and IGRP) and port numbers of TCP/IP-based applications. Like standard access lists, IP extended access lists use wildcard masks as well.

CLI Configuration

The primary difference in the configuration of standard and extended access lists is that the extended access list has more parameters. IP extended access lists use the range of 100 through 199 to identify the access list. An example of an IP extended access list follows:

```
Router(config)#access list 125 permit tcp any
    host 10.1.1.5 eq 80
```

In the example, the arguments are as follows: The access list number is *125*, the rule for this entry is to *permit any* source address with a destination address of *10.1.1.5* if it is establishing an HTTP (*eq 80*) connection. All other traffic will be denied because of the implicit *deny all* entry. When signifying the port number, use *eq* for *equal to, lt* for *less than, gt* for *greater than,* or *neq* for *not equal.* The command to apply an extended access list to an interface is the same command used to apply the IP standard access list to the interface. It can be applied to packets coming *in* to the router or going *out*. See the following example:

```
Router(config-if)#ip access-group 125 out
```

 Test Tip: When filtering ports, you can use terms as well as numbers (that is, 80 = WWW, 20 + 21 = FTP, 25 = SMTP).

In the next example, all FTP traffic (program = port 21 and data = port 20) is being denied from subnet 131.1.5.0 to subnet 131.1.6.0. The final entry of the access list is a *permit any;* without the *permit any* all hosts would be subject to the implicit *deny* all. Only FTP traffic will be filtered between the two subnetworks as a result of this access list. The final option available is to place the word *log* at the end of the access list, which would in turn send a message to the console if a packet matches an entry, as follows next:

```
Router(config)#access list 101 deny tcp
    131.1.5.0 0.0.0.255 131.1.6.0 0.0.0.255 eq
    21 log

Router(config)#access list 101 deny tcp
    131.1.5.0 0.0.0.255 131.1.6.0 0.0.0.255 eq
    20 log

Router(config)#access list 101 permit ip any
    any
```

In this example, the administrator used the wildcard mask of 0.0.0.255 to compare the first three octets of the source and destination network. The access list must now be grouped on an interface. When applying access lists to interfaces, remember the following:

- IP extended access lists should be applied as close to the source as possible.

- IP standard access lists should be applied as close to the destination as possible.

 Test Tip: The CCNA Exam may have several questions about access lists. Memorize the ranges of IP access lists. Also, look for the keyword *only* in the question. If the access list is to "only" filter one protocol, there must be a *permit any* entry.

6.3   NAMED ACCESS LISTS AND NETWORK ADDRESS TRANSLATION (NAT)

Named access lists are used to manage access lists in the network. A named IP access list has basically the same role in a network as an IP numbered access list. However, if using named access lists, there is no limitation in the amount of access lists used on a router. Remember, when using numbered access lists, only 100 access lists can be set for both IP standard and IP extended access lists. Granted, 100 access lists may be more than enough in most networks, but every network is different and an organization might need to set up many access lists.

Manageability is an additional benefit to using named access lists. Managing a network's access lists is much easier if they are named logically. For example, when trying to determine what access lists are on a router and what they are permitting or denying, it is easy to type

```
Router#show access-list
Standard IP access list 10
    deny 10.1.1.0, wildcard bits 0.0.0.255
    permit any
```

This command shows the access lists configured on the router. Notice the identity of the access list is simply a number. If using named access lists, a much more descriptive name can be used and the preceding entry would look like this:

```
Router#show access-list
Standard IP access list DenyKioskLAN
    deny 10.1.1.0, wildcard bits 0.0.0.255
    permit any
```

This is much more manageable, especially if there are many access lists to monitor.

CONFIGURING NAMED ACCESS LISTS

When creating a named access list, the access list can be either an IP standard access list or an IP extended access list. The command to create the named access list is slightly different than the command to create a numbered access list. For example, *ip access-list [standard | extended] given_name* is the proper command to use. Notice the first parameter of the command is *ip* not simply *access-list*, which is used for a numbered access list. Also, denoting which type of IP access list is being created—*standard* or *extended*—is mandatory. And finally, the name of the access list must be placed at the end.

CLI Configuration

Let's go through the steps of building a named access list. In this example, we will set up a standard named access list that blocks users from our Kiosk LAN from accessing our Corporate LAN.

```
Router#config t
Router(config)#ip access-list standard
    DenyKioskLAN
```

After the preceding command is entered, the router changes modes to the standard NACL (Named Access Control List) mode:

```
Router(config-std-nacl)#
```

Once in the preceding mode, continue with the access list entry:

```
Router(config-std-nacl)#deny 10.1.1.0 0.0.0.255
```

The preceding *deny* statement denies all packets that match the 10.1.1.0 subnet, which we can assume is the Kiosk LAN. The command to apply this access list to the router's interface is *ip access-group DenyKioskLAN out*. Be sure to be in the interface configuration mode when applying the named access list.

You can create IP extended access lists with a named access list as well. Remember the extended access lists can block data based on many other rules than can standard access lists. Extended access lists can block based on source, destination, protocol, and port when trying to filter specific traffic such as e-mail (port 110 and 25), web (port 80), DNS (port 53), and many others.

NETWORK ADDRESS TRANSLATION (NAT)

Network address translation or NAT is the process of converting private IP addresses of the LAN into public addresses on the WAN. NAT is discussed here primarily because NAT statements are done utilizing Cisco access lists. There are generally two types of NAT statements used, dynamic and static. Dynamic NAT statements allow the router to convert a pool of private addresses to a single public address. This is usually used when you have multiple clients on the inside of the router that need access to the Internet. Static NAT statements force the router to do a one-to-one mapping of a single private address to a single public address. Static NAT statements are popular when you have a service such as a web server running on the inside of a network that you would like people to have access to.

Configuring Network Address Translation

When creating network address translation statements there is certainly a sequence that must be adhered to. Remember that NAT is one of the core services that allow users to get to the Internet and allow the Internet to get to your services. There are many different situations where NAT can be applied. Here you will learn the basic NAT sequence.

CLI Configuration

In this example a NAT setup will be completed for a dynamic environment where the users on the local area network need to get to the Internet.

In the first step define which interface is the inside interface and which is the outside interface. In most situations the Ethernet interface will be the inside interface. However in some situations the router may have two Ethernet interfaces one for the inside and one for the outside network. In this example the inside interface is F0/0 and the outside interface is S0/0.

```
Router#config t
Router(config)#Interface f0/0
Router(config-if)#ip nat inside
Router(config-if)#interface s0/0
Router(config-if)#ip nat outside
```

The following command identifies the pool of addresses with a name of Public, which will be used on the outside interface.

```
Router(config)#ip nat pool Public 64.42.1.1
      64.42.1.1 netmask 255.255.255.0
```

Next the inside NAT statement must be created in this statement. Notice that access list 50 is referenced. Therefore, access list 50 must be created too. The access list will permit the hosts on the internal network.

```
Router (config)#ip nat inside source list 50
      Public overload
```

In the above command the overload statement means more than one internal IP address can be translated into the single public address on the outside interface. Finally, create the access list for the internal hosts.

```
Router(config)#access-list 50 permit 10.1.0.0
      0.0.255.255
```

 Test Tip: If a NAT question arises and it mentions a NAT pool, the router is using dynamic NAT. If the NAT statement reads static it is normally a 1-to-1 translation.

6.4 MONITORING AND REMOVING ACCESS LISTS

Several commands are available to monitor and verify whether any access lists are configured on the router and on specific interfaces. The commands allow you to verify IPX access lists.

Test Tip: Before taking the CCNA Exam, have a strong understanding of the following commands.

ACCESS LIST VERIFICATION

The commands to verify whether or not access lists are configured on the router are similar for IP and named access lists. To verify if any access lists are on the router type

```
Router#show access-list
```

This command lists all access lists and the parameters of each. However, the *show access-list* command does not show you what interface the access list is assigned to. To see the parameters of an individual access list, use this command:

```
Router#show access-list 101
```

This command shows the configuration of access list 101 but not the interface it is assigned to. To view the access lists for a specific protocol such as IP, use the following command:

```
Router#show ip access-list
```

This command shows any IP access lists. It does not show the interface that the access list is assigned to. To verify whether any access lists are configured on an interface and what the access list identification numbers are, use the following command:

```
Router#show ip interface
```

The preceding command gives information about the interfaces, including any access lists assigned to the interface, but not the parameters of the access list. Finally, the *show runnig-config* command shows interfaces and access lists applied to them but not the parameters of the access lists.

 Test Tip: To view the interface applied to an access list, use *show running-config* or *show ip interface.* To see the settings within the access lists, use *show access-list, show access-list [number],* or *show ip access-list.*

CHAPTER SUMMARY

This chapter covered the procedures of applying access lists to a router. The topics included IP standard and extended access lists as well as named access lists. Wildcard masking was explained as well as monitoring and verifying the existence of access lists on a router. Use the knowledge test to prepare for the CCNA Exam.

KNOWLEDGE TEST

Choose one answer for all questions unless directed to do otherwise.

1. What are the IP standard and extended access list identification numbers?
   a. 800–899, 900–999
   b. 900–999, 1000–1099
   c. 100–199, 200–299
   d. 1–99, 100–199

2. When working with access lists to control traffic into a VTY line, which command is used to apply the access list to the VTY line?
   a. *Access-group*
   b. *IP access-group*
   c. *Access-class*
   d. *IP access-class*

3. Which command would deny all hosts from the 121.0.0.0 network after being applied to an interface?
   a. *Router(config)#access-group 25 deny 121.0.0.0 255.255.255.255*
   b. *Router(config)#access-list 25 deny 121.0.0.0 0.255.255.255*
   c. *Router(config)#access-group 25 deny all 121.0.0.0 0.255.255.255*
   d. *Router(config)#access-list 25 deny all 121.0.0.0 0.255.255.255*

4. What criteria are used for filtering packets with an extended IP access list? (Choose all that apply.)
   a. Source address
   b. Subnet mask of destination
   c. Destination address
   d. Socket type
   e. Protocol type

5. Write the commands that would create access list 159 and prevent only WWW traffic from host 192.168.1.25/24 to host 10.10.100.254/16 while allowing all others access.
   Line 1. _____
   Line 2. _____

6. Write the command that will create access list 160 and allow the 10.1.32.0/20 subnet access to the FTP server with the address of 192.168.68.1/24.
   Line 1. _____

7. Which command will show the details of IP extended access list 101?
   a. *Router#show extended ip access-list 101*
   b. *Router#show ip access-list 101*
   c. *Router#show ip access-list 101 extended*
   d. *Router#show 101 ip access-list*

8. What command would be used to view all access lists configured on a router? (Choose all that apply.)
   a. *Router#show running-config*
   b. *Router#show ip access-list*
   c. *Router#show ipx access-list*
   d. *Router#show any access-list*
   e. *Router#show access-list*

9. Which command would apply access list 129 to filter traffic as it enters the router from Fast Ethernet 0?
   a. *IP access-group 129 out*
   b. *IP access-group 129 in*
   c. *Access-group 129 out*
   d. *Access-group 129 out*

10. Which command would be used to allow clients from the 192.16.9.0 network to access a web server over HTTP with an address of 141.19.1.7? (Choose all that apply.)
    a. *Router(config)#access-list 18 permit TCP 192.16.9.0 0.0.0.255 host 141.19.1.7 eq 80*
    b. *Router(config)#access-list 118 permit TCP 192.16.9.0 0.0.0.255 host 141.19.1.7 eq 80*
    c. *Router(config)#access-list 118 permit TCP 192.16.9.0 0.0.0.255 141.19.1.7 any eq 80*
    d. *Router(config)#access-list 118 permit TCP 192.16.9.0 0.0.0.255 141.19.1.7 0.0.0.0 eq 80*
    e. *Router(config)#access-list 18 permit UDP 192.16.9.0 0.0.0.255 host 141.19.1.7 eq 80*

11. Write the command to allow all Internet traffic access to the SMTP server, which has an IP address of 172.16.5.100.
    Line 1. _____

12. What are the rules that apply to all access lists? (Choose all that apply.)
    a. Access lists must have an identifying number to differentiate between access list types.
    b. Access lists use the range 0–99 more frequently than 1000–1099.
    c. Access lists have an implicit *permit all* as the last entry.
    d. Routers are limited to one access list per protocol, per interface, per direction.
    e. Access lists have an implicit *deny all* (*any*) as the last entry.
    f. Routers are limited to one access list per address, per interface, per direction.

13. What is the command sequence that will allow you to create an access list on Serial 0/0 named PUBLIC that will allow Internet users to access only your web server with an address of 172.16.90.1?

a. *Router(config)#ip access-list standard public*
   Router(config-std-nacl)#permit tcp any host 172.16.90.1 eq 80
   Router(config-std-nacl)#exit
   Router(config)#Interface S0/0
   Router(config-if)#IP access-group public in

b. *Router(config)#ip access-list extended public*
   Router(config-ext-nacl)#permit tcp any host 172.16.90.1 eq 80
   Router(config-ext-nacl)#exit
   Router(config)#Interface S0/0
   Router(config-if)#IP access-group public in

c. *Router(config)#ip access-list extended public*
   Router(config-ext-nacl)#permit tcp any host 172.16.90.1 eq 80
   Router(config-ext-nacl)#exit
   Router(config)#Interface F0/0
   Router(config-if)#IP access-group public in

d. *Router(config)#ip access-list extended public*
   Router(config-ext-nacl)#permit any host 172.16.90.1 eq 80
   Router(config-ext-nacl)#exit
   Router(config)#Interface S0/0
   Router(config-if)#IP access-group public in

14. What will the *show access-list* command list?
   a. The specifics of an IP access list
   b. All access lists with no parameters
   c. The interfaces that each access list is configured on
   d. All access lists with all parameters on the router

15. Named access lists can only be applied as inbound access lists.
   a. True
   b. False

16. When using wildcard masks, what is the value of 0.0.0.0 255.255.255.255 equivalent to?
   a. Check all hosts on all networks.
   b. Do not check any hosts on any networks.
   c. Check some hosts on some networks.
   d. Check all IPX addresses.

17. What is the *access-class* command used for?
   a. Applies an access list to the auxiliary port
   b. Applies an access list to the serial interface
   c. Applies an access list to a Token Ring interface
   d. Applies an access list to the VTY lines

18. What command would be used to deny TFTP traffic from host 10.1.1.89 to host 203.45.90.23?

    a. *Router(config)#access-list 100 deny UDP 10.1.1.89 0.0.0.0 203.45.90.23 0.0.0.0 eq 69*

    b. *Router(config)#access-list 10 deny UDP 10.1.1.89 0.0.0.0 203.45.90.23 0.0.0.0 eq 69*

    c. *Router(config)#access-list 100 deny TCP 10.1.1.89 0.0.0.0 203.45.90.23 0.0.0.0 eq 69*

    d. *Router(config)#access-list 100 deny UDP 10.1.1.89 255.255.255.255 203.45.90.23 255.255.255.255 eq 69*

19. Access lists are only used to permit or deny data into serial and Fast Ethernet ports.

    a. True

    b. False

20. If your router has an access list applied to an interface without any identified access list entries, the interface will forward all packets.

    a. True

    b. False

CHAPTER 7

Routing in a Wide Area Network

OBJECTIVES

The following topics are discussed in Chapter 7:

- Choose WAN services to meet customer requirements.
- Implement simple WAN protocols.
- Perform simple WAN troubleshooting.
- Evaluate key characteristics of WANs.

INTRODUCTION

In the current business world, many companies have multiple offices spread across national and international boundaries. To transmit data between offices, companies look to service providers to carry their data because it is too expensive to install their own national or global network. A service provider in the networking industry is similar to a service provider in the telephone industry carrying long-distance telephone calls from one region of the globe to another. Most of the larger telephone service providers offer data-carrying services. Cisco routers offer mechanisms that can be used to relay a company's LAN signals to a service provider's wide area network (WAN). This chapter discusses four layer 2 protocols that Cisco routers use to transmit data over a WAN: High-Level Data Link Control (HDLC), Point-to-Point Protocol (PPP), Integrated Services Digital Network (ISDN), and Frame Relay.

7.1 WIDE AREA NETWORKING

Before discussing the protocols used to transmit data, a brief discussion about wide area network (WAN) terminology and the three primary connection types is in order.

WAN TERMINOLOGY

WANs are used to connect multiple LANs to one another so an organization can maintain a seamless integration of data between sites. To accomplish this, companies usually look to WAN service providers to provide low-cost data transmission from one LAN to another. To lease these services from a service provider, some terms to be aware of are

- **Customer Premises Equipment (CPE).** The devices owned or leased by the subscriber. CPE is located at the customer's premises.

- **Demarc** or **Demarcation.** The point where the responsibility of the data changes hands. The subscriber turns the responsibility of the data media and communication equipment over to the service provider, or vice versa.

- **Local loop.** The cable run that connects the subscriber to the central office.

- **Central Office (CO).** The service provider's switching facility that receives the subscriber's data before forwarding them to their ultimate destination. The CO is often referred to as the point of presence (POP).

- **Toll network.** This is the service provider's collection of switches, cable, and links that are often represented as a cloud. The mechanisms that are in the WAN provider's cloud are not discussed in this chapter.

Figure 7.1 shows how these components of a WAN are designed.

These terms describe the hardware components that allow data to be transferred between destinations. The final term, *encapsulation,* is the means of adding control and addressing information to a protocol data unit (PDU). WAN protocols encapsulate data at layer 2 of the OSI model before forwarding the data out of the interface of a router. Several WAN protocols provide encapsulation for data transport, including

- **HDLC.** Cisco's default encapsulation for point-to-point connections using a *synchronous transmission,* which maintains precise timing between communicating stations.

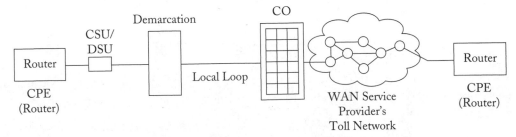

Figure 7.1 *WAN components working together*

- **PPP.** Replaced the Serial Line Internet Protocol (SLIP) and provides encapsulation for point-to-point connections using synchronous or *asynchronous transmissions.* Asynchronous transmissions do not require precise timing between stations.

- **Frame Relay.** Grew out of the older X.25 standard, and transmits data over a packet-switched network using virtual circuits.

- **Asynchronous Transfer Mode (ATM).** Uses fixed-length cells of 53 bytes to transmit voice, video, and data over a packet-switched network.

WAN CONNECTION TYPES

A WAN connection type is comprised of the components (such as wire, switches, and routers often referred to as a cloud) that the service provider uses to forward data from one subscriber's location to another. The three WAN connection types to be aware of are leased (dedicated) lines, packet-switching connections, and circuit-switched connections. A brief description of each follows:

- **Leased lines.** Leased lines or dedicated connections are typically used if an organization needs a guaranteed connection that is always available and not shared with other subscribers. The encapsulation methods that are available on a leased line are PPP, HDLC, and SLIP. Leased lines are considered point-to-point connections.

- **Packet-switched connections.** Packet-switched connections offer an end-to-end connection that allows multiple subscribers to use the same wire at any given time. The packet-switched connections maintain a virtual point-to-point or point-to-multipoint connection by using different virtual circuits for each subscriber. Subscribers typically pay a different price based on the bandwidth allocated to them by the provider. Packet-switched encapsulation consists of Frame Relay, X.25, and ATM.

- **Circuit-switched connections.** Circuit-switched connections are used on a per-connection basis and are normally implemented in a dial-up modem or ISDN environment where the connection is only made available when data needs to be transmitted. Circuit switching works best for organizations that only need periodic WAN connectivity. Encapsulation used over a switched circuit is normally PPP, SLIP, or HDLC.

7.2 HIGH-LEVEL DATA LINK CONTROL (HDLC) ENCAPSULATION

HDLC is a bit-oriented protocol. Bit-oriented protocols can use single bits to represent control information, which results in less overhead. HDLC can travel over synchronous lines. Synchronous communication occurs when the sending and receiving devices use a clocking mechanism to regulate the transmission.

HDLC FEATURES

HDLC is the default WAN protocol that Cisco routers use when sending data out of the serial port. HDLC is an ISO standard, but all of its implementations are proprietary to the manufacturer of the device, including Cisco routers. Cisco's version of HDLC does not offer authentication services and can transport multiple network layer protocols such as IP or IPX. HDLC is best to use when connecting two Cisco devices in a point-to-point topology over leased lines.

HDLC CONFIGURATION

When configuring a serial interface on a Cisco router, the default encapsulation is HDLC. However, if the default configuration has been changed and it is time to revert back to HDLC, use the following command at the interface configuration mode:

```
Router(config-if)#encapsulation hdlc
```

Use the *show interface* command to verify that HDLC is correctly configured on an interface.

7.3 POINT-TO-POINT PROTOCOL (PPP) ENCAPSULATION

PPP encapsulation is an industry standard and can be implemented between Cisco and non-Cisco devices. PPP can be used for router-to-router connections or for hosts to dial into networks over asynchronous telephone lines. PPP works over synchronous, asynchronous, and ISDN lines. PPP supports authentication between devices.

PPP FEATURES

PPP uses the Network Control Protocol (NCP) to support the encapsulation of multiple network layer protocols. NCP has built-in functionality for IP and IPX called IPCP and IPXCP, which are the control protocols for each network layer protocol, respectively.

PPP uses the Link Control Protocol (LCP) as well to set up the link between two devices making a PPP connection. Some of the LCP options include

- **Authentication.** Uses the password authentication protocol (PAP) or the challenge handshake authentication protocol (CHAP), or both.
- **Compression.** Uses the Stacker or Predictor compression protocol.
- **Error detection.** Uses the Quality and Magic Number protocol.
- **Multilink.** Divides up the networking load over multiple links using the Multilink protocol. This feature is available with Cisco IOS 11.1 or better.

Session Establishment

PPP uses three phases for session establishment:

1. **Link establishment phase.** The link is established through sending and receiving LCPs.

2. **Authentication phase (optional).** If configured, the protocols used are PAP or CHAP.

3. **Network layer protocol phase.** During this final phase, the PPP devices send NCP packets between each other to determine which network layer protocols they will be using for the current session.

Authentication

Authentication protocols supported by PPP are PAP and CHAP. A description of both follows:

- **PAP.** An authentication protocol that uses a two-way handshake. The calling router transmits its user name and password to the receiving router after the initial PPP link establishment, which in turn accepts or denies the connection. It is, therefore, a two-way session establishment. One of the limitations of PAP is that it sends the password across the line once, at the beginning of the session, in clear text format.

- **CHAP.** Normally the preferred method of authentication between two devices using PPP because CHAP uses a three-way handshake and encrypts the user name and password. When using CHAP, the router that is being called initiates the challenge after the initial PPP link is established. The calling router then responds with the user name and password. The called router now has the option of accepting or denying the authentication information. The host router periodically challenges the guest router, randomly requesting the user name and password.

PPP CONFIGURATION

To set the encapsulation of an interface to PPP, use the encapsulation command that follows the interface configuration mode:

```
Router(config-if)#encapsulation ppp
```

Configuring Authentication

To configure authentication between two routers, use the following command from the local router:

```
Router(config)#username [RemoteRouter
     Hostname] password [password]
```

Each router must be configured with the remote router's host name after the *username* argument. Both routers must have the same password configured as well. The password is in clear text; use *service password-encryption* to encrypt it. For example, NorthRouter and SouthRouter are to use PPP. On the NorthRouter, type

```
NorthRouter(config)#username SouthRouter
     password OurPassword
```

On the SouthRouter, type

```
SouthRouter(config)#username NorthRouter
     password OurPassword
```

To configure the routers to use PAP or CHAP, or both, enter the interface configuration mode and type the following command:

```
Router(config-if)#ppp authentication [chap |
     pap | chap pap | pap chap]
```

If both PAP and CHAP are configured, the router will try the authentication method that was configured first. If it fails the router will then try the second. Use the *debug ppp authentication* command to view authentication exchanges between routers.

7.4   INTEGRATED SERVICES DIGITAL NETWORK (ISDN)

ISDN is a wide area connection standard offered by existing telephone service providers and implemented over existing telephone lines. It typically uses PPP to encapsulate network layer protocols to traverse the WAN. ISDN requires specialized equipment to access the ISDN network. Cisco supports this equipment in different implementations. For example, ISDN service modules can be purchased through Cisco and integrated into existing routers within the internetwork. In addition to that, Cisco sells ISDN-based routers that are primarily used for access to an ISDN network. In this section, ISDN features, channels, configuration, and dial-on-demand routing (DDR) is examined.

ISDN FEATURES

ISDN is used to send voice, video, and data over a digital line using a dial-up method. However, it is not a traditional dial-up line because it dials into an ISDN service provider and offers higher rates of speed when compared to traditional dial-up technology. ISDN uses PPP or HDLC as its encapsulation protocol in addition to ISDN protocols. An ISDN connection may require additional hardware that does not always come packaged with a Cisco router. In this section, ISDN hardware components, reference points, and protocols are described.

ISDN Hardware Components

Certain hardware components are needed to connect to an ISDN network. ISDN terminology represents these connections as listed here:

- **Terminal Endpoint 1 (TE1).** A TE1 is a component, such as a PC or a router, with an ISDN adapter installed in it.

- **Terminal Endpoint 2 (TE2).** A TE2 is a component within the ISDN that does not have an integrated ISDN adapter in it. These components often need an additional hardware component, such as an external ISDN adapter, which is considered a terminal adapter.

- **Terminal Adapter (TA).** A component external to a TE1 that allows access into the ISDN network.

- **Network Termination Device 1 (NT1).** NT1 is the device that connects the CPE with the service provider. This device could be a Channel Service Unit/Data Service Unit (CSU/DSU) converting the signals between the LAN and the WAN.

- **Network Termination Device 2 (NT2).** NT2 is the ISDN switching device and may or may not be located at the CPE.

The key to making this work successfully is to check with the ISDN provider as to which components it will provide the business with and which components must be purchased separately.

Reference Points

Each connection in an ISDN configuration is given a reference point to describe its logical connection within the network design. It is important to understand these reference points because routers can support different interface types, and there may be a need for additional equipment in the ISDN design. The four reference points are

- **Reference Point "R".** Represents the connection between the TE2 and a terminal adapter.

- **Reference Point "S".** Represents the connection between the TE1 or the TA and the NT2. S and T reference points are electrically the same, so they can be represented as S/T.

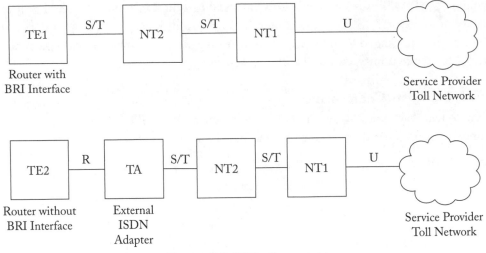

Figure 7.2 *ISDN reference points*

- **Reference point "T".** Represents the connection between an NT1 and the NT2. S and T reference points are electrically the same, so they can be represented as S/T.

- **Reference point "U".** Represents the connection between the NT1 and the ISDN network. If the router has a built-in NT1 component, it can connect directly to the ISDN.

In Figure 7.2, view the hardware and reference points used in an ISDN connection.

ISDN Protocols

ISDN uses three sets of protocols that are published by the International Telecommunication Union (ITU):

- **E-series protocols.** These protocols recommend telephone network standards:

  - E.163 for international telephone numbering plan.
  - E.164 for international ISDN addressing.

- **I-series protocols.** These protocols deal with concepts and terminology:

  - I.100 supports general ISDN concepts.
  - I.200 is used for the service aspects of ISDN.
  - I.300 deals with network aspects.
  - I.400 sets the standards for the User Network Interface (UNI).

- **Q-series protocols.** Q-series protocols work with layer 2 and layer 3 signals:
  - Q.931 defines the layer 3 functionality between terminal and ISDN switches.
  - Q.921 defines the data-link processes used by the Link Access Procedure on channel D (LAPD) protocol.

Test Tip: E = Telephone network standards; I = Concepts; Q = Signals.

ISDN CHANNELS

ISDN uses multiple channels of signaling to transmit voice, video, and data. ISDN is a synchronous communication standard and reserves one channel of the communication medium for signaling. ISDN supports two communication standards: *Basic Rate Interface (BRI)* and *Primary Rate Interface (PRI)*.

Basic Rate Interface (BRI)

BRI consists of three signaling channels. Two of the channels are called *Bearer* or *B* channels and are used to transmit data. The third channel is a *Delta* or *D* channel and is used for control and signaling, including call setup and termination. The two B channels can carry up to 64 Kbps of data, so while using BRI ISDN, the data rate is 128 Kbps. The D channel can carry 16 Kbps of control and signaling information and is not included in the aggregate total of bandwidth available. The D channel works with the LAPD protocol, which is a data-link protocol that complies with the signaling standards of ISDN.

Primary Rate Interface (PRI)

PRI can handle more data than the BRI. PRI has different standards throughout the world; for example, in North America and Japan, it can handle up to 23 B channels at 64 Kbps and 1 D channel using 64 Kbps. In Australia and Europe, PRI uses 30 B channels with 64 Kbps and 1 D channel at 64 Kbps. Configuration of PRI is not discussed in this book.

ISDN CONFIGURATION

If the router has a BRI, additional hardware is not necessary because the device is a TE1. If the router does not support the BRI standard internally, additional hardware such as a TA must be purchased. The TA needs to be connected to the router's serial port with a serial cable. For successful communication to take place, it is important to know the type of ISDN switch the service provider is using. During configuration, the Cisco router is configured to send data to a specific type of ISDN switch. A successful connection may not be possible if the incorrect ISDN switch type is listed in the router.

CLI Configuration

Configuring ISDN involves three steps: configure the encapsulation used on the interface, identify the switch type that the service provider is using, and set up a service profile identifier (SPID), which is an identifier given by the service provider. To configure the ISDN interface with the PPP encapsulation, first enter the BRI configuration mode:

```
Router(config)#interface bri0
```

Next, set the encapsulation:

```
Router(config-if)#encapsulation PPP
```

After specifying the encapsulation, the router must be configured with the type of switch it is connecting to at the service provider's location. Several types of ISDN switches are available and Cisco has many commands to represent the different switches. The following are three popular U.S. BRI switch types and the Cisco commands that support them:

Switch Type	Cisco Command
AT&T basic rate switch	*basic-5ess*
Northern Telecom DMS-100 basic rate switch	*basic-dms100*
National ISDN-1	*basic-ni1*

Configure the ISDN switch type at the global configuration mode or the interface configuration mode. If configured at the global configuration mode, all ISDN interfaces on the router use the same ISDN switch type. The command to set up the ISDN switch type follows:

```
Router(config-if)#isdn switch-type basic-ni1
```

Once configured, the final step is to configure SPID (if required). Check with the service provider to determine whether or not a SPID is required. If required, the provider issues a number to the customer. SPIDs may be required for each B channel on the ISDN connection. To specify the SPIDs, use the following command:

```
Router(config-if)#isdn spid1 [SPID assigned by
     service provider]
Router(config-if)#isdn spid2 [SPID assigned by
     service provider]
```

DIAL-ON-DEMAND ROUTING (DDR)

DDR is a low-cost method of sending data on an as-needed basis over an ISDN line or public-switched telephone network. DDR is used to connect two or more

Cisco routers to one another. The DDR connection can be configured to forward data only when they meet specified criteria. These data are called interesting data or interesting traffic. When interesting data enter the router, it initiates a call to the destination router, forwards the interesting data, and then terminates the session. This saves money because there is no need to pay for an expensive dedicated or leased line.

DDR Connection

There are five steps that take place when a DDR connection is made to forward data:

1. The router receives a data packet and must determine whether there is an entry in its routing table for the destination network that is identified in the data packet.

2. If the router has an entry in the routing table to the destination network, it determines whether the data are interesting (interesting data are a configurable option).

3. The router must get the dialer information from the dialer map (which specifies the next hop address), the host name of the remote router, and the number to dial to make a connection.

4. The router transmits the traffic.

5. The router terminates the connection.

DDR Configuration

Three tasks must be performed when configuring DDR:

1. Define static routes so the router knows the interface to send the data out of when making a DDR connection.

2. Specify what data are interesting so the router knows when to make a DDR connection.

3. Configure the dialer information so the router knows what number to dial to make a connection.

CLI Configuration

The first step in configuring DDR is to ensure that static routes are configured to avoid sending route updates. Use the *ip route* command to specify static routes. The second task is to specify what data are interesting. This defines what data coming into the router will cause a DDR connection to be initiated. The command used is *dialer-list* at the global configuration mode. Here is an example that defines all IP traffic as interesting:

```
Router(config)#dialer-list 1 protocol ip
    permit
```

Next, apply the dialer list to an interface using the *dialer-group* command:

```
Router(config)#interface bri0
Router(config-if)#dialer-group 1
```

The *dialer-group* command value must match the value specified in the dialer list.

The final step is to use the dialer string command to specify the telephone number to dial when interesting data triggers a connection. See the following:

```
Router(config-if)#dialer string 5551212
```

This example dials the phone number 5551212 when interesting traffic reaches the router. To test the setup, send interesting data to the router.

Test Tip: There are three requirements to set up an ISDN BRI:
1. IP Address Mask
2. Encapsulation
3. Define when to call (based on Interesting Data) and who to call [number of provider]

Optional DDR CLI Commands

There are two additional DDR commands to be aware of. One of them is

```
Router(config-if)#dialer load-threshold 255
    [outbound | inbound | either]
```

This command sets the amount of bandwidth available for a connection. The load can be calculated using the inbound, outbound, or either optional arguments. The default setting is outbound. The threshold value is between 1 and 255 and represents a percentage of the bandwidth available. If the value of 255 is used, then 100% of bandwidth is allocated to the connection.

The other command sets an idle session to timeout after 30 seconds of idling and is as follows:

```
Router(config-if)#dialer idle-timeout 30
```

VERIFYING ISDN

Several *show* and *debug* commands can be used to verify the ISDN connection. See Table 3.1 in Chapter 3 for a list of them.

7.5 FRAME RELAY

Frame Relay is an ITU and ANSI standard used to forward frames through a public data network (PDN). The PDN is comprised of many Frame Relay devices that forward frames from one location to another. A Frame Relay service provider is needed to send data into the PDN. After the data are sent into the Frame Relay cloud, the service provider's Frame Relay switches forward the data to the destination through virtual circuits.

FRAME RELAY FEATURES

The Frame Relay protocol is a layer 2 encapsulation protocol that sends data through the serial port of a Cisco router to a Frame Relay service provider. Frame Relay providers allow customers to buy the amount of bandwidth needed. The amount of bandwidth allocated to the customer in bits per second is called the *Committed Information Rate (CIR)*. This section covers how to get the Frame Relay frames from the router to the service provider's network. The provider's responsibility is to ensure that the data received are forwarded to the destination. Some of the features of Frame Relay are virtual circuits, Data-Link Connection Identifiers (DLCI), and the Local Management Interface (LMI).

Virtual Circuits

A *virtual circuit* is a logical connection between two DTEs in a Frame Relay network. The service provider's Frame Relay switches provide the means to create a virtual circuit between two routers. The two types of virtual circuits are *permanent virtual circuits (PVC)* and *switched virtual circuits (SVC)*.

- **Permanent virtual circuit (PVC).** A PVC uses the same path all the time to get data through the PDN from one DTE (router) to another DTE (router). It is configured in advance, is always available to the subscriber, and is normally used for a connection that is consistently sending data across the Frame Relay connection.

- **Switched virtual circuit (SVC).** SVC is dynamically created at the outset of a transmission and torn down at the conclusion of the transmission, much like the process of setting up a telephone connection. SVCs are used for sporadic transmission of data and are less popular than PVCs.

Data-Link Connection Identifier (DLCI)

A DLCI is a unique number within a PDN that is provided by the service provider. It represents the connection between the local router (DTE) and the service provider's Frame Relay switch. It is only significant to the local router. When a DLCI is given to a subscriber, the subscriber applies the DLCI to its local router's interface. The service provider's Frame Relay switches use the DLCI to connect the local router with a remote router through the PVC. The remote router is given a separate DLCI. Both routers are then responsible to determine the destination router's IP address by creating a static DLCI-to-IP address map or by dynamically using the *Inverse Address Resolution Protocol (Inverse ARP)*. After the routers know the IP address of their destination router (which is at the other end of the PVC), they send data to the Frame Relay switch, which forwards the data to the correct DLCI.

Test Tip: The DLCI of the local router is mapped to the IP address of the remote router.

Local Management Interface (LMI)

LMI is a signaling standard between the router and the Frame Relay switch. It manages the connection and the status of virtual circuits between the local router and the Frame Relay switch. LMI supports multicast addressing, multicasting, connection keepalives, and virtual circuit status messages. Three types of LMIs are supported by Cisco routers:

- **Cisco.** Developed by the "gang of four": Cisco systems, Northern Telecom, Stratacom, and Digital Equipment Corp.

- **ansi.** ANSI standard.

- **q933a.** ITU standard.

Although Cisco routers beginning with IOS version 11.2 can autosense the LMI, it is possible to configure the router with a specific LMI. When a router receives LMI status messages, it updates the virtual circuit status. The following are three possible states that a virtual circuit can be in:

- **Active state.** The virtual circuit between the local and remote routers is fully operational.

- **Inactive state.** The remote router is not functioning.

- **Deleted state.** No LMI information is being passed. The line is down or addresses are not mapped correctly.

Test Tip: "Cisco" is the default LMI for Cisco routers.

Congestion Control

Frame Relay uses several features to control congestion on the WAN:

- **Discard Eligibility (DE) Bit.** One of the fields of the frame relay frames is the *DE* field. When the DE field is set to one, this indicates that the frame being sent is bursting over the CIR and may be discarded in preference to other frames. If Subscriber A is bursting over the CIR and Subscriber B forwards data onto the line, Subscriber A's bursting data may be prevented from being sent. There are prevention methods to keep from losing the data. For example, if the data is bursting with the DE bit on and it happens to be discarded, the upper layer protocol services, such as TCP, will request retransmission of the lost segments. The frame switch can also buffer the data until the line goes back into a noncongested state.

- **Backward Explicit Congestion Notification (BECN).** In Frame Relay operations, the Frame Relay devices have the capability to report line congestion to other Frame Relay devices in the network. For example, the Frame Relay device can use the *BECN* to inform the sending Frame Relay switch that the line is congested and to slow down the sending of frames.

- **Forward Explicit Congestion Notification (FECN).** The *FECN* works in the same fashion as the BECN, but the FECN informs the destination Frame Relay device that the line the frame has just traveled is congested.

 Test Tip: Three congestion control mechanisms: FECN, BECN, DE Bit.

FRAME RELAY CONFIGURATION

Several commands must be configured correctly to ensure data transmission using Frame Relay. Such commands include confirming LMIs, mapping DLCIs, using Inverse ARP, using subinterfaces, and differentiating between point-to-point and multipoint configurations.

CLI Configuration

The first step in configuring Frame Relay is to ensure that the interface Frame Relay is going to be configured on has an IP address. Next, set the Frame Relay encapsulation type from the interface configuration mode:

```
Router(config-if)#encapsulation frame-relay
    cisco
```

The two types of Frame Relay encapsulation are *cisco* and *ietf*. If both routers are Cisco routers, use *cisco*. Use the *ietf* argument if connecting to a non-Cisco router.

 Test Tip: If connecting two Cisco routers, the encapsulation type is *cisco*. If connecting a Cisco router to a non-Cisco router, the encapsulation type is *ietf*.

The next step is to configure the LMI. Remember, the LMI can be autosensed with IOS 11.2 or better. The options available are *cisco, ansi,* or *q933a*. The Cisco

LMI standard is used in the following command:

```
Router(config-if)#frame-relay lmi-type cisco
```

The next command is the *bandwidth* command, which is based on the line speed purchased from the service provider:

```
Router(config-if)#bandwidth 56
```

The final step in configuring Frame Relay is to ensure that the DLCIs are mapped to the correct IP addresses. This is explained in the next section.

Inverse Address Resolution Protocol (Inverse ARP)

Inverse ARP is enabled by default on the Frame Relay configured Cisco routers. This allows for dynamic mapping of DLCIs between Cisco routers in a Frame Relay network. Each end of a virtual circuit is given a DLCI by the service provider. If router R1 has an IP address of 192.168.20.1 and router R2 has an IP address of 192.168.15.1, each router must be able to map its local DLCI to the IP address of the remote router. For example, if router R1 has a DLCI of 100 and router B has a DLCI of 75, each router would maintain a table mapping their DLCI to the remote router's IP address to ensure connectivity. Those entries are stored in the Frame Relay map table. There is also an entry to describe the connection between the two routers as active, inactive, or deleted. The routers are able to learn the state of the connection by the LMI status packets that are sent between the routers. Figure 7.3 shows a Frame Relay network with the DLCI-to-IP address mapping in the Frame Relay map for each router involved.

The command to enable Inverse ARP in the event it has been disabled is

```
Router(config-if)#frame-relay inverse arp ip
    100
```

In this command, the argument specifies IP as the protocol. Other options are available, including IPX, AppleTalk, DECnet, VINES, and XNS. The *100* at the end of the command specifies the local DLCI. Enabling Inverse ARP ensures that the Frame Relay router will build its Frame Relay map of DLCIs-to-IP addresses dynamically. It is possible to configure the Frame Relay map statically if one of the routers in the Frame Relay connection does not support Inverse ARP, or to cut down on broadcast messages. The command for this is as follows:

```
Router(config-if)#frame-relay map ip 125.0.0.5
    100 broadcast
```

In this command, *ip* is the protocol being used. The IP address of the destination router is *125.0.0.5* and the DLCI mapped to the local router is *100*. The *broadcast* argument is optional and allows broadcast messages to be forwarded to the address.

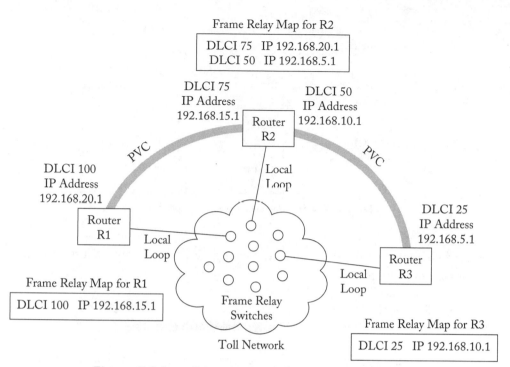

Figure 7.3 *Frame Relay network with IP address to DLCI mappings*

 Test Tip: If the router does not support Inverse ARP, the DLCI map must be configured statically.

Subinterfaces

Frame Relay allows multiple connections to be supported through a single interface by using subinterfaces. Subinterfaces subdivide an interface into multiple logical interfaces, allowing each subinterface to connect to a different remote router. This allows flexibility in the growth of a Frame Relay network without having to purchase several routers each time a new site is introduced. Frame Relay subinterfaces support two types of connections: *point-to-point* and *multipoint*.

Point-To-Point   In this configuration, the administrator configures multiple subinterfaces on an interface. Ensure that any network layer addresses assigned to the physical interface are removed and the Frame Relay encapsulation has been set at the interface. Each subinterface gets its own IP address and the service provider assigns each IP address a DLCI (Figure 7.4).

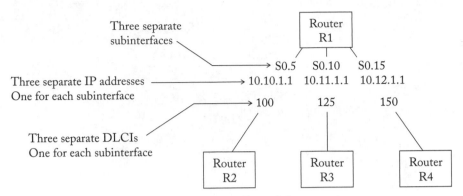

Figure 7.4 *Point-to-point Frame Relay connection*

Use the following command to create and configure Frame Relay subinterfaces in a point-to-point fashion:

```
Router(config-if)#interface serial 0.5 point-
    to-point
```

In this command, the *serial 0* is the physical interface that is being configured, the *.5* is the subinterface, and a value must be between 1 and 4294967293.

After the subinterfaces are created, configure DLCI on each subinterface to distinguish it from the physical interface. See the following command:

```
Router(config-subif)#frame-relay interface-
    dlci 100
```

Test Tip: To configure multiple subinterfaces, simply increase the interface parameter; for example, interface serial0.1, interface serial0.2, interface serial0.3, and so on.

Multipoint   Multipoint subinterface connections are different from point-to-point subinterface connections because each subinterface shares the same network layer address. However, they each have a different DLCI (Figure 7.5).

To configure a multipoint connection, the command is as follows:

```
Router(config-if)interface serial 0.15
    multipoint
```

If the multipoint interface is configured with Inverse ARP, use the DLCI command shown in the point-to-point section.

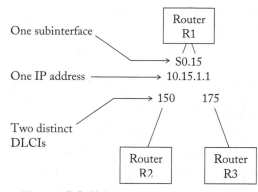

Figure 7.5 *Multipoint Frame Relay connection*

Frame Relay multipoint configuration is not recommended because Frame Relay uses the split horizon algorithm, and without multiple IP addresses the router will not forward route update data out the same interface that it learned it from. Using a single network layer address for all subinterfaces may defeat the purpose of subinterfaces in certain networks.

Monitoring and Verifying Frame Relay

The commands used to monitor and verify Frame Relay functionality are entered from the privileged EXEC mode; for example, the *show interface* command shows encapsulation type of the interface, LMI and DLCI information, and the line and protocol status of the interface. The *show frame-relay lmi* command shows traffic statistics exchanged between the router and the Frame Relay switch. The *show frame-relay pvc* gives information on each PVC configured, including its DLCI and its status. The *show frame-relay map* shows the static or dynamically mapped DLCI-to-network layer addresses the router knows about, as well as the status of the connection. You can clear this map using the *clear frame-relay-inarp* command.

Finally, the *debug frame-relay lmi* command can be used to troubleshoot the Frame Relay connection. The output of this command shows whether an LMI packet is an *out packet,* which is a frame going from the router to the Frame Relay switch or an *in packet,* which is a frame coming from the Frame Relay switch. In each frame, be aware of a field called the *status field*. The status field has three possible values for a DLCI connection:

- **0x0 – Inactive.** The switch knows about the DLCI but is not operational yet.
- **0x2 – Active.** The connection is operational.
- **0x4 – Deleted.** Not currently configured or deleted.

Test Tip: 0x0 = Inactive; 0x2 = Active; 0x4 = deleted.

CHAPTER SUMMARY

This chapter explained WAN technologies and PPP, ISDN, DDR, and Frame Relay. It is important to have a basic understanding of these technologies when dealing with Cisco routers. Several configuration commands were covered for each technology but not all of them. This was only an introduction to WAN routing. Switching technologies will be covered in depth in Chapter 8. Take some time to go over the knowledge test to prepare for the CCNA Exam before going on to the next chapter.

KNOWLEDGE TEST

Choose one answer for all questions unless directed to do otherwise.

1. One of the routers in your Frame Relay configuration does not support Inverse ARP. Which configuration must you complete to overcome this obstacle?
   a. Enable the Boot P protocol on the DHCP server.
   b. Configure a static DLCI-to-IP address map.
   c. Change the routing algorithm to a distance-vector algorithm.
   d. Disable all dynamic routing algorithms.

2. What command would allow you to see LMI traffic exchanged between the local router and the service provider's Frame Relay switch?
   a. *Show frame-relay lmi*
   b. *Show lmi frame relay*
   c. *Show frame-relay ip statistics*
   d. *Debug frame-relay lmi*

3. Your configuration has two PPP-configured routers. You want to use CHAP to authenticate the routers. The routers' names are East and West. The East router has a password of newengland. How would you set the user name and password on router West to allow router East to authenticate to router West?
   a. Username East password east
   b. Password newengland username east
   c. Username west password newengland
   d. Username east password newengland

4. DLCIs must be configured while using Frame Relay. What are the characteristics of DLCIs? (Choose all that apply.)
   a. DLCIs map MAC addresses to IP addresses.
   b. DLCIs are locally significant.
   c. DLCIs are mapped to remote network addresses.
   d. DLCIs must be mapped to IP addresses using the Boot P protocol.
   e. DLCIs can be mapped to IP addresses dynamically or statically.

5. You want to configure Frame Relay subinterfaces in a point-to-point configuration in your TCP/IP network. What steps are included in the configuration? (Choose all that apply.)
   a. Set the encapsulation for the interface to Frame Relay.
   b. Identify and create the subinterfaces.
   c. Configure the subinterface encapsulation with the *multipoint* argument.
   d. Delete the IP address for the serial interface.
   e. Configure each subinterface with its own IP address.
   f. Configure each subinterface with the same IP address.

6. What statements are used to describe ISDN? (Choose all that apply.)
   a. ISDN provides two 56 Kbps lines and one 16 Kbps line with the BRI.
   b. ISDN supports voice and data.
   c. ISDN uses Frame Relay as its encapsulation method.
   d. ISDN offers basic rate services and primary rate services.
   e. BRI offers more speed over PRI.
   f. ISDN provides end-to-end digital connectivity.
   g. ISDN supports voice only.
   h. ISDN supports data only.

7. What channels will be available to you while using the BRI?
   a. 23 B channels and 1 D channel
   b. 30 B channels and 1 D channel
   c. 2 D channels and 1 B channel
   d. 2 B channels and 1 D channel

8. ISDN has three series of protocols associated with it. Choose the correct protocol and standard combinations. (Choose three.)
   a. Q series = Telephone network standards
   b. Q series = Signaling standards
   c. Q series = Concepts and terminology
   d. E series = Telephone network standards
   e. E series = Signaling standards
   f. E series = Concepts and terminology
   g. I series = Telephone network standards
   h. I series = Signaling standards
   i. I series = Concepts and terminology

knowledge **TEST**

9. When configuring two routers to use Frame Relay and one of the routers is a Cisco router but the other one is not, what type of Frame Relay encapsulation should you use?
   a. Cisco
   b. IETF
   c. ANSI
   d. q933a

10. What command is used to set the encapsulation type to the PPP on an interface?
   a. *Encapsulate PPP*
   b. *PPP encapsulate*
   c. *Encapsulation ppp*
   d. *PPP encapsulation*
   e. *Enable ppp*
   f. *Protocol ppp*

11. What are the possible Frame Relay encapsulation types?
   a. Cisco
   b. ANSI
   c. IETF
   d. q933a
   e. I series

12. What command do you use to configure Frame Relay on an interface?
   a. *Protocol encap frame-relay*
   b. *Frame encapsulation*
   c. *Encapsulation frame-relay*
   d. *Enable frame-relay*

13. To view the DLCI-to-network address map, what command should be used?
   a. *Show frame-relay pvc*
   b. *Show frame-relay map*
   c. *Show frame-relay dlci map*
   d. *Show frame-relay lmi*

14. Which command would you use to configure a subinterface on a Frame Relay configured router? (Choose all that apply.)
   a. *Interface s0.1 multipoint*
   b. *Interface s.0.1 point-to-point*
   c. *Interface s.0.1 multipoint*
   d. *Interface s0.1 point to point*
   e. *Interface s0.1 multi-point*
   f. *Interface s0.1 point-to-point*

15. Which WAN encapsulation protocols support multiple network layer protocols? (Choose all that apply.)
    a. PPP
    b. HDLC
    c. IP
    d. IPX

16. What is DDR best suited for? (Choose all that apply.)
    a. Permanent connections
    b. Connections that require enough bandwidth to handle a high volume of data
    c. Connections that consistently broadcast data
    d. Connections that require the periodic transfer of data
    e. Connections that transfer low rates of data

17. Which encapsulation methods work best over a synchronous serial line such as a leased line? (Choose all that apply.)
    a. PPP
    b. Frame Relay
    c. ATM
    d. X.25
    e. HDLC

18. Which command can be used to check the encapsulation method used on an interface?
    a. *Show encapsulation*
    b. *Debug encapsulation*
    c. *Encapsulation method*
    d. *Show interface*

19. What command can you use to verify PPP authentication method?
    a. *Debug ppp authentication*
    b. *Verify ppp authentication*
    c. *Show ppp authentication*
    d. *PPP authentication verification*
    e. *Debug authentication*

20. What is the purpose of the D channel in an ISDN configuration? (Choose all that apply.)
    a. Call setup
    b. High-speed data transfer
    c. Call termination
    d. Signaling
    e. All of the above

CHAPTER 8

Layer 2 Switching in a Local Area Network

OBJECTIVES

The following topics are discussed in Chapter 8:

- Design a simple LAN using Cisco technology.
- Configure a switch with VLANS and interswitch communication.
- Implement a LAN.
- Customize a switch configuration to meet specified network requirements.
- Perform an initial configuration on a switch.
- Perform LAN and VLAN troubleshooting.
- Troubleshoot a device as part of a working network.
- Describe the Spanning Tree process.

INTRODUCTION

This chapter examines networking in a LAN beginning with a description of Ethernet standards, which are some of the most popular LAN standards in the industry today. We will discuss hardware components such as bridges and switches that are used to segment a LAN to achieve better throughput on the network, as well as virtual LANs (VLAN) and how to configure them on Cisco switches. There are many types of Cisco switches. This text focuses working on the 1900 series switch and the 2900 series switch.

8.1 DESIGNING AN ETHERNET LAN

Ethernet is a layer 2 protocol that organizes data into frames before sending them onto the wire in a network. This protocol was developed by Digital, Intel, and Xerox in the 1970s and later standardized by the IEEE in the 802 project as 802.3. Both Ethernet and 802.3 define the physical as well as the data-link layer standards to follow when using them in a network.

ETHERNET STANDARDS

This section defines Ethernet standards at the physical and data-link layers. A brief discussion about how Ethernet can operate in half-duplex or full-duplex mode will follow the Ethernet standards.

Physical Layer

Signaling methods are defined at the physical layer. Ethernet uses a *baseband* signaling method when sending data on the network. Baseband is a digital transmission that consumes the entire bandwidth of the line that it is placed on. The physical layer standards are as follows:

- **10BaseT.** Sends data at a rate of 10 Mbps using a baseband transmission over category 3 unshielded twisted-pair (UTP) wire. Each cable segment can be no more than 100 meters. Each connection is point to point, connecting to a central location such as a hub or a switch. The physical topology is a star. An RJ-45 connector is used to connect a node to the wire.

- **10Base2.** Sends data at a rate of 10 Mbps using a baseband transmission. Each cable segment can be 185 meters with a total of 30 nodes on the segment. It also is known as thinnet or thin Ethernet because it uses a thin coaxial cable (RG58u). 10Base2 requires 50 ohms of resistance on each end of the wire. The physical topology is a bus. A British Naval Connector (BNC) is used to connect a node to the wire.

- **10Base5.** Sends data at a rate of 10 Mbps using a baseband transmission. Each cable segment can be 500 meters with a total of 100 nodes on the segment. It also is known as thicknet or thick Ethernet because it uses a thicker coaxial cable (RG8 or RG11) than does 10Base2. When used, 10Base2 is implemented as a network backbone. The physical topology is a bus. To connect a node to the wire, an auxiliary unit interface (AUI) is used from the node to a transceiver connected directly to the wire.

The two additional types of Ethernet are Fast Ethernet and Gigabit Ethernet. Fast Ethernet's (802.3u) three standards are as follows:

- **100BaseTX.** Sends data at a rate of 100 Mbps using a baseband transmission over category 5 UTP wire. Each cable segment can be no more than 100 meters. Each connection is point to point, connecting to a central location such as a hub or a switch. The physical topology is a star. An RJ-45 connector is used to connect a node to the wire.

- **100BaseFX.** Sends data at a rate of 100 Mbps using a baseband transmission over fiber-optic wire. Cable segments can be up to 400 meters. The physical topology is point to point. A duplex media interface connector ST (MIC) is used to connect a node to the wire.

Finally, Gigabit Ethernet can transmit data at 1000 Mbps using UTP or fiber-optic wire. The fiber-optic wire can carry the data longer than the UTP, which has a limitation of 100 meters. Gigabit Ethernet is normally implemented as a network backbone but is now carrying data to the desktop of users.

Data-Link Layer

The data-link layer defines the method by which the nodes access the wire, referred to as the media access method. Three media access methods are used to allow nodes on a network to transmit data onto the wire: *polling, token passing,* and *contention.* Ethernet is based on a logical bus technology and uses the contention method. Because only one signal can be on the wire at a time and stations have to contend for the wire, many data collisions occur. When data collisions occur, neither signal is sent successfully. The Carrier Sense Multiple Access with Collision Detection (CSMA/CD) access method was created to address this problem. CSMA/CD is used by Ethernet to assist in data transmission. It allows a node to sense the carrier (wire) to determine whether a signal is already on the wire. If the wire is occupied by another signal, the node continuously senses the wire until the wire is free. The node transmits its signal after the wire is free.

Half-Duplex Mode vs. Full-Duplex Mode

Ethernet can transmit data in half-duplex mode or full-duplex mode. Remember that half duplex means only one station can transmit at a time, and full duplex means both stations can transmit at the same time. Ethernet NICs normally have an autodetect feature that allows the board to determine whether it is in half- or full-duplex mode. If either station is in half-duplex mode, both stations must communicate in this mode. Communicate can occur in full-duplex mode when two nodes have a direct connection between them (which occurs when nodes are directly connected to a layer 2 switch). Nodes connected to a hub rather than a switch use half duplex because a hub does not create a direct connection between nodes. The network in half-duplex mode is only using 30 to 40 percent of the bandwidth due to collisions. If a full-duplex connection is negotiated between two end nodes, 100 percent of the bandwidth (in each direction) is used. The collision detection circuit of CSMA/CD in full-duplex mode is disabled and two separate circuits of cable are used to send and receive data.

8.2 SWITCHING TECHNOLOGIES

Several types of switches are used in networks today. Switches operate at layer 2 or layer 3 of the OSI model. Layer 2 switches work at the data-link layer of the OSI model, whereas layer 3 switches operate at the network layer and perform functions that are closely related to routers. For the CCNA Exam and the rest of this textbook, the term *switch* refers to layer 2 switching.

A layer 2 switch is a network device that allows data to be filtered and forwarded between two segments of wire based on the MAC address. The benefits of segmenting a LAN with switches include increasing the number of collision domains and decreasing the size of collision domains in the network. Remember, a collision domain is a segment of wire where multiple machines compete for the wire and many data collisions occur. Reducing the size of collision domains and increasing the number of collision domains increase the network bandwidth.

Test Tip: Switches and bridges perform the same role in a network. Be aware that they both create multiple collision domains, reduce the size of collision domains, and segment an existing network.

THREE PURPOSES OF A SWITCH

A switch has three purposes in a network: it learns the MAC addresses of all nodes connected to it dynamically, makes decisions about where to forward incoming data, and avoids switching loops through the use of the Spanning-Tree Protocol (STP).

Learning MAC Addresses

Layer 2 switches know which stations are connected to them by the using the MAC address. When switches are initially placed in a network, their MAC table is empty. They must learn the MAC address of each node connected to each of their ports (interface). Switches can have many ports and build a MAC address database, also known as a MAC table, as they learn the MAC addresses of the nodes attached to them.

Switches listen for frames on all ports to build their MAC table. When a switch receives a frame on a specific port, it opens the frame and reads the source field of the frame, which includes the MAC address of the source (sending) node. After the switch learns the source address, it links the source address with the port that the frame was received on by adding the entry to its MAC table.

Forwarding and Filtering Decisions

After the table is built, the switch can make intelligent decisions about which port to send each frame that enters the switch. Before forwarding frames, the switch examines the destination field of the frame and compares the destination field MAC

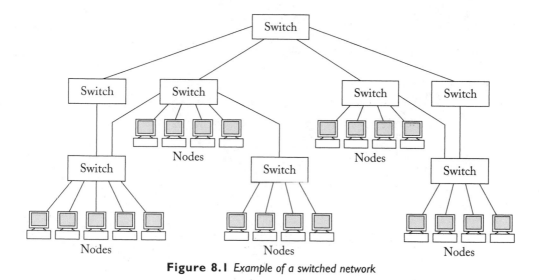

Figure 8.1 *Example of a switched network*

address with its MAC table. If an entry is found in the MAC table, the frame is sent to that port and subsequently to the node. If an entry is not found, the packet is *flooded* to every port in the switch, except the port it was received on. Flooding is the process of sending a frame out to every port on a switch. Flooding occurs when

- A broadcast or multicast message is received and is destined for all nodes.
- The switch does not know the destination address of a frame.
- The MAC table is full and the destination address of a frame is not listed in the table.

Avoiding Loops

When designing a switched network, it is usually beneficial to create redundant paths to critical parts of the network. Each node will only have a point-to-point connection with one switch, yet a switched network normally has many switches that help make up the backbone. Figure 8.1 shows a switched network with redundant switches.

Having redundant paths through more than one switch allows the network to continue to operate after the failure of one switch or a single cable. The following are two concerns to be aware of when designing a bridged network with redundant paths:

- **Broadcast storms.** Broadcast storms occur when switches forward frames continuously between redundant paths, causing network congestion. Figure 8.2 shows how two broadcast storms could occur in one large, switched network.

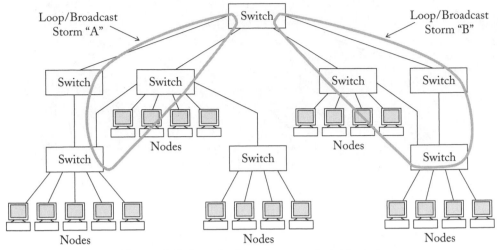

Figure 8.2 *Example of broadcast storm/switching loop*

- **Multiple copies of a frame.** When multiple copies of the same frame arrive at different ports of the same switch, unexplained results could occur because it would cause MAC table instability.

To avoid these problems, Digital Equipment Corporation designed the *Spanning-Tree Protocol,* which was later standardized by the IEEE as 802.1d. The protocol is enabled by default on Cisco switches.

Spanning-Tree Protocol (STP)

STP was created initially to avoid the looping problems associated with bridged networks. However, the technology between bridges and switches is so similar that STP works with switched networks as well. In the context of this section, the terms *switch* and *bridge* are used interchangeably because STP works in the same fashion with both devices. Some of the terms to be aware of when discussing STP are

- **Root Bridge.** One bridge in a network that is designated by the other bridges in a network. The root bridge is selected by sending bridge protocol data units (BPDU) between each switch. These packets are forwarded continuously and elect the root bridge based on the priority number of a bridge. This is a configurable value and the default is 32768. If two switches are both using the default value, then the switch with the lower MAC address is selected as the root bridge. All ports on the root bridge are designated ports.

- **Designated Port.** One port per cable segment that is allowed to send data onto the segment.

- **Nonroot Bridge.** Bridges in the network that are not elected as the root bridge.

- **Root Port.** A port on a nonroot bridge that has the lowest cost path from the nonroot bridge to the root bridge. There is only one root port per non-root bridge and the lowest cost path is based on bandwidth; for example, a 10 Gbps link has a cost of 2 (1 in the older version of STP), a 1 Gbps link has a cost of 4 (1 in the older version of STP), a 100 Mbps link has a cost of 19 (10 in the older version of STP), and a 10 Mbps link has a cost of 100 (100 in the older version of STP). Catalyst 1900 switches use the older version of STP to calculate costs.

- **Nondesignated Port.** A port on a nonroot bridge that does not forward data. This port is in a blocking state and breaks up the loop. Multiple nondesig-nated ports can be on a LAN segment because there is only one designated port per segment.

 Test Tip: 1 root bridge per network; 1 designated port per cable segment; 1 root port per nonroot bridge.

View Figure 8.3 to see how the switches can avoid the loops seen in Figure 8.2 after given their respective roles of root bridge, designated ports, nonroot bridge, root port, and nondesignated port.

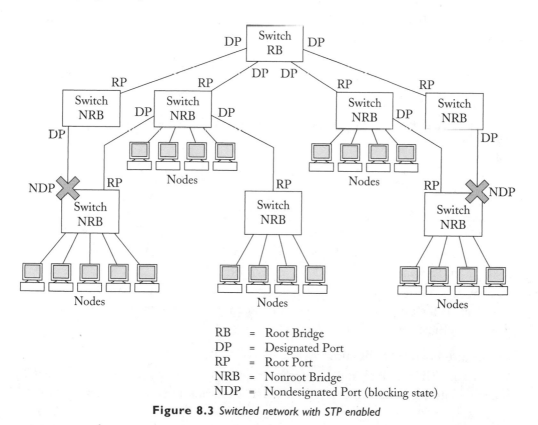

RB	=	Root Bridge
DP	=	Designated Port
RP	=	Root Port
NRB	=	Nonroot Bridge
NDP	=	Nondesignated Port (blocking state)

Figure 8.3 *Switched network with STP enabled*

A bridge port can be in four possible states while using STP: *blocking, listening, learning,* and *forwarding.* In normal bridge (switch) operations, the ports are in either the forwarding or blocking states. During convergence, however (which is the process of all ports trying to achieve either the forwarding or blocking states), ports make the transition between the listening and learning states. Following are the definitions of each state:

- **Blocking state.** The blocking state is the first state a port is in when it is turned on. While in a blocking state, the port will not forward any data but will receive BPDUs.

- **Listening state.** The listening state is a transitional state the port goes into on its way to the forwarding state. During the listening state, it is actually listening for BPDUs to determine whether are any loops are occurring. If there are no loops, the port transits to the next state.

- **Learning state.** The learning state is the state in which a port learns MAC addresses and builds its MAC table.

- **Forwarding state.** The port when it enters the forwarding state.

The network is fully converged after each port on all switches in the network is in the forwarding or blocking state. Any topology changes force the ports back into the listening and learning states. It takes less than a minute (50 seconds) for a port to go from the blocking state to the forwarding state. The time it takes to go from the listening state to the learning state, or from the learning state to the forwarding state, is considered the forward delay.

 Test Tip: Blocking → Listening → Learning → Forwarding.

SWITCHING METHODS

You need to know three switching methods for the CCNA Exam: *store-and-forward switching, cut-through switching,* and *fragment-free switching.* Each method uses a different process for forwarding frames. When comparing switching methods, the *latency* and *error rate* of the method can be compared. Latency refers to the time it takes to forward a frame; the lower the latency, the more efficient the switching method. Error rate is the number of bad frames forwarded by a switch; the lower the error rate, the more efficient the switch.

Store-and-Forward Switching

When a switch is in store-and-forward mode, the entire frame received by the switch is copied into the switch's memory. The switch performs an error check on the frame's

Cyclic Redundancy Check (CRC) to determine whether there are any errors in the frame. The frame is forwarded out of the destination port if there are no errors. This type of switching has a low error rate but the latency varies based on frame size.

Test Tip: Keywords that identify store-and-forward switching are *variable latency, error check,* and *entire frame.*

Cut-Through Switching

A cut-through switch does not copy the entire frame into memory. Therefore, it operates at wire speed. It copies the destination MAC address of the frame (the first 6 bytes) and immediately forwards it to its destination. It does not perform the CRC check for errors. The switch is primarily concerned with the destination address of the frame. After it is read into memory, the switch looks in the MAC table and immediately forwards the frame to the outgoing port. Cut-through switching has a reduced latency period but a higher error rate than store-and-forward switching. If the error rate becomes too high, the switch can be forced into store-and-forward mode.

Test Tip: Keywords that identify cut-through switching are *low latency, forwards frame immediately,* and *operates at wire speed.*

Fragment-Free Switching

Because most data collisions occur in the first 64 bytes of a frame, fragment-free switching reads the first 64 bytes of a frame and forwards it to the destination if there are no errors. Fragment-free switching is a modified version of cut-through switching with better error checking and virtually no increase in latency. It is the default for catalyst 1900 switches.

Test Tip: Keyword that identifies fragment-free switching is *first 64 bytes.*

8.3   SWITCH CONFIGURATION

This section describes how to set a basic configuration on a 1900 and a 2900 series switch. Although there are three methods to configure a switch, the CCNA Exam is primarily concerned with the administrator's ability to work with the CLI. Therefore, this is the primary method shown in this book.

CONFIGURATION METHODS

The three configuration methods available to configure a switch are: the command line interface (CLI), the menu-driven screens, and the Web-enabled interface. To configure the switch through the Web-enabled interface, enter the IP address of the switch in a Web browser and the screen to configure the switch that should appear. By default, the switch does not have a valid IP address, so this will not work until the switch has been configured with an IP address. To configure the switch with an IP address, use one of the other two options available. The CCNA Exam focuses on using the CLI to configure switches.

General Configuration (1900 Series)

For the initial configuration of the switch, connect a console cable to the RJ-45 port on the back of the switch and use a terminal emulation program such as Hyper Terminal in Windows to view the screens. After the switch is powered on and it runs through its POST, a screen that looks similar to the one shown here will appear:

```
         User Interface Menu
   [M] Menus
   [K] Command Line
   [I] IP Configuration
 Enter Selection:
```

Notice the three options. If you press M, the switch enters the menu-driven mode. If K, the switch enters the IOS CLI mode. The I option is available only until the IP configuration of the switch is configured. The switch should be given an IP address for management purposes. By default, the switch's IP address is 0.0.0.0.

There are several different modes to be aware of, but for the most part, they are similar to a router's modes. For example, the > symbol at the command prompt represents user EXEC mode. The # symbol represents privileged EXEC mode. The word *(config)#* represents the global configuration mode and *(config-if)#* represents the interface configuration mode. The CLI does not have a default name for the switch. The switch command prompt is represented as the symbols just mentioned until a host name is configured. The command sequence to change the switch host name is as follows:

```
>enable
#configure terminal
(config)#hostname Switch01
Switch01(config)#
```

Changes that are made to the switch's running configuration file are automatically saved to the NVRAM. The switch can have its NVRAM configuration copied to a

TFTP server. The command is:

```
Switch01#copy nvram
      tftp://10.1.1.20/switch01.cfg
```

To copy the file back to the switch, use this command:

```
Switch01#copy tftp://10.1.1.20/switch01.cfg
      nvram
```

If using this method to save the startup configuration file, the IP address in the command is the IP address of the TFTP server and the file name should be the name of the file the configuration will be saved as. To reset to the factory settings, use the *delete nvram* privileged EXEC command.

IP Configuration

Use the *show ip* command to view the IP configuration information set on the switch, including the IP address, subnet mask, default gateway, the VLAN and management domain the switch belongs to, and the DNS server address. To set the switch's IP address, use the following command:

```
Switch01(config)#ip address 192.168.1.10
      255.255.255.0
```

You can use Telnet or the switch's Web-enabled interface Visual Switch Manager (VSM) to configure the switch after the IP address of the switch is set. To reset the IP address to 0.0.0.0, use the *no ip address* global configuration command. You can also set a default gateway address for the switch. The default gateway address should be the address of the router in the internetwork. The command is as follows:

```
Switch01(config)#ip default-gateway
      192.168.1.1
```

Configuring Duplex Modes

To configure the duplex modes of a switch, first enter the interface configuration mode of the interface to be configured and then use the *duplex* command to set the mode. The Catalyst 1912 switch has 12 10BaseT ports identified as e0/1-e0/12 and 2 100BaseTX ports (port A = f0/26 and port B = f0/27). The 100BaseTX ports are uplinks and use crossover cables to connect to other devices. The Catalyst 1924 switch has 24 10BaseT ports (e0/1-e0/24) and 2 100BaseTX uplink ports (port A = f0/26 and port B = f0/27). Each switch also has an AUI port identified as e0/25. To set the duplex mode on any of these ports, use the *duplex* interface configuration command with one of the following parameters:

- **auto.** Sets the interface for autonegotiation.
- **full.** Sets full-duplex mode (default for 100BaseTX).
- **full-flow-control.** Sets full-duplex mode with flow control.
- **half.** Sets half-duplex mode (default for 10BaseT).

The command looks like this:

```
Switch01(config-if)#duplex full
```

Managing MAC Tables

The switch can learn MAC addresses dynamically, permanently, or statically. The administrator configures the latter two MAC entries. By default, entries in the MAC table are dynamically learned by the switch. The MAC table can maintain up to 1,024 addresses. Addresses that are not in use are dropped from the MAC table to make room for addresses that are being used. To assign specific addresses to ports to avoid having them dropped, use the *mac-address-table permanent* global configuration mode command. This is useful if it is imperative that some node's addresses always have entries in the MAC table; for example, set permanent entries for network servers that are often used by all nodes in the network. The next command allows for all frames destined for the MAC address 3333.0000.2222 to be forwarded out of Ethernet port e0/5:

```
Switch01(config)#mac-address-table permanent
      3333.0000.2222 e0/5
```

To delete the permanent addresses, use the *no* parameter before the command. To further restrict access to a port, use the *mac-address-table restricted static* global configuration command. This example allows specific port-to-port communication. For example, the next command allows all stations connected to Ethernet port e0/2 to send data to the restricted node with the MAC address of 5555.5555.5555 on port e0/1:

```
Switch01(config)#mac-address-table restricted
      static 5555.5555.5555 e0/1 e0/2
```

To remove the entry, use the *no* parameter before the entry. To view the MAC table, use the *show mac-address-table* command.

Port Security

Port security can be configured on an individual interface to limit the number of stations that can be connected to a switch port. By default, a switch port can handle up to 132 entries. Using the *port secure* interface configuration command can reduce that number and provide a measure to stop users from connecting unauthorized hubs with additional nodes to the network. The command is as follows:

```
Switch01(config-if)port secure max-mac-count
   [1-132]
```

General Configuration (2900 Series)

The Catalyst 2900 series switch is configured in the same manner as the 1900 series. The switch can be configured through the CLI or by using Cisco's VSM. To use the VSM, you need an IP address on the switch and a web browser to connect to it. The CCNA Exam concentrates using the CLI for configuration, so we will discuss the CLI commands here. When a 2900 series switch is booted, it goes through a POST process similar to all Cisco devices. After the POST process is complete, the switch prompts for autoconfiguration of an IP address, subnet mask, default gateway, and enable mode secret password. The switch is also automatically made a member of VLAN 1. All these settings can be changed through the CLI if required.

Many of the configuration commands for the 2900 series switch are considerably different than the 1900 series switch commands; however, some are similar. For example, setting a privileged mode password is the same:

```
2900_Switch(config)#enable secret password delmar
```

The preceding command sets the enable mode secret password to *delmar.*

IP Configuration

Configuring the IP address of a 2900 series switch is certainly different than configuring a 1900 series switch. For example, to set the IP address on a 1900 series switch, the command is simply *IP address 10.1.1.1 255.0.0.0* from the global configuration mode. When configuring a 2900 series switch, the command is a bit different:

```
2900_Switch#config t
2900_Switch(config)#interface vlan 1
2900_Switch(config-if)#ip address 10.1.1.1
   255.0.0.0
```

Notice in the preceding command sequence that the switch had to be in the VLAN 1 interface mode, which is the default interface for the switch. Every switch should have an IP address, to make it easy to configure all switches in the internetwork from one location. A requirement to remotely manage all switches is to have Telnet configured on all switches. To configure Telnet on a switch, use the following commands:

```
2900_Switch(config)#line vty 0 4
2900_Switch(config-line)#password Thomson
2900_Switch(config-line)#end
```

From any location in the network, it is now possible to manage this switch.

Port Configuration

Additional port configuration commands on a 2900 series switch allow you to manipulate speed and duplex modes, block flooded unicasts and multicasts, control broadcasts, secure ports, and add ports to specific VLANs. To change the speed and duplex mode of a switch port, use the following commands (be sure to choose one of the mandatory options in brackets):

```
2900_Switch(config)#int fa0/1
2900_Switch(config-if)#speed [10 | 100 | auto]
2900_Switch(config-if)#duplex [full | half | auto]
```

To prevent the unnecessary flooding of unicast and multicast packets from the interface configuration mode, use these commands:

```
2900_Switch(config-if)#port block unicast
2900_Switch(config-if)#port block mulicast
```

To prevent a port from forwarding broadcast storm packets, it is important to first generate a baseline of how many packets are sent from the port. This is because the *port storm-control threshold* command forces the port to stop forwarding packets when the threshold is reached. If there is no baseline to go by, inaccurate thresholds could cause major problems in the network. The command is

```
2900_Switch(config-if)#port storm-control
    threshold rising [0 - 4294967295]
falling [0 - 4294967295]
```

In the preceding command, the *rising* parameter determines when to shut down the port and the *falling* parameter dictates when the port will begin forwarding packets again.

Securing the ports is a two-part process. The first part is to allow the MAC table to be built, which can be done dynamically or statically. After the MAC table is built, secure the port and specify the action that is taken by the port if the security is breached. To add a secure address, use the global configuration *mac-address-table secure* command as seen here:

```
2900_Switch(config)#mac-address-table secure
    mac address port vlan vlan ID
```

After the addresses are either statically entered or dynamically learned, configure the port security from the interface configuration mode. Be sure to identify the number of addresses the port can learn as well as what action the port will take if the security is violated.

```
2900_Switch(config-if)port security max-mac-
    count [1-132]
2900_Switch(config-if)port security action
    [shutdown | trap]
```

After a switched network is up and running, you might need to have one port of one switch become a member of a separate VLAN from all other ports in the switch. To do this from the interface configuration mode, use the *switchport access* command. To make a port a member of VLAN 10 if the switch it is on is a member of VLAN 1, use the following command:

```
2900_Switch(config-if)#switchport mode access
2900_Switch(config-if)#switchport access vlan 10
```

You can also make a port a member of multiple VLANs with the *switchport multi interface* configuration mode command.

8.4 VIRTUAL LAN (VLAN)

A VLAN is a means of logically grouping together nodes that are (or are not) physically located near one another. Each VLAN is configured as its own broadcast domain with support for a separate Spanning Tree. VLANs can be implemented on a single switch or multiple switches connected together. Each port can only belong to one VLAN, unless the port is configured as a *trunk*. A trunk is a way of extending VLANs between switches using the switch's uplink to connect it to another switch. VLANs can be either statically or dynamically assigned. However, if dynamic assignment is used, the Catalyst 1900 switch must be configured to receive dynamic

VLAN membership information from a VLAN membership policy server (VMPS), which is not covered in this textbook nor on the CCNA Exam. VLAN terminology and VLAN configuration are explained in this section.

VLAN TERMINOLOGY

You should become familiar with several terms to understand VLANs. The two terms that are explained here are Inter-Switch Link (ISL) and VLAN Trunking Protocol (VTP).

Inter-Switch Link

ISL is a layer 2 protocol proprietary to Cisco. The protocol carries data between two Cisco devices such as switches, routers, and ISL-capable network adapter boards. ISL tags all frames that travel through ISL-enabled components. This process is called *frame tagging* and ISL encapsulates the layer 2 header by adding the VLAN ID to the frame. It also recalculates the CRC of a frame. ISL is normally configured on the ports of a switch that trunks (connects) two switches together. For example, the Fast Ethernet ports on the Catalyst 1900 are the uplinks of a switch and would be configured with ISL when trunking VLANs between switches. An additional trunking protocol is available: the *IEEE 802.1Q* frame tagging protocol. If you are trunking a Cisco switch with a non-Cisco switch, 802.1Q must be used.

VLAN Trunking Protocol

VTP is a management protocol used to simplify the management of VLANs. Switches that can be managed with VTP must be members of the same *management domain*. A management domain is established by identifying a group of switches that will share the same configuration. By default, the switch is configured in a no-management-domain state. A switch can be configured as one of three possible VTP configuration modes: *VTP server, VTP client,* or *transparent*.

- **VTP server mode.** A switch configured as a VTP server can create, delete, and modify VLANs as well as management domain configuration information. When changes are made to the domain, they are all forwarded out of the ISL trunk connections of the switch and saved to NVRAM of the VTP server. The switch also synchronizes its VLAN configuration with information learned from other switches.

- **VTP client mode.** A switch configured as a VTP client cannot make changes to the domain and does not save any changes in NVRAM. The switch also synchronizes its VLAN configuration with information learned from other switches.

- **VTP transparent mode.** A switch configured with the VTP transparent mode can create, delete, and modify VLANs. However, the changes are not forwarded to other switches; they only pertain to the local switch and are saved in NVRAM. The switch will not synchronize its VLAN configuration with information learned from other switches. It will forward the information learned through advertisements from other switches.

VTP PRUNING

To avoid the unnecessary flooding of data in a VTP management domain, *VTP pruning* is implemented. VTP pruning consists of using VTP advertisements to determine whether frames are being sent to switches that are not configured for specific VLANs. VTP pruning is disabled by default. View Figure 8.4 to see a pruned VLAN.

VLAN CONFIGURATION

To configure VLANs, it is important to understand what the default VLAN settings of a switch are and how to change them. The default switch settings are explained in this section. How to set up a management domain and add switches to the management domain are covered as well as how to configure VLANs inside a management domain, how to trunk switches, and how to configure ports as members of VLANs.

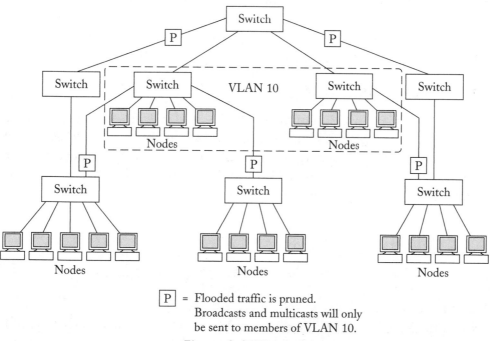

P = Flooded traffic is pruned.
Broadcasts and multicasts will only
be sent to members of VLAN 10.

Figure 8.4 *VTP pruning*

Default Settings

The default VLAN settings for a switch include

> Domain Name = None
>
> VTP mode = Server
>
> VTP Password = None
>
> VTP pruning = Disabled
>
> VTP Trap = Enabled

To create a VTP management domain, use the *vtp* global configuration command. The *vtp* command allows all the settings listed to be changed with one command. See the following command:

```
Switch01(config)#vtp server domain VTP1 trap
    enable password Securepassword pruning
    enable
```

In this command, the switch is put into *server* mode; other options include *client* or *transparent*. The domain name is VTP1 (case sensitive), pruning is enabled, and the password *Securepassword* is set. All passwords on all the switches in the same management domain must be the same. The *trap* parameter allows for an SNMP message to be sent each time a VTP message is sent (every 5 seconds). Once configured, the *show vtp* command provides all that information, including the IP address, the number of VLANs, the version, and the max number of VLANs, which is 1005.

ADDING VLANs (1900 SERIES)

The switch must be in VTP transparent or VTP server mode to add, change, or delete VLANs. The *vlan* global configuration command is used to create a VLAN. Each VLAN must be uniquely identified with at least a number. VLAN configuration is different between a 1900 switch and a 2900 switch. The command listed here show how a 1900 series switch is configured:

```
Switch01(config)#vlan vlan10
```

To give a VLAN a name, use this command:

```
Switch01(config)#vlan vlan10 name ccnaproject
```

Trunking

Because the VLAN created may cross multiple switches, it is important to be able to trunk the switches together. The *trunk* interface configuration command is used to configure trunking. When configuring a trunk, ISL is being enabled on the switch interface. The Catalyst 1900 supports Dynamic ISL, which allows for ISL trunk negotiation between local and remote switches. To trunk the Catalyst 1900 series switch, use the Fast Ethernet ports. These ports are the uplinks for the switch and a crossover cable is necessary to connect them to one another. First, enter the interface that will be trunked:

```
Switch01(config)#interface f0/26
```

Then use the *trunk* command with one of the following five options:

- **on.** Sets ISL trunk mode and negotiates the remote port into trunk mode.
- **off.** Disables port trunk mode and negotiates the remote port into nontrunk mode.
- **desirable.** Forces the local port to negotiate with the remote port. If the remote port is in the on, desirable, or auto state, trunk mode will be configured.
- **auto.** Forces the local port to negotiate with the remote port. If the remote port is in the on or desirable state, trunk mode will be configured.
- **nonnegotiate.** Permanent trunk mode with no negotiation.

See the following example:

```
Switch01(config-if)#trunk on
```

Use the *show trunk* command with the *A* or *B* parameter to verify the configuration. The A or B refers to the port used. Port A refers to f0/26 and port B refers to f0/27.

Port Assignment

Now that there is a VLAN created and trunking has been configured, it is time to add ports to the VLAN. To statically configure a port to be a member of a VLAN, use the *vlan-membership* interface configuration command. Each port can only be a member of one VLAN. Use the following command:

```
Switch01(config)#interface e0/2
Switch01(config-if)#vlan-membership static 10
```

Use the *show vlan-membership* privileged EXEC command to see VLAN membership for all ports on the switch.

ADDING VLANs (2900 SERIES)

The commands to configure VLANs on a Catalyst 2900 series switch are different than those of the 1900 series switch. For example, configuring VLANs on the 1900 series switch is done from the global configuration mode. Adding VLANs to a 2900 series router is done from the VLAN database mode. The number chosen for the VLAN must be between 1 and 1001. For an example see the following:

```
2900_Switch#vlan database
2900_Switch(vlan)#
```

Once in the VLAN database mode, add the VLAN and name it if required:

```
2900_Switch(vlan)vlan 150 name Marketing
```

To remove the VLAN, use the *no* parameter before the preceding command. To add ports to the VLAN, use the *switchport mode access* and the *switchport access vlan 150* interface configuration mode commands.

Trunking

The trunking commands on a 2900 series switch are slightly different from those of a 1900 series switch. However, the premise is the same. To enable trunking on a 2900 series switch, first determine the type of trunk that will be enabled. The two options are ISL, which is Cisco's proprietary trunking protocol, or 802.1q, which is the IEEE standardized trunking protocol. If all the devices in the network are Cisco devices, ISL will work fine. If any devices are non-Cisco devices, use the 802.1q encapsulation protocol. The command sequence to turn trunking on is shown here:

```
2900_Switch(config)#int fa0/1
2900_Switch(config-if)#switchport mode trunk
2900_Switch(config-if)#switchport trunk
    encapsulation [isl | dot1q]
```

A trunk sends data from all VLANs listed in the switch's VLAN database. You can disallow VLAN traffic over certain trunks. The following commands allow VLAN traffic from VLAN 150 but not VLAN 1:

```
2900_Switch(config-if)#switchport trunk
    allowed vlan add 150
2900_Switch(config-if)#switchport trunk
    allowed remove vlan 1
```

To disable the trunk, use the *no switchport mode* command from the interface configuration mode.

Finally, if a switch is configured with multiple VLANs, the VLANs act as separate broadcast domains. Therefore, if two PCs are plugged in to the same switch but are members of different VLANs, they will not be able to communicate with one another without the use of a router. To route between those two VLANs, configure an ISL-capable Cisco router's Ethernet interface with two subinterfaces and set up a trunk port to connect the switch to the router. This allows the router to route for the two VLANs and is considered a *router on a stick*.

CHAPTER SUMMARY

In this chapter, you learned about switching technologies and how to configure Catalyst 1900 and 2900 series Cisco switches. Virtual LANs were also covered in this chapter. Following this summary is the final knowledge test to help you prepare for the CCNA Exam. Go through every knowledge test several times until you are extremely comfortable with the answers before taking the CCNA Exam. GOOD LUCK!

KNOWLEDGE TEST

Choose one answer for all questions unless directed to do otherwise.

1. Which type of switching method is being used if the switch reads the first 64 bytes of a frame before forwarding it?
   a. Fragment-free
   b. Store-and-forward
   c. Sort-and-forward
   d. Cut-through

2. In what situation will a switch flood the network with a frame that it received? (Choose all that apply.)
   a. When in an idle state for 30 seconds or longer
   b. When the destination address of the frame is not in the MAC table
   c. When a broadcast frame is received by the switch
   d. During normal operations
   e. When the MAC table is full

3. Which of the following statements are true about switching methods? (Choose all that apply.)
   a. The cut-through switching method's latency is based on the size of the frame entering the switch.
   b. The fragment-free switching method has zero latency.
   c. The cut-through switching method works at the speed of the wire with little or no latency through the switch.
   d. The store-and-forward switching method's latency is based on the size of the frame.

4. Frame tagging consists of which of the following statements? (Choose all that apply.)
   a. Encapsulating a frame and adding a network ID to the header
   b. Encapsulating a frame and adding a VLAN ID to the header
   c. Placing a checkpoint in a frame sent from a node already in the MAC table
   d. Replacing the CRC of a frame

5. What are the three purposes of a switch?
   a. Split horizon
   b. Avoiding loops
   c. Network identification
   d. Address learning
   e. Filtering and forwarding frames
   f. Routing packets between networks

6. What are the four STP port states?
   a. Learning
   b. Listener
   c. Blocked
   d. Forwarding
   e. Listening
   f. Forwarder
   g. Blocking

7. What benefits would your network have by replacing all 10 Mbps hubs with 10 Mbps Catalyst switches? (Choose all that apply.)
   a. Increase the number of broadcast domains.
   b. Decrease the number of broadcast domains.
   c. Increase the number of collision domains.
   d. Decrease the number of collisions domains.
   e. Increase the bandwidth between stations that are directly connected to the switch.
   f. Allow for full-duplex operations between nodes directly connected to the switch.

8. What is the default IP address of a switch?
   a. 0.0.0.0
   b. 192.168.1.1
   c. 10.0.0.1
   d. 255.255.255.255

9. Which command sequence would allow you to configure a 2900 series switch with VLAN 20 named Sales?
   a. *2900#config t*
      2900(config)#vlan 20 name sales
   b. *2900#config t*
      2900(config)#vlan name sales eq 20

   c. *2900#vlan database 1*
     2900(vlan)#vlan 20 name sales
   d. *2900#vlan database*
     2900(vlan)#vlan 20 name sales

10. Which switching method only reads the address portion of a frame when it enters the switch before forwarding it?
   a. Cut-through
   b. Fragment-free
   c. Store-and-forward
   d. Sort-and-forward

11. By default, implementing a switched network increases the number of collision domains. Which switching technology allows for a decrease in the size of broadcast domains?
   a. STP
   b. Filtering and forwarding
   c. VLANs
   d. VTP pruning

12. What command is used to set a port on a switch to full-duplex mode?
   a. Mode full-duplex
   b. Duplex full
   c. Switch full
   d. Port full

13. Which statements are true about half-duplex Ethernet? (Choose all that apply.)
   a. CSMA/CD is turned on in half-duplex mode.
   b. CSMA/CD is turned off in half-duplex mode.
   c. On a 10 Mbps link, communicating nodes have 10 Mbps of bandwidth available to them.
   d. Half-duplex transmission is mandatory if nodes are directly connected to a hub that is connected to a switch.
   e. Half-duplex transmission is mandatory if nodes are directly connected to a switch.
   f. Because separate circuits are used by communicating end nodes in half duplex, collisions will not occur.

14. Which statement is true about store-and-forward switching? (Choose all that apply.)
   a. Only the header of a frame is read before the switch forwards the frame.
   b. The switch reads the frame into RAM and calculates the CRC before forwarding the frame.
   c. Both latency and the error rate are decreased.
   d. Both latency and the error rate are increased.
   e. Latency is increased, whereas the error rate is decreased.

knowledge TEST

15. STP was developed:
    a. To prevent bridges from forwarding information out of ports that the information was received
    b. To prevent routing loops in a routed internetwork
    c. To avoid loops in a bridged network with redundant paths
    d. To assist in the depletion of IP addresses

16. What are the three VTP modes a switch can be in?
    a. Server, client, virtual
    b. Server, host, transparent
    c. Sever, host, volatile
    d. Server, client, transparent

17. What command is used to view the MAC table of a switch?
    a. *Show table*
    b. *Show mac-table*
    c. *Show mac-address-table*
    d. *Verify mac-table*

18. Which statements are true about VTP pruning? (Choose all that apply.)
    a. It is enabled by default.
    b. It is disabled by default.
    c. It is used to allow two Spanning Trees to work simultaneously on the same segment of wire.
    d. It increases available bandwidth.
    e. It increases the amount of needless traffic on a network.

19. For a VLAN to span two or more switches, what must be configured?
    a. A switch's duplex feature
    b. A VTP management domain
    c. A VPMS must be installed
    d. An ISL trunk connection

20. After entering the interface configuration mode for a port on a switch, which command would assign the port to VLAN 10?
    a. *vlan-membership 10*
    b. *vlan-membership static 10*
    c. *vlan static 10*
    d. *vlan 10 static-membership*

Abbreviated CLI Commands

This appendix contains a short list of commonly used abbreviated commands. See Table 3.1 in Chapter 3 to learn what the commands will accomplish.

Command	Abbreviation
Router>enable	*En*
Router#show interfaces	*sh int*
Router#show interfaces Ethernet 0	*sh int e0*
Router#show startup-config	*sh start*
Router#show running-config	*sh run*
Router#show version	*sh ver*
Router#Copy startup-config running-config	*copy st run*
Router#Copy running-config startup-config	*copy run st*
Router#Copy running-config tftp	*copy run tftp*
Router#configure terminal	*config t*
Router#configure network	*config n*
Router(config)#configure memory	*config m*
Router(config)#erase startup-config	*erase start*
Router#interface ethernet 0	*int e0*
Router#interface serial 0	*int s0*

CCNA 640-801 Exam Preparation

OBJECTIVES

At the end of this appendix, you should be prepared to identify and answer the different styles of questions on the CCNA 640-801 Exam.

INTRODUCTION

This appendix contains information to prepare you for the CCNA Exam. In March 2002, Cisco announced that its exams would be given in a new format consisting of skill-based questions. It was developed to test real-world skills needed to become a CCNA.

Cisco is not the first vendor to use certification exams that are geared toward real-world experience. The goal of these exams is to ensure that CCNA candidates have the formal training or experience with the product before becoming certified to use it. Don't let this trouble you. If you know and understand the product, you should be able to pass the exam regardless of how the questions are presented.

TYPES OF QUESTIONS

In the CCNA Exam, Cisco uses three types of questions in addition to the traditional multiple-choice questions as seen in the knowledge tests throughout this book: Drag and Drop, Fill in the Blank, and Router Simulation.

DRAG-AND-DROP QUESTIONS

Drag-and-drop questions are designed for the examinee to use the mouse to click on and drag the correct answer to its correct location. These questions normally have several items to move, and the instructions are to place the correct answer in the correct blanks. See the following example:

QUESTION:
As data travel down the OSI model, they are encapsulated for transport over the network. Below you will find a diagram of the OSI model. Place the correct encapsulation type at the appropriate layer of the OSI model. Encapsulation types may be used more than once.

ANSWER COLUMN	OSI MODEL
FRAMES	Layer 7. _____
DATA	Layer 6. _____
BITS	Layer 5. _____
SEGMENTS	Layer 4. _____
PACKETS	Layer 3. _____
	Layer 2. _____
	Layer 1. _____

The goal is to place the mouse cursor over the type of encapsulation and drag it to its appropriate layer. You should know that in this example you would place the DATA encapsulation type in three areas: Layers 7, 6, and 5; SEGMENTS are at Layer 4; PACKETS are at Layer 3; FRAMES are at Layer 2; and BITS are at Layer 1.

FILL-IN-THE-BLANK QUESTIONS

Fill-in-the-blank questions normally request that the examinee type a command or other answer (without being provided with any choices) to complete the question. For example:

QUESTION:
What command allows you to go from User EXEC mode to privileged EXEC mode?

Router>_____

ANSWER:

Router>enable

Although Cisco routers allow you to enter a partial command (for example, *en* for *enable*), you should type out the complete command during the exam. Take nothing for granted when you are taking the exam unless the question specifically asks you for the shortcut command. Table 3.1 in Chapter 3 should help tremendously with these questions. It has many commands that you can be tested on within the limits of the CCNA test objectives.

SKILLS-BASED QUESTIONS

The router simulation questions are the bread and butter of this exam. They test your knowledge of working with Cisco equipment.

A router is not a complex piece of equipment to work with. The commands used to configure a router are simple and make sense logically. It stands to reason that if you know how to configure a router, are familiar with the commands to use, and do not get nervous when given a router simulation question, you will get these questions right. Again, Table 3.1 will come in handy for these questions. However, you have to remember that there is normally a sequence of commands that you have to go through to complete a task. The router simulation questions do not remind you that there is a sequence to run through. For example, if the question asks you to configure an interface, there are several steps to go through before you can even start configuring the interface: you must enter privileged mode, enter the global configuration mode, and then from there you can enter the interface mode.

There are several skills-based questions in the following pages that will prepare you for what the CCNA Exam uses to test your knowledge. These examples are not exactly what you will see on the CCNA Exam; however, they are a good way to benchmark your skills and gain some confidence before taking the exam. Remember as you are taking the actual exam, you will be working in a Windows HyperTerminal session. The following figure shows a HyperTerminal window. Directions will be provided to you during the exam. Be sure to read them.

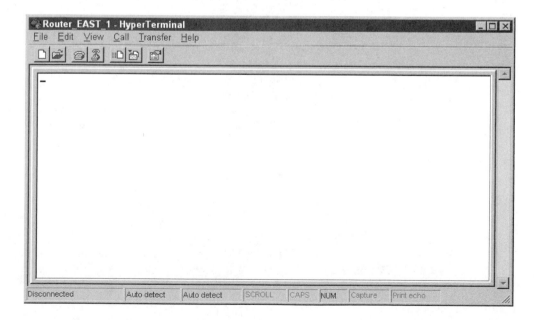

In the following scenarios, read the tasks in the objective column and write down the answers (including the router configuration mode) in the answer column. If you want to run through these scenarios for a second and third time, write your answers on a separate sheet of paper. Assume that your HyperTerminal session has been established; after pressing the Enter key, your command prompt is Router_name>. Figure B.1 shows the topology that you will be working with for scenarios 1, 2, and 3.

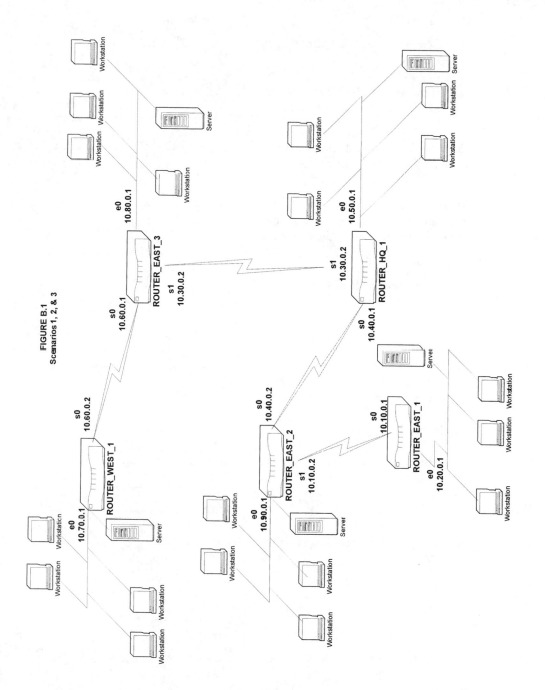

FIGURE B.1
Scenarios 1, 2, & 3

Scenario 1

Objectives

1. Log in to Router_East_1 privileged EXEC mode.

2. Set the enable secret password to *Delmar* from the correct mode.

3. View the hardware and software configurations of the router.

4. Give the serial 0 interface an IP address of 10.10.0.1 with a subnet mask that supports 254 subnets.

5. Set the clock rate of serial 0 to 64 Kbps.

6. Enable serial 0.

7. Give the Ethernet 0 interface an IP address of 10.20.0.1 with a subnet that supports 254 subnets.

8. Enable Ethernet 0.

9. View the interfaces to ensure they are both up.

10. Save the running configuration to NVRAM.

Answers

_____

_____

_____

_____

_____

_____

_____

_____

_____

_____

_____

_____

_____

_____

_____

Answers to Scenario 1

1. *ROUTER_EAST_1>enable*

2. *ROUTER_EAST_1#configure terminal*
   ROUTER_EAST_1 (config)#enable secret Delmar

3. *ROUTER_EAST_1 (config)#exit*
   ROUTER_EAST_1#show version

4. *ROUTER_EAST_1#configure terminal*
   ROUTER_EAST_1 (config)#interface serial 0
   ROUTER_EAST_1 (config-if)#ip address 10.10.0.1 255.255.0.0

5. *ROUTER_EAST_1 (config-if)#clock rate 64000*

6. *ROUTER_EAST_1 (config-if)#no shutdown*

7. *ROUTER_EAST_1 (config-if)#interface ethernet 0*
   ROUTER_EAST_1 (config-if)#ip address 10.20.0.1 255.255.0.0

8. *ROUTER_EAST_1 (config-if)#no shutdown*

9. *ROUTER_EAST_1 (config-if)#exit*
   ROUTER_EAST_1 (config)#exit
   ROUTER_EAST_1#show interfaces

10. *ROUTER_EAST_1#copy running-config startup-config*

Scenario 2

Objectives   Answers

Note: In this scenario the host name of the router has not been configured yet.

1. Log in to ROUTER_HQ_1
   privileged EXEC mode.   _____

2. Set the enable secret password to   _____
   DelmarHQ.
                                                  _____

3. Configure the console not to   _____
   time out.
                                                  _____

4. Change the command history   _____
   buffer to permanently remember
   100 commands.   _____

                                                  _____

5. Set a banner message of the day   _____
   that reads: This is the HQ router,
   unauthorized access is a punishable   _____
   offense.
                                                  _____

6. Set the console password to   _____
   DelmarHQ.
                                                  _____

7. Set the Telnet (VTY line 0 4) pass-   _____
   word to *DelmarHQ.*
                                                  _____

                                                  _____

8. Configure the router's host name to   _____
   be ROUTER_HQ_1.
                                                  _____

9. View the running config.   _____

                                                  _____

10. Save the running config to TFTP   _____
    server 10.50.0.100.
                                                  _____

                                                  _____

Answers to Scenario 2

1. *Router>enable*

2. *Router#configure terminal*
   Router(config)#enable secret DelmarHQ

3. *Router(config)#line console 0*
   Router(config-line)#exec-timeout 0 0

4. *Router(config-line)#exit*
   Router(config)#exit
   Router#history size 100

5. *Router#configure terminal*
   Router(config)#banner MOTD # This is the HQ Router,
   *   unauthorized access is a punishable offense. #*

6. *Router(config)#line console 0*
   Router(config-line)#login
   Router(config-line)#password DelmarHQ

7. *Router(config-line)#line vty 0 4*
   Router(config-line)#login
   Router(config-line)#password DelmarHQ

8. *Router(config-line)#exit*
   Router(config)#hostname ROUTER_HQ_1

9. *ROUTER_HQ_1(config)#exit*
   ROUTER_HQ_1#show running-config

10. *ROUTER_HQ_1#copy running-config tftp*
    Enter 10.50.0.100 when prompted for the IP address and accept
    *   the default file name.*

Scenario 3

Objectives	Answers
1. Log in to ROUTER_EAST_3 privileged EXEC mode.	_____
2. Set the static host name to IP address mapping for ROUTER_HQ_1 with addresses: 10.30.0.2; 10.40.0.1; 10.50.0.1.	_____ _____ _____
3. Verify the host name you created is in the name cache.	_____ _____
4. Disable DNS lookup.	_____
5. Ping the host name ROUTER_HQ_1.	_____
6. Configure a static route to the 10.70.0.0 network; use a subnet mask that allows for 254 subnets and 10.60.0.2. as next hop.	_____ _____
7. Telnet to ROUTER_WEST_1 no password is required.	_____ _____
8. Configure static routes to the 10.80.0.0 network; use a subnet mask with 254 hosts and 10.60.0.1 as next hop. Verify the route table.	_____ _____ _____ _____ _____
9. Disconnect from ROUTER_WEST_1.	_____
10. Save the running config of ROUTER_EAST_3 to NVRAM.	_____

Answers to Scenario 3

1. *ROUTER_EAST_3>enable*

2. *ROUTER_EAST_3#configure terminal*
   ROUTER_EAST_3(config)#ip host ROUTER_HQ_1 10.30.0.2 10.40.0.1
   10.50.0.1

3. *ROUTER_EAST_3(config)#exit*
   ROUTER_EAST_3#show hosts

4. *ROUTER_EAST_3#no ip domain-lookup*

5. *ROUTER_EAST_3#ping ROUTER_HQ_1*

6. *ROUTER_EAST_3#configure terminal*
   ROUTER_EAST_3(config)#ip route 10.70.0.0 255.255.0.0 10.60.0.2

7. *ROUTER_EAST_3(config)#exit*
   ROUTER_EAST_3#10.60.0.2

8. *ROUTER_WEST_1>enable*
   ROUTER_WEST_1#configure terminal
   ROUTER_WEST_1(config)#ip route 10.80.0.0 255.255.0.0 10.60.0.1
   ROUTER_WEST_1(config)#exit
   ROUTER_WEST_1#show ip route

9. *ROUTER_WEST_1#cxit*

10. *ROUTER_EAST_3#copy running-config startup-config*

Use Figure B.2 as a reference for Scenario 4.

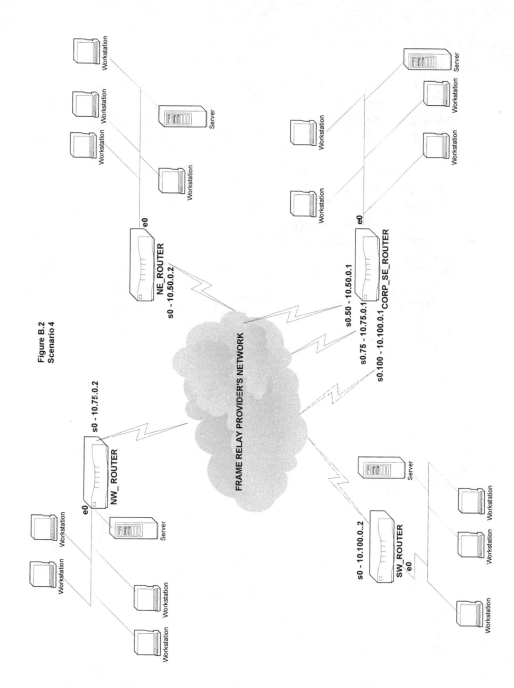

Figure B.2
Scenario 4

Scenario 4

Objectives   **Answers**

1. Log in to CORP_SE_ROUTER privileged EXEC mode.
   _____

2. Remove the IP address set for
   serial 0.
   _____
   _____
   _____

3. Configure Frame Relay default
   encapsulation for serial 0.
   _____

4. Configure three point-to-point
   subinterfaces on serial 0 with the
   following parameters:
   s0.50, 10.50.0.1, 255.255.0.0,
      DLCI 120
   s0.75, 10.75.0.1, 255.255.0.0,
      DLCI 125
   s0.100, 10.100.0.1, 255.255.0.0,
      DLCI 130.
   _____
   _____
   _____
   _____
   _____
   _____
   _____
   _____
   _____
   _____
   _____
   _____
   _____

5. Configure RIP routing for
   CORP_SE_ROUTER networks.
   _____
   _____
   _____
   _____
   _____
   _____

6. Create a standard IP access list
   to allow packets from the three
   networks configured.
   _____
   _____
   _____

7. Group the access list on the
   Ethernet 0 interface of the router.
   _____
   _____

8. Save the running config to NVRAM.
   _____
   _____

Answers to Scenario 4

1. *CORP_SE_ROUTER>enable*

2. *CORP_SE_ROUTER#configure terminal*
   CORP_SE_ROUTER(config)#interface serial 0
   CORP_SE_ROUTER(config-if)#no ip address

3. *CORP_SE_ROUTER(config-if)#encapsulation frame-relay*

4. *CORP_SE_ROUTER(config-if)#interface serial 0.50 point-to-point*
   CORP_SE_ROUTER(config-subif)#ip address 10.50.0.1 255.255.0.0
   CORP_SE_ROUTER(config-subif)#frame-relay interface-dlci 120
   CORP_SE_ROUTER(config-fr-dlci)#exit
   CORP_SE_ROUTER(config-subif)#interface serial 0.75 point-to-point
   CORP_SE_ROUTER(config-subif)#ip address 10.75.0.1 255.255.0.0
   CORP_SE_ROUTER(config-subif)#frame-relay interface-dlci 125
   CORP_SE_ROUTER(config-fr-dlci)#exit
   CORP_SE_ROUTER(config-subif)#interface serial 0.100 point-to-point
   CORP_SE_ROUTER(config-subif)#ip address 10.100.0.1 255.255.0.0
   CORP_SE_ROUTER(config-subif)#frame-relay interface-dlci 130

5. *CORP_SE_ROUTER(config-fr-dlci)#exit*
   CORP_SE_ROUTER(config-subif)#exit
   CORP_SE_ROUTER(config-if)#exit
   CORP_SE_ROUTER(config)#router rip
   CORP_SE_ROUTER(config-router)#network 10.50.0.0
   CORP_SE_ROUTER(config-router)#network 10.75.0.0
   CORP_SE_ROUTER(config-router)#network 10.100.0.0

6. *CORP_SE_ROUTER(config-router)#exit*
   CORP_SE_ROUTER(config)#access list 5 permit 10.50.0.0 0.0.255.255
   CORP_SE_ROUTER(config)#access list 5 permit 10.75.0.0 0.0.255.255
   CORP_SE_ROUTER(config)#access list 5 permit 10.100.0.0 0.0.255.255

7. *CORP_SE_ROUTER(config)#ethernet 0*
   CORP_SE_ROUTER(config-if)#ip access-group 5 out

8. *CORP_SE_ROUTER(config-if)#exit*
   CORP_SE_ROUTER(config)#exit
   CORP_SE_ROUTER#copy running-config startup-config

Answers to
Knowledge Test Questions

Chapter 1

1. **D.** The correct process of encapsulation is data created by the upper layer protocols, segments created by the transport layer, packets created at the network layer, frames created at the data-link layer and bits transmitted on the wire by the physical layer.

2. **B.** De-encapsulation is the reverse of encapsulation. Encapsulation is the process of adding control information to a data stream as it travels down the OSI model of the sending machine. De-encapsulation is stripping off the control information on the way up the OSI model of the receiving machine.

3. **A.** See Table 1.1.

4. **A.** The network layer's primary responsibility is to route packets between independent networks operating with distinct and separate logical addresses.

5. **B.** Flow control, acknowledgments, and windowing are all features of the transport layer.

6. **C and E.** Sequencing segments and establishing virtual circuits are done at the transport layer. Formatting the data is done at the presentation layer.

7. **B and D.** Connection-oriented communication occurs at the transport layer and segments are sequenced rather than frames, which are a function of the data-link layer. Windowing is the process of sending one acknowledgment for multiple segments, not multiple acknowledgments for one segment.

8. **False.** The physical address is the MAC address, which is associated with the network adapter board. The cable address is considered a network, protocol, hierarchical, or logical address.

9. **B and D.** Bridges forward broadcasts to all segments of wire they are attached to on the network. A bridge cannot connect networks that use different access methods; that is a feature of a router.

10. **False.** Repeaters only lengthen the duration of a signal on a single cable run. All transmissions are forwarded to all segments of the wire attached to the repeater. Therefore, repeaters do not break up the collision or broadcast domain.

11. **C.** SAP stands for service access point, and SNAP stands for subnetwork access point; they are defined by the LLC of the data-link layer. The MAC layer defines how data are transmitted onto the wire. Acknowledgments are a function of the transport layer.

12. **D.** Baseband transmission means only one signal can be on the wire at one time.

13. **C.** With full-duplex transmission, both transmitters can communicate at the same time. Half-duplex means only one transmitter can transmit at a time. Simplex is unidirectional wherein communication occurs in only one direction at a time.

14. **A and D.** Dividing up broadcast domains is a feature of a router. Switches operate in full-duplex mode.

15. **B.** In a physical bus topology, all nodes connect to a single wire called a backbone. In a physical ring topology, all nodes are connected in a ring fashion. In a physical mesh topology, all nodes are connected to one another for redundancy.

16. **B.** The three types of access methods are polling, contention, and token passing.

17. **E.** Routers operate at the network layer, and CSUs/DSUs operate at the physical layer of the OSI model.

18. **B and D.**

19. **B, D, E, F, G, H.** See Table 1.2.

20. **B and E.** MAC addresses are 48 bits long represented by 12 hexadecimal digits. A portion of the address is assigned to the board manufacturer by the IEEE. Another portion of the address is assigned by the board manufacturer to the individual network adapter board.

Chapter 2

1. **D.** The application layer of the TCP/IP model is equivalent to the three upper layers of the OSI model.

2. **C.** Internet Control Message Protocol (ICMP). IP is responsible for addressing. TCP is used for connection-oriented communication, and ARP is used for IP-to-MAC address resolutions.

3. **D.** TCP is connection oriented. UDP is connectionless.

4. **B.** False. Although TFTP does use UDP as its transport protocol, it uses port 69.

5. **B.** FTP uses TCP ports 20 and 21, DNS uses UDP and TCP port 53, and TFTP uses UDP 69.

6. **B.** False. DNS uses port 53 over a TCP connection for zone transfers. It does, however, use port 53 over UDP for name queries.

7. **A.** For practice, convert the other three. B is 201, C is 219, D is 225.

8. **D.**

9. **C.** Class A has the least amount of networks but the most hosts per network. Class B has more networks than class A but less hosts per network. Class B also has more hosts per network than class C but less networks. Classes D and E do not apply.

10. **A.**

11. **D.** 19 consecutive 1s would look like this: 11111111.11111111.11100000.00000000, which in decimal equals 255.255.224.0.

12. **B, C, and F.** If the first 4 bits of the third octet are added together, 240 will be the value of the third octet. The complete mask is 255.255.240.0. If the IP address and the subnet mask are both converted to decimal, it will be evident that the host portion of the IP address is 2.245. The network portion will be identified as 64 because the 64 bit of the IP address falls within the subnet mask:

	Network	**Host**
IP address:	01010101.00000001.0100	0010.11110101
Subnet mask:	11111111.11111111.1111	0000.00000000

Because the network and host are in the same octet, they must be added together for a value of 66 in the third octet. In decimal, this number can be deceiving because it serves two purposes but is only one number. However, when looking at it in binary, it is clear what portion of the address is used for the network ID and what portion of the address is used for the host ID. Remember, where the 1s stop in the subnet mask, the hosts begin in the IP address.

13. **A.**

14. **B.** It is not possible. Although 2^2 gives a total of 4 networks, 2 network addresses must be subtracted for administrative purposes. Only 2 valid network numbers will be available. 3 bits of the fourth octet would be required, which would allow for 6 valid network IDs. That would only leave 5 bits for hosts. 2^5 equals 32 minus 2, allowing for 30 hosts on each of the 6 networks.

15. **D.** 2^6 equals 64 minus 2 gives a total of 62 valid network IDs. 2^5 equals 32 network IDs; however, 2 addresses must be subtracted for administrative purposes, leaving the total number of networks available to 30. If 6 bits are used for network IDs, that leaves 10 bits for hosts, 2 bits in the third octet, and 8 bits in the fourth octet. 2^{10} equals 512 minus 2 would be 510 hosts per network.

16. **B.** To determine the answer, convert the IP address and the subnet mask to binary.

	Network	Host
IP address	10100101.01100100.001	00000.00101100
Subnet mask	11111111.11111111.111	00000.00000000

Using the preceding chart, the network ID in the third octet in the IP address row is 32. The hard part is determining what the hosts are. If none of the 0s in the third octet is used for hosts, the host IDs will begin with 1 in the last octet and go to 254. It is safe to assume that the beginning network and host address will be 165.100.32.1. If the network grew to more than 254 hosts, it would be necessary to start using the same octet that the network ID is in (the third octet) for host IDs. In binary, this is how it would look:

Third Octet Only	Network	Host
	001	00001 = 33
	001	00010 = 34
	001	00011 = 35
	001	00100 = 36

This continues until the number 63 in the third octet is reached. At that time, the next bit to turn on would be 64, which is in the network portion of the octet. So the next network ID would begin with 64. The last host on the 32 network would be 63.254. It is important to realize that every host ID shown in the same octet as the network ID (32, 64, 96, 128, 160, 192) would be able to use the fourth octet as well. In this example, it is possible to have 2^{13} of hosts per network, which equals 8,192 minus 2.

17. **C.** In this example, use 27 bits as the subnet mask. The procedure is the same as shown in answer 16, but the fourth octet is to be used. The network ID is 32 and the hosts are 33–62 in the fourth octet. 63 in the fourth octet would mean that the host portion of the address would consist of all ones (1s), which is an illegal address.

	Network	Host
IP address	10100101.01100100.00100000.001	00011
Subnet mask	11111111.11111111.11111111.111	00000

18. **A.** Class A default subnet mask is 255.0.0.0. Class C default subnet mask is 255.255.255.0.

19. **B.** 2^9 minus 2 equals 510.

20. **A.** RARP resolves MAC addresses to IP addresses.

Chapter 3

1. **D.** NVRAM is type RAM that does not lose its data when the router is powered off. The startup-configuration file is stored in NVRAM. The running-configuration file is the active configuration located in physical RAM. The IOS is stored in flash RAM, and ROM stores a mini IOS as well as POST instructions.

2. **C.** To set passwords on individual terminal lines, you must start at global configuration mode, then focus on the line you want to configure, log in to the line, and then create the password. Remember that setting passwords on VTY lines and auxiliary lines is similar to this.

3. **B.** When configuring the bandwidth on a serial interface, you must type the value as kilobits per second rather than bits per second as with the *clock rate* command.

4. **B.** In this question, the only correct command is B. There is no *tftp-startup* command. To back up to a TFTP server, use the command *copy running-config tftp;* the router will then prompt you for the address of the TFTP server.

5. **A and D.** The command to enter the privileged EXEC mode from the user EXEC mode is *enable. En* is the least amount of characters you can use to uniquely identify the *enable* command.

6. **A.** When determining what arguments are available with a specific command, ensure a space is in between the command and the "?".

7. **A.** *Show version* gives you the IOS version, the configuration register value, the uptime of the router, basic hardware information (amount of RAM and processor speed), as well as what IOS and configuration file is running.

8. **B.** After typing this command, the CLI will prompt you for the name of the TFTP server you want to store the file on.

9. **D.** The configuration register will be set to 0x2101 if you use the *boot system rom* command. Answers B and C will look for an IOS file stored in NVRAM, and A will boot directly into ROM Monitor mode.

10. **D.** The command *sh int e0* is the abbreviated form of *show interface Ethernet0.* Either command will have the same output. Remember, if you type *show interfaces,* you will be able to see the line and protocol status of all the router's interfaces.

11. **D.** The *banner motd* command must be typed at the global configuration mode. The message that will be displayed must be typed in between two delimiting characters—in this example the @ symbol.

12. **B.** The only valid command is the *no shutdown* command. You must be in the interface configuration mode to turn the interface on or off.

13. **C.** You can set an encrypted password to enter the privileged EXEC mode from the global configuration mode. *Enable secret* and *enable password* commands cannot be used in conjunction with one another. The commands are used in an either/or situation.

14. **A.** The *boot system* command allows you to specify where the IOS should be loaded from. The values in the configuration register change based on the input of this command. You can use the *show version* command to view the configuration value. When using this command, you can specify whether or not the router boots from a file in flash RAM, boots from ROM, or boots from a TFTP server.

15. **D.** The command *history buffer* is set with the *terminal history* command. Use the *show history* command to view the commands in the buffer. The default setting is to remember 10 commands and the maximum is 256 commands.

16. **B.** CDP is a layer 2 protocol proprietary to Cisco. It allows Cisco products (for example, switches and routers) to identify one another while independent of the layer 3 protocol being used. The devices that are connected are considered neighbors and the *show cdp neighbors* command gives a list of all the connected neighbors the router knows about.

17. **A.** Ctrl+A moves the cursor to the beginning of the CLI. Ctrl+B moves the cursor back one word. Ctrl+P navigates the last command in the command history buffer. Ctrl+C is invalid.

18. **C.** After you learn the names and addresses of the devices connected to your router through the *show cdp neighbors* command, you can view detailed statistics about each neighbor with the *show cdp entry [address]* command.

19. **D.** In this command, the router looks for an image named IOS1 on a TFTP server with an address of 192.168.1.25.

20. **D.** All passwords entered between the *service password-encryption* and *no service password-encryption* will be encrypted. Remember that you must follow the same steps to set the passwords. But you enter the respective modes and set the passwords in between the two commands described.

Chapter 4

1. **C.** The 16th network is considered unreachable because RIP has a maximum hop count of 15. IGRP has a default maximum hop count of 100 and can be increased to 255.

2. **B.** OSPF is a link-state routing algorithm. BGP is an EGP, and RIP and IGRP use distance-vector routing algorithms.

3. **A and E.** Although low overhead and holddown timers are features of RIP, they are not considered disadvantages.

4. **C.** To enable a routing protocol, you must enter the router configuration mode through the global configuration mode.

5. **B and E.** IGRP is a proprietary protocol developed by Cisco. It uses a maximum hop count of 100 by default and can be extended to 255. IGRP is a distance-vector routing algorithm that uses a composite metric for routing. The metric can consist of five components: bandwidth, delay, reliability, load, and MTU.

6. **B.** A router must know all the answers; however, to forward the packet, it must know where the packet is destined.

7. **B and C.** Static routing has less processor overhead and is well suited for small internetworks. When an internetwork gets too large to manually configure routes, it is time to implement dynamic routing.

8. **C.** Enter router configuration mode through the global configuration mode.

9. **C, E, F, and I.** IGRP broadcasts the routing table every 90 seconds. Link-state routing algorithms only send the routing table changes after the initial convergence. RIP learned routes have an administrative distance of 120. All static routes have an administrative distance of 1. RIP only uses the hop count as its routing metric.

10. **B and C.** RIP uses four mechanisms to avoid routing loops: split horizon, route poisoning, holddown timers, and triggered updates. Triggered updates work with holddown timers.

11. **A.** To view routing updates, use the *debug ip rip* command; to stop debugging, use the *no debug all* command.

12. **B.** The *show IP route* command shows the routing table that is using IP routing. Information available from that command includes known networks, the routing protocol they came from, the administrative distance and metric to the network, the address of the next hop router, when each route was updated last, and the interface the router will use to send packets to each network.

13. **C.** You must include the addresses of all directly connected networks when configuring RIP. This allows the router to start the RIP routing process on the identified networks.

14. **D.** Route poisoning advertises the route with a hop count of 16. Holddown timers ensure that a route cannot change for the worse within a specified amount of time. Triggered updates allow routers to send routing tables before the route table update timer is complete.

15. **C.** The *show ip protocols* command displays the routing protocol being used. It also shows details of the protocol such as when updates are sent, when the next update is due, how long before routes will be flushed, and the administrative distance.

16. **A.** The proper commands are *debug igrp transactions* and *debug igrp events*.

17. **D.** Split horizon does not advertise the route from the interface where it was learned.

18. **B and E.** OSPF is an example of a link-state routing algorithm. Link-state routing algorithms have a higher processor overhead than static routing because they are dynamic. Link-state algorithms send changes to their routing tables only.

19. **B.** The command to use to ensure packets are not dropped is the *ip classless* command. The command is used because routers use classful addressing by default. After you enter this command, the router will be able to successfully use classless routes that are external to the internetwork.

20. **A.** Routes can be updated before a holddown timer expires if the route has the same or better metric than the current metric. However, if the update has a worse metric than the current update, the holddown timer will prevent the update from taking place.

Chapter 5

1. **C.** Link-state routing protocols only send updates on the network when network links it knows about change. Distance-vector–based routing protocols send updates that include the entire routing table at a predetermined interval.

2. **B.** The proper command to set the OSPF process on a router is *router ospf 1*. The command is done from the global configuration mode and puts the prompt into the *Router(config-router)#* mode. The process ID is locally significant on a router and any number can be used. If OSPF is configured on a separate router in the same internetwork, the same process ID does not have to be used.

3. **B and E.** EIGRP bases its metric on four values: bandwidth, delay, reliability, and load. Adjacencies and neighbor relationships do not factor into the route-calculation process.

4. **A.** The protocol-dependent modules of EIGRP allow for the support of multiple network layer protocols such as IP, IPX, and AppleTalk. RTP guarantees the delivery of routing updates and DUAL helps create and maintain the routing table.

5. **D.** *Show ip eigrp topology* command shows the network topology. The routes show up as passive routes when using this command. The *show ip route* command shows the actual routing table.

6. **D.** The correct answer places the router into the proper mode and assigns the router to AS 871. B is incorrect because the router *eigrp* command is given in the wrong mode. C is invalid because it is unnecessary to give a host address when setting up EIGRP.

7. **C.** The *show ip eigrp interfaces* command also lists the average SRTT, packets waiting in the queue, and the maximum number of seconds the router will send multicast EIGRP packets.

8. **B.** OSPF is an IGP that works within an AS. Large autonomous systems can be divided up by areas while using OSPF.

9. **B.** The process ID is locally significant to each router in the OSPF network. This means that routers in an OSPF network can all utilize different process IDs.

10. **C.** To determine the cost of the route, divide 100,000,000 by the bits per second. In this case, a 56 Kbps line has 56,000 bits per second. The cost would be 1786. This would be considered a poor route.

11. **B, C, and D.** Link-state routing algorithms also have a fast convergence time, use complex metrics that demand more from the processor, and only send route table updates when changes in the network occur.

12. **B, D, and E.** The neighbor database lists all the router's neighbors. The topology database stores a listing of network links, routers advertising the links, and the types of links. The routing table maintains a list of all known networks and the path to get data there.

13. **B.** Designated router and backup designated router elections will not be held in a point-to-point or a point-to-multipoint OSPF network.

14. **A = 2, B = 1, C = 4, D = 3.**

15. **B.** The administrative distance for EIGRP is 90.

16. **A, C, and D.** Adjacencies are set up automatically during the convergence process and in a single AS, you do not have to set the AS in the command.

17. Hello Packets, Database Description Packets, Link State Requests, Link State Announcements, and Link State Updates.

18. Hello Packets, Update Packets, Query Packets, Reply Packets, and ACKs.

19. **A.** *Show ip eigrp traffic* gathers statistics on the overall routing traffic of an EIGRP router.

20. **D.** The *show ip ospf neighbor* command shows the contents of the router's neighbor table.

Chapter 6

1. **D.**

2. **C.** *Access-class* is the command used to apply an access list to a VTY line. VTY lines allow Telnet access. The IP *access-group* command is used to apply an access list to an interface.

3. **B.** The command identifies 121.0.0.0 as the source network, and the wildcard mask 0.255.255.255 compares the first octet of the address. If a packet is sent from the 121.0.0.0 network, it will be applied to the access list and denied access.

4. **A, C, and E.** Sockets are used with the IPX/SPX suite, not the TCP/IP suite.

5. The proper command would be:

```
Line 1. IP access-list 159 deny TCP host
    192.168.1.25 host 10.10.100.254 eq 80
Line 2. IP access-list 159 permit any
```

The alternate command if using wildcard masks would be:

```
Line 1. IP access-list 159 deny TCP 192.168.1.25
    0.0.0.0 10.10.100.254 0.0.0.0 eq 80
Line 2. IP access-list 159 permit any
```

6. In this command, you have to block an entire subnet. To determine what the subnet is, look at the subnet mask. In this question, the mask is in CIDR format /20, which means the mask is 255.255.240.0. If 240 is the subnet mask that is broken up, determine what your networks are incrementing by. The lowest on bit in 240 is the 16 bit. Because the 16 bit is the lowest on bit, that is what the networks increment by. So to determine the wildcard mask for that specific octet, subtract 1 from 16 as that is the block of address in that range. So the wildcard mask is 0.0.15.255.

The proper command is:

```
Line 1. IP access-list 160 permit TCP 10.1.32.0
    0.0.15.255 host 192.168.68.1 eq ftp
```

7. **B.** The *show ip access-list access [list number]* command shows the access list entries included in the access list. It does not show what interface the access list is applied to.

8. **A and E.** It is possible to learn what access lists are configured on the router by reading through the running configuration. The running configuration identifies interfaces and the access lists that are configured on them. It does not show the individual access list entries contained in each access list. The *show access-list* command shows all access lists and the entries within them. It does not show what interfaces the access lists are applied to.

9. **B.** The *IP access-group* command would be used and the parameter for inbound traffic is *In*.

10. **B and D.** A is incorrect because it is set to use access list 18, which is a standard access list. C is incorrect because the argument *any* should be placed before the destination address not after it. E is incorrect because HTTP uses TCP, not UDP.

11. The proper command would be:

    ```
    IP access-list 100 permit TCP any host
    172.16.5.100 eq 25
    ```

12. **A, D, and E.**

13. **B.** A is incorrect because it establishes a standard access list, C is incorrect because it applies the access list to the Fast Ethernet 0/0 interface, and D is incorrect because the access list does not have the *TCP* parameter included.

14. **D.** This access list shows all parameters of all access lists. To see the interfaces they are applied to, use the *show IP interface* command or *show run* command.

15. **B.** Named access lists operate the same as numbered access lists.

16. **B.** The wildcard mask 0.0.0.0 255.255.255.255 is equivalent to the *any* command. It states that any host on any network does not have to be compared with entries in the access list.

17. **D.** The *access-class* command is used to apply an IP standard access list to VTY lines to control access to the router with the Telnet application.

18. **A.** B is incorrect because it is using an access list number of 10, which is used for IP standard access lists. C is wrong because TFTP uses UDP, not TCP. D is wrong because the wildcard masks are incorrect. When a wildcard mask has 255.255.255.255, it states that no comparisons against the access list will be made.

19. **B.** This is false because access lists are used for many different reasons in Cisco routers. This book only touches on the very basics of what an access list can be used for. They have many roles in a network to include Network Address Translation (NAT), Telnet (VTY Line) access, and DDR to name a few.

20. **B.** False because the access list drops all packets that do not have an entry because of the implicit *deny*. Access lists must contain at least one entry or all packets will be dropped.

Chapter 7

1. **B.** The two methods of creating a Frame Relay map is dynamically using inverse ARP (which is the default) or statically using the *frame-relay map* command.

2. **D.** The *debug frame-relay lmi* command shows the actual output of LMI packets being sent and received. The *show frame-relay lmi* command only reports statistics of LMI messages sent and received.

3. **D.** When authenticating with PPP, the host router must be configured with the guest router's host name and by specifying it with the *username password* command. The password on each router also is required to be the same.

4. **B, C, and E.** Although the DLCI is assigned to the local router, it is mapped to the network address of a remote router. DLCIs are normally assigned by the Frame Relay service provider and should be unique to the network.

5. **A, B, D, and E.** To configure point-to-point subinterfaces, encapsulate the serial interface, delete the IP address of the serial interface, create subinterfaces using the point-to-point Frame Relay configuration, and assign IP addresses to each subinterface. If configuring a multipoint Frame Relay configuration, do not delete the IP address on the serial interface.

6. **B, D, and F.** ISDN offers two rates: BRI and PRI. BRI offers two 64 Kbps lines for transferring data and one 16 Kbps line for transferring control and signal information. PRI offers much more bandwidth. Because ISDN is not a packet-switching technology, it does not use Frame Relay to encapsulate data. ISDN can encapsulate data using PPP or HDLC. ISDN supports voice and data; the data that it can carry includes video and special services.

7. **D.** PRI offers 23 B channels and 1 D channel at 64 Kbps each in North America and Japan, as well as 30 B channels and 1 D channel at 64 Kbps each in Europe, Australia, and other parts of the world.

8. **B, D, and I.**

9. **B.** There are only two types of Frame Relay encapsulation Cisco routers use: Cisco (default) and IETF. ANSI and q933a are LMI standards.

10. **C.**

11. **A and C.** I series is an ISDN protocol standard. ANSI and q933a are LMI types.

12. **C.**

13. **B.**

14. **A and F.** The command must identify the serial interface, which is the *s0* argument, then the subinterface number after a dot (.), which is *1*, and then the type of subinterface configuration your router will be configured for. The two to choose from are *multipoint* or *point-to-point*.

15. **A and B.** Cisco's implementation of HDLC does support multiple network layer protocols because of an additional protocol field in the HDLC frame itself. Many other implementations of HDLC do not support multiple network layer protocols.

16. **D and E.**

17. **A and E.** ATM, Frame Relay, and X.25 are all packet-switching technologies and work best in a PDN that uses packet-switching technologies.

18. **D.** The *show interface* command is very useful and reports statistics on the status of the lines as well as protocols and encapsulation methods configured. If using Frame Relay encapsulation, it also reports data about the DLCI and LMI configuration.

19. **A.**

20. **A, C, and D.** The D channel only supports 16 Kbps of data; therefore, it is not capable of handling high-speed data transfer.

Chapter 8

1. **A.** Fragment-free switching, which is the default switching method for Cisco's Catalyst 1900 switches, allows the collision window to pass before forwarding the frame.

2. **B, C, and E.** Switches also may flood the frame if it is a multicast frame.

3. **C and D.** Although fragment-free switching latency is reduced, it is not completely eliminated.

4. **B and D.** Frame tagging occurs at layer 2 of the OSI model, and Cisco switches use ISL to monitor VLAN membership.

5. **B, D, and E.** Split horizon and routing packets between networks are features of a router.

6. **A, D, E, and G.**

7. **C, E, and F.** It is possible to increase the number of broadcast domains with switches. However, to do that you must implement VLANs. Increasing the number of collision domains actually reduces the amount of data collisions between end nodes.

8. **A.**

9. **D.** Before creating the VLAN in a 2900 series switch, you must first enter the VLAN database configuration mode. In a 1900 series switch, the command sequence is slightly different because it is done from the global configuration mode.

10. **A.** Cut-through switching forwards the frame as soon as it knows the frame's destination. It has the lowest latency and the highest error rate of the three switching methods discussed.

11. **C.** Implementing virtual LANs increases the number of broadcast domains. However, if the number of broadcast domains are increased, the amount of stations in each broadcast domain will be decreased, thus increasing the amount of available bandwidth throughout the entire switched network.

12. **B.** The command is issued from the interface configuration mode.

13. **A and D.** The additional answers are all features of full-duplex mode.

14. **B and E.** Store-and-forward switching has the highest latency and the lowest error rate of the three switching methods discussed.

15. **C.** The technology used with bridges is very similar to the technology used by switches. Therefore, the STP works with switches as well as bridges. Bridges are essentially software based, whereas switches are hardware based. Switches use application-specific integrated circuits (ASIC) to build and maintain the MAC table as well as help with forwarding and filtering decisions.

16. **D.**

17. **C.**

18. **B, C, and D.**

19. **D.** Cisco switches use Cisco's proprietary ISL protocol to enable a trunk between two or more switches.

20. **B.** The command is *vlan-membership*. However, membership can be assigned statically or dynamically. In this command, membership is assigned statically. The network must include a VMPS to assign VLAN membership dynamically.

Password Recovery Procedures

The ability to recover passwords on a Cisco router is just as important as the ability to set passwords on a Cisco router. Although passwords should be documented and accessible by administrators in the network, there may be times where the password is simply inaccessible. These practices are not condoned in the field, but are often the case. Whatever the reason may be, it is important to know that router passwords can be recovered. The steps to recovering a password are listed here and can be used on a multitude of Cisco routers (not just the 2600):

1. Use the power switch to turn off the router and then turn it back on.

2. From a standard Windows 98/2000/XP operating system connected to the Console port of the router, press the Ctrl+Break keys during boot (preferably within 60 seconds of the power-up). The router will end at the Rommon prompt.

3. From the rommon 1> prompt type *confreg 0x2142*. (Note the 0 before the x is a zero.) The router now boots from Flash without loading the startup configuration from the NVRAM, which is what the 2142 sets the configuration register to.

4. After pressing Enter, your prompt should like this: *rommon 2>*. Type **reset** to reload the router configuration. The router reboots, but ignores its saved configuration.

5. After the router is rebooted, type **no** after each setup question.

6. At the user mode prompt, type **enable**. In the privileged mode, type **copy start run** to load the configuration file that you just bypassed into memory. However, you are already in privilaged mode, so you do not need to enter the privileged mode password.

7. Go to the global configuration mode by typing **Config t**.

8. Reset the enable mode password by typing **enable secret -your new password-**.

9. You must now enter your interfaces and turn them on with the *no shutdown* command because when you copy the configuration from NVRAM to memory, the interfaces are not turned on.

10. Now reset your configuration register in the global configuration mode by using the *config-register 0x2102* command.

11. Finally, from the privileged mode, type **copy run start** to commit the changes. Be sure to document the new password.

ABR.   Area Border Router. An OSPF router that has interfaces in multiple areas to include a connection to the backbone area (Area 0).

Access layer.   The first layer in Cisco's three-layered hierarchical model. Users interact with the internetwork at this layer.

Access list.   Set of test conditions set by the administrator to determine whether or not a router will accept a packet.

Acknowledgment.   Also known as an ACK. It is a confirmation of the receipt of data during peer transport-layer communication.

Active hub.   Network component that acts as a central device for multiple nodes to connect to. Active hubs require power and regenerate data signals before forwarding them. Another term for an active hub is a *multiport repeater*.

Adjacency.   A term used to describe the relationship between two neighboring routers.

ANSI.   American National Standards Institute. ANSI is the American division of the ISO.

Area.   A self-contained routing management domain used with OSPF, which is part of the larger autonomous system.

AS.   A logical grouping of networks connected together by an interior gateway protocol such as OSPF.

ASBR.   Autonomous System Border Router. ASBRs sit at the edge of an autonomous system.

ATM.   Asynchronous Transfer Mode. A packet-switching technology that configures fixed-length packets 53 bytes in size called cells.

Backbone area.   Logical area (considered "Area 0") of the OSPF network in which all other areas must be connected.

Backbone router.   An OSPF router that has at least one interface in Area 0 (the backbone area).

Bandwidth.   Measurement in terms of bits per second. Represents the capacity of data transmittable over a network link.

Baseband.   Communication technique using a digital signal, which is capable of handling one signal on the cable at any given time.

BGP.   Border Gateway Protocol. An exterior gateway protocol used to connect two autonomous systems together.

BPDU.   Bridge Protocol Data Unit. Packets sent between bridges (or switches) in a Spanning-Tree Protocol network.

BRI.   Basic Rate Interface. ISDN standard that calls for two Bearer channels of 64 Kbps and one Delta channel of 16 Kbps.

Bridge.   Network device that works at the data-link layer of the OSI model and is responsible for segmenting an existing network into multiple collision domains through the use of a MAC table.

Broadband.   Communication technique using an analog signal, which is capable of handling multiple signals on the cable at any given time.

Broadcast domain.   Logical grouping of network components that will all receive a broadcast signal sent from any node in the group. Routers are capable of creating multiple broadcast domains because they do not normally forward broadcast signals.

Broadcast message.   A data message sent to all nodes that are associated with the same network address.

CDP.   Cisco Discovery Protocol. Cisco's proprietary protocol that allows Cisco devices the capability to transfer hardware and software information to one another.

CHAP.   Challenge Handshake Authentication Protocol. PPP authentication protocol that uses a three-way encrypted handshake.

CIDR.   Classless Inter Domain Routing. Provides an efficient method of allocating IP addresses. CIDR was developed to prevent the depletion of IP version 4 addresses. CIDR allocates addresses based on powers of 2 rather than using the classful IP addressing scheme; for example, Class A, B, C, and so on.

CIR.   Committed Information Rate. A Frame Relay network's minimum amount of bandwidth, in bits per second, provided to the customer.

CLI.   Command Line Interface. The prompt available for the user to issue commands on a Cisco router.

CO.   Central Office. WAN service provider's switching facility. Also known as point of presence (POP).

Collision domain.   Logical grouping of network components that must compete for access to the network cable to send data. Switches and bridges can create separate collision domains through the use of MAC tables. A broadcast domain can contain several collision domains, but a collision domain cannot span multiple broadcast domains.

Configuration register.   A hexadecimal value that specifies how Cisco routers behave during initialization.

Connectionless communication.   A data transfer standard that does not represent the reliable transmission of data. The opposite of connection-oriented communication. UDP is an example.

Connection-oriented communication.   A data transfer standard that represents the reliable transmission of data. TCP uses acknowledgments and flow control to achieve connection-oriented status.

Convergence.   The process routers in an internetwork go through while learning about all networks. The internetwork is fully converged when all routers know about all other routers' paths to all networks.

Core layer.   The third layer in Cisco's three-layered hierarchical model. This layer forwards data between distribution layer devices.

Count to infinity.   A routing loop that can occur while using a distance-vector routing algorithm.

CPE.   Customer Premises Equipment. Devices owned or leased by the subscriber of a WAN service. The devices are installed at the customer's site. Examples include terminals, modems, and telephones.

CRC.   Cyclic Redundancy Check. The value of a mathematical algorithm run through a frame and appended to the end of the frame before transmission.

CSMA/CD.   Carrier Sense Multiple Access with Collision Detection is a media access method that allows the sending station to sense the wire before transmission to determine whether it is clear to send.

CSU/DSU.   Channel Service Unit/Data Service Unit. Network device that modulates LAN signals into WAN signals before sending the data to the public network.

Cut-through switching.   A switching method used that works at wire speed, only reading the destination address into RAM before forwarding the frame.

DARPA.   Defense Advanced Research Projects Agency. A U.S. government agency developed to advance defense capabilities. Currently known as ARPA.

Data circuit equipment (DCE).   In terms of routing, the DCE receives signals from a router and forwards them to the public network. DCE makes up a portion of the

DTE/DCE communication channel. A typical DCE device is a CSU/DSU. DTE/DCE communication is governed by the RS232c standard.

Datagram.　Term given to a logical grouping of data after it has been encapsulated by the network layer of the OSI model; also known as a packet.

Data packet.　Packet of data sent by a router that consists of information being sent from one node on a network to another node on a separate network.

DDP.　Database Description Packet. During the formation of an adjacency in OSPF operations, routers send DDPs to one another to learn the status of each other's current link-state database.

DDR.　Dial-on-Demand Routing. A method used by a router to open an ISDN connection on demand and forward data based on predefined rules.

Dead Timer.　In OSPF operations the dead interval is the amount of time a router will wait before a route is declared dead.

De-encapsulation.　The process a protocol data unit goes through as it travels up the OSI model. Protocols at each layer of the model strip peel layer information off the PDU before forwarding it to the next layer in the model.

Default routing.　A router configuration method that specifies that the router must forward all packets out of a specified interface.

Demarc.　The location between the CPE and the WAN service provider's equipment. Also known as demarcation.

Designated port.　Port on a bridge (or switch) in a Spanning-Tree Protocol network that is in the forwarding state.

Distance-vector routing algorithm.　Algorithm that states that routers must forward their entire routing table to adjacent routers for route updates.

Distribution layer.　The second layer in Cisco's three-layered hierarchical model. This layer provides route determination and local security policies.

DLCI.　Data Link Connection Identifier. A numeric value that represents a virtual circuit in Frame Relay networks.

DNS.　Domain Name System. Application layer protocol of the TCP/IP suite used for domain name resolution. DNS uses the services of both TCP and UDP to transport data.

DTE.　Data terminal equipment. In terms of routing, the DTE is normally the router. It makes up a portion of the DTE/DCE communication channel. The DTE forwards data to the DCE, which forwards the data to a public network. DTE/DCE communication is governed by the RS232c standard.

Dynamic routing. A router configuration process of allowing routing protocols to update routing tables.

EGP. Exterior Gateway Protocol. A category of routing protocols that includes BGP. EGPs are normally used to connect two autonomous systems together.

EIGRP. Enhanced Interior Gateway Routing Protocol. Cisco proprietary hybrid routing protocol that has features of link state routing as well as distance-vector routing protocols.

Encapsulation. The process a protocol data unit goes through as it travels down the various layers of the OSI model. Protocols at each layer of the model add layer specific information to the PDU before sending it to the next layer.

Ethernet. Networking standard created by Digital, Intel, and Xerox. It uses a baseband transmission and the CSMA/CD media access method. Ethernet has several physical layer standards such as 10BaseT, 10Base2, and 10Base5.

FC. Feasibility Condition. In EIGRP, the feasibility condition states that if a route learned from a neighbor has a lower metric than the current feasible distance to the same destination network, the learned route will then become the router's FD.

FD. Feasible Distance. In EIGRP operations, the FD is the route to a destination network that has the lowest metric among all known paths.

FDDI. Fiber Distributed Data Interface. Networking standard that uses fiber-optic wire and a token passing media access method.

Flash RAM (Flash Memory). Location where the IOS software image is stored.

Flow control. Method of ensuring that a receiving machine is not overwhelmed with data being sent to it during a network transmission.

Fragment-free switching. A switching method that checks the integrity of the first 64 bytes of a frame before forwarding the frame to its destination.

Frame. A logical grouping of data after they have been encapsulated by the data-link layer of the OSI mode.

Frame Relay. A packet-switched protocol, often used in a WAN that operates at the data-link layer of the OSI reference model.

FS. Feasible Successor. A list of possible next hop routers (to a known destination) in an EIGRP network.

FTP. File Transfer Protocol. Application layer protocol of the TCP/IP suite used for transferring files. FTP uses the connection-oriented services of TCP for transport.

Full duplex. A data transmission process that allows two end stations to have the entire communication channel available to them. Each station is capable of sending and receiving data at the same time. Communication can occur in both directions by both stations at the same time.

Function group. A term used to identify hardware components in an ISDN.

Global configuration mode. The router configuration mode that allows changes that affect the entire router to be made. Examples include passwords, host names, and banners.

Half duplex. A data transmission process that allows one station to transmit while the other station receives data. Communication can occur in both directions, but only one station at a time.

HDLC. High-Level Data Link Control. A data-link layer protocol that was developed for transmitting data over serial lines.

Hello-Interval. In EIGRP operations, the Hello-Interval is how often routers send hello packets to maintain the neighbor relationship.

Hello packet. Hello packets are exchanged between routers to establish and maintain neighbor relationships with other routers. OSPF and EIGRP use hello packets.

Hello timer. In OSPF routing, the hello timer is the amount of time a router waits before sending hello packets to its neighbors.

Holddown timers. A timer used in distance-vector routing that will not allow a router to accept an additional route change unless it has a better cost.

Holdtime Interval. In EIGRP routing, the holdtime interval is the maximum time a router will keep a neighbor relationship alive without receiving a hello packet.

Hop. The process of a packet being forwarded by a router.

IEEE. Institute of Electrical and Electronics Engineers. IEEE is a nonprofit association that is a leading authority in technical areas.

IGP. Interior Gateway Protocol. A category of routing protocols normally used within an autonomous system. Examples are OSPF, RIP, and IGRP.

IGRP. Interior Gateway Routing Protocol. Cisco proprietary distance-vector routing protocol.

Interface. The component of a router that allows the router to physically connect to and send data onto the network cable.

Internal area router. An OSPF router that has all interfaces within the same OSPF area.

Inverse ARP. Inverse Address Resolution Protocol. Protocol used by Frame Relay that associates network addresses to DLCIs.

IP. Internet Protocol. The network interface layer protocol of the TCP/IP suite primarily responsible for network addressing.

IP address. Addressing scheme used by IP in the TCP/IP suite. 32 bits represented in dotted decimal notation. An IP address is broken into four octets of 8 bits each.

IPCP. IP Control Protocol. Protocol used by PPP to establish IP communication.

IP extend access list. A set of test conditions that filters data based on the source and destination IP address as well as TCP and UDP port numbers.

IP standard access list. A set of test conditions that filters data based on the source IP address.

IPX. Internetwork Packet eXchange. The IPX/SPX network layer protocol primarily responsible for network addressing.

IPXCP. IPX Control Protocol. Protocol used by PPP to establish IPX communication.

IPX extended access list. A set of test conditions that filters data based on the source and destination IPX address as well as protocol types and socket numbers.

IPX SAP filter. A set of test conditions that filters IPX SAP advertisements on router interfaces to cut down on unnecessary traffic.

IPX standard access list. A set of test conditions that filters data based on the source IPX address.

ISDN. Integrated Services Digital Network. A communication standard that allows telephone companies to carry voice, video, and data over existing telephone lines.

ISL. Inter-Switch Link. A proprietary to Cisco, data-link layer protocol that carries data between ISL components such as switches, routers, and ISL-capable network adapter boards.

ISO. International Organization for Standardization. ISO is a network of the national Standards Institutes of 148 countries.

LCP. Link Control Protocol. Protocol used by PPP to establish, test, and tear down a connection.

Link-state routing algorithm. Routing algorithm that states routers must only forward the status of its own links to all routers in the internetwork.

LMI. Local Management Interface. A set of signaling standards that was applied to the Frame Relay protocol to enhance it.

Local loop. The cable that connects the subscriber to the CO.

Logical bus topology.   Explains that when data are placed on the cable in a network by one station, they will be partially read by all nodes on the local segment.

Logical ring topology.   Describes that when data are placed on the network, they will travel from one station to another until the destination station is reached and the data are read.

Logical topology.   The rules of how data flow on a network.

LSA.   Link State Announcements. LSAs are used by OSPF routers to advertise the routes they know about as well as the status of them. Five types of LSAs are sent by Cisco OSPF routers.

LSR.   Link State Request. In OSPF operations, during the exchange of DDPs if a receiving router's database is different from the sending router's database, the receiving router will send a LSR to the router with the new information.

LSU.   Link State Update. The packet that carries the link state announcement in OSPF operations.

MAC address.   Physical address burned into the ROM of a NIC, 48 bits long, and represented in hexadecimal notation.

MAC table.   A database consisting of MAC addresses of nodes known by the bridge or switch storing the table.

Management domain.   A method used to administer a group of switches that maintain the same configuration parameters.

Media access method.   How data are placed on the wire by a node in a network. There are three popular methods: Contention, Token Passing, and Polling.

Metric.   A value associated with the cost of a path to a network in a router's routing table.

MTU.   Maximum Transmission Unit. The maximum size a packet can be on all links of a network.

Multiport repeater.   See *active hub*.

NCP.   Network Control Protocol. A control protocol used by PPP. It provides functionality to PPP so it can encapsulate multiple network layer protocols.

Neighbor database.   In OSPF and EIGRP operations the neighbor database maintains a listing of all known routers.

Neighbor relationship.   Neighbor relationships are formed between routers in OSPF and EIGRP networks. This is the first step routers take in their attempt to build their databases.

Netware Core Protocol.   The IPX/SPX protocol suite upper layer protocols.

Network adapter board.   Also known as a network interface card or NIC. A hardware component that allows for a node to physically connect to and send data onto a network cable.

Network address.   A hierarchical addressing scheme that allows for two identifications: host (node) and network (cable). Also known as logical address, protocol address, or layer 3 address.

Node.   Any device attached to the network, including workstations, servers, printers, and so on.

Nondesignated port.   A port on a nonroot bridge in a Spanning-Tree Protocol network that is placed in the blocking state.

Nonroot bridge.   A bridge (or switch) in a Spanning-Tree Protocol network that is not elected as the root bridge.

NVRAM.   Nonvolatile Random Access Memory. A type of RAM that will not lose its settings when power is turned off.

Octet.   Represents a series of 8 bits (byte) in an IP address.

OSI model.   Open Systems Interconnect Reference model. A seven-layered conceptual networking model primarily used to ensure interoperability between multiple vendors.

Packet.   A logical grouping of data after it has been encapsulated by the network layer of the OSI model. Also known as a datagram.

PAP.   Password Authentication Protocol. PPP authentication protocol that uses an unencrypted two-way handshake.

Passive hub.   Network component that acts as a central device for multiple nodes to connect to. Passive hubs do not require power and do not repeat data signals before forwarding them. They are primarily responsible for wire management.

PDU.   Protocol data unit. A unit of information that refers to data being transmitted between peer layer protocols during network communication.

Peer layer communication.   Virtual communication between peer layers of the OSI model on two different end nodes in a networked environment.

Physical topology.   Physical design of a network.

Polling.   Media access method used by mainframes. The centralized unit (mainframe) polls all nodes in the network based on priority and gives them the opportunity to transmit data.

Port (TCP). A decimal value that represents application layer protocols in the TCP/IP suite.

PPP. Point-to-Point Protocol. A dial-up protocol used over synchronous or asynchronous lines.

Preamble. A series of 1s and 0s included in the header of a frame to notify the destination station of the forthcoming data.

PRI. Primary Rate Interference. ISDN standard that allows for 23 Bearer channels at 64 Kbps and 1 Delta channel at 64 Kbps.

Privileged EXEC mode. An administrative mode of the router in which configuration changes and debugging can take place. Also known as privileged mode.

Protocol suite. A group of closely related protocols that allow for network communications to occur. Also known as a protocol stack.

PVC. Permanent virtual circuit. A virtual circuit used in a Frame Relay network. Normally configured and maintained on a permanent basis.

RAM. Random-Access Memory. The location where the IOS and the running-configuration file are loaded into during boot-up and executed from while the device is powered on.

Reference point. A term given to a logical connection between ISDN components.

Reliability. A metric used when calculating the cost to a destination network. It is concerned with the reliability of the link and is a configurable option.

Repeater. Network component that works at the physical layer of the OSI model. A repeater's primary purpose is to extend the distance a signal can travel.

RIP. Routing Information Protocol. Distance-vector routing protocol that broadcasts its entire routing table to its neighbors every 30 seconds. RIP has a version to Route IP and a version to Route IPX.

ROM. Read-Only Memory. A chip inside the router that contains a code to load the bootstrap program, initialize the Power-On Self-test (POST), and find and load the IOS.

Root bridge. The bridge (or switch) in a Spanning-Tree Protocol network is designated by peer bridges and determines which interfaces of neighboring bridges will be designated ports and which will be nondesignated ports.

Root port. Port on a nonroot bridge with the lowest cost path to the root bridge.

Route poisoning. A process used by distance-vector routing algorithms to prevent routing loops. Route poisoning advertises a downed route as unreachable after it learns that a specific network is down.

Routed protocol.   The network layer protocol responsible for transmitting the data throughout a network.

Router.   Network component that operates at the network layer of the OSI model. Routers are primarily concerned with network addressing and allow two or more networks to interconnect with one another. Routers create multiple broadcast domains.

Routing algorithm.   The rules followed by routing protocols while gathering and distributing route information.

Routing loop.   An event that occurs when two routers forward inaccurate information to one another in an endless loop.

Routing protocol.   Algorithm-based protocol that generates routing paths, the costs associated with those paths, and updates routing tables.

Routing table.   Table of information stored in a router's memory that lists all network routes that the router knows about, including those that are available through other routers.

Running-configuration file.   The configuration file located in RAM that executes while a router is powered up.

RXBOOT mode.   A diagnostic mode of the router used for maintenance. Also known as ROM Monitor mode.

Segment.   A logical grouping of data after it has been encapsulated at the transport layer of the OSI model.

Sequencing.   A process of placing segments in sequence order and adding a sequenced value to them before passing them down to the network layer. It allows for the segments to be reordered when they get to the destination machine.

Setup mode.   The router mode that the router will boot into if there is no configuration file in NVRAM.

Simplex.   A transmission process that allows for one-way communication.

SMTP.   Simple Message Transport Protocol. An application layer protocol of the TCP/IP suite used to send e-mail.

SNMP.   Simple Network Management Protocol. An application layer protocol of the TCP/IP suite used to monitor network components.

Socket.   A virtual pipe created for two nodes to send data through. It consists of a service type (TCP, UDP), an IP address, and a port number.

Spanning-Tree Protocol.   STP. Hierarchical bridging protocol that prevents bridging loops.

SPID.   Service profile identifier. An identifying number assigned to an ISDN subscriber by an ISDN provider.

Split horizon.   A method used to prevent routing loops in distance-vector algorithms. Split horizon does not allow routers to advertise information about a specific route out of the interface in which the information was learned.

SPX.   Sequenced Packet eXchange. The IPX/SPX transport layer protocol. It can be compared with TCP.

Startup-configuration file.   The configuration file placed in RAM when a router is powered up. It is stored in NVRAM and acts as a backup to the running-configuration file.

Static routing.   The process of manually adding route information to a routing table.

Store-and-forward switching.   A switching method that receives a frame, copies it into its buffers, verifies the integrity of the frame by checking its CRC, and then forwards it to the destination address of the frame.

Stub area.   An area of an OSPF network that has one area border router acting as the default router for all packets leaving the area.

Subinterface.   The subdivision of a router interface that allows for multiple logical connections.

Subnet.   A subdivision of a current IP network.

Subnet mask.   A number that is configured along with an IP address to identify which portion of the IP address can be assigned to networks and which portion can be assigned to hosts.

Successor.   The successor is a router in an EIGRP network that is selected as the next hop router to a destination network. The successor becomes both the FD and the AD.

SVC.   Switched virtual circuit. A virtual circuit that is created when transmission of data begins and terminated when the transmission is over.

Switch.   A network component that works at layer 2 or layer 3 of the OSI model. Layer 2 switches are responsible for segmenting a network into multiple collision domains. Layer 2 switches maintain a MAC table and can support full-duplex transmissions. Layer 3 switches perform functions similar to routers.

TCP.   Transmission Control Protocol. The transport layer protocol of the TCP/IP protocol suite primarily responsible for connection-oriented, reliable, end-to-end communication.

Telnet.   TCP/IP suite terminal emulation protocol.

TFTP.   Trivial File Transfer Protocol. Application layer protocol of the TCP/IP suite used for transferring small files. TFTP uses UDP for transport. TFTP servers are often used to store router configurations.

Three-way handshake.   A process TCP goes through during the session establishment phase of data transfer. It consists of sending a series of requests and acknowledgments to establish a session.

Tick.   Timing mechanism (1/18 of a second) that determines how long it will take for a packet to reach a destination network.

Token.   A unit of data that primarily consists of control information that allows machines to communicate in a token passing network.

Token passing.   Media access method in which a token is generated and passed from node to node on the network. A node is only allowed to send data when it has control of the token.

Token Ring.   Networking standard created by IBM. Token Ring uses the token passing media access method.

Toll network.   A collection of a WAN service provider's switches and cables that are used to forward data. Often represented as a WAN cloud.

Triggered update.   Allows a distance-vector routing algorithm to send update information to its neighbors without having to wait for its predetermined time to send.

Trunking.   The process of linking two switches together with ISL.

UDP.   User Datagram Protocol. A transport layer protocol of the TCP/IP suite primarily responsible for unreliable connectionless communication.

Update packet.   Packet of data generated by a router and sent to other routers in the network. Update packets help routers learn about other networks in the internetwork.

User EXEC mode.   A read-only view of the router's configuration file. Also known as user mode.

VLAN.   Virtual LAN. Logical grouping of nodes that may or may not be physically located to one another.

VTP.   VLAN Trunking Protocol. A VLAN management protocol used to administer VLAN management domains.

VTP pruning.   A method of cutting down on unnecessary traffic in a VLAN management domain.

Wildcard mask.   A method used with access lists to identify IP addresses.

Windowing.   A process used by TCP to specify the number of segments that may be received during a data transfer before responding with an acknowledgment.

INDEX